THE STORY OF
STORY
MAGAZINE

THE STORY OF

STORY

MAGAZINE

A MEMOIR BY

MARTHA FOLEY

*Edited, and with an Introduction
and Afterword by*

JAY NEUGEBOREN

W · W · NORTON & COMPANY
London   New York

Published simultaneously in Canada by George J. McLeod Limited,
Toronto. Printed in the United States of America.

All Rights Reserved

First Edition

Portions of the Introduction by Jay Neugeboren appeared, in
different form, in *the New York Times Book Review*, February 21,
1979.

Library of Congress Cataloging in Publication Data

Foley, Martha.
The story of Story magazine.
Includes index.
1. Foley, Martha.   2. Editors--United States--
Memoir   3. Story (Vienna and New York, 1931–   )
I. Neugeboren, Jay, ed.   II. Title.
PN149.9.F6A37   070.4'092'4 [B]   79–28331
ISBN 0–393–01348–0

1 2 3 4 5 6 7 8 9 0

CONTENTS

INTRODUCTION   7

One: Beginnings   29

Two: Whit and the New York Tabloids   47

Three: Paris in the Twenties   61

Four: Tales from the Vienna Woods   82

Five: *STORY!*   101

Six: Marriage   127

Seven: David   139

Eight: *Aufwiedersehn,* Vienna!   157

Nine: Majorca   174

Ten: *STORY* in America   200

Eleven: Hollywood and the War Years   222

AFTERWORD   242

INDEX   275

INTRODUCTION

৶

There was never any memorial service for Martha Foley—no funeral, no condolences sent or received. At the time of her death on September 5, 1977, at the age of eighty, she was living in a two-room furnished apartment in Northampton, Massachusetts. The only items in the apartment that were her own were some books, a multivolume Kraus reprint of *STORY* Magazine, a typewriter, and a used file cabinet that she'd bought from a local barbershop. And yet for half a century, this woman, whose death —and life—went virtually unnoticed and unsung, had been a major force in American literature. Editor of the annual *Best American Short Stories* for the previous thirty-seven years, and before that co-founder and co-editor of *STORY* magazine and of the Story Press, she had labored ceaselessly to find friends and homes for the American short story—for what Ted Solotaroff in his introduction to the 1978 *Best Stories* calls "the most beleaguered of our literary forms and the waif of the magazine and publishing industry."

On the night of her death, Judy Stark, who during Martha's four years in Northampton had been doing typing for her, telephoned to tell me that Martha was in the intensive-care unit at Cooley-Dickinson Hospital. Martha died shortly after midnight.

Introduction

In the morning, Judy asked if I would come to the apartment to help with arrangements, as Martha had named no next of kin and apparently had no living relatives. I'd never met Judy before, though Martha had spoken of her often, and with great warmth. With Judy were two of my neighbors from North Hadley— Josephine Apanell and Bernice Jarvis—sisters who had, once a week for the previous four years, cleaned house for Martha and driven her around town on errands. The four of us sat together in the tiny apartment, going through Martha's telephone book, talking to lawyers about procedures, making final arrangements. At about 9:30 that morning the realtor for the building showed up and began asking questions—wanting to know when the apartment would be cleaned out and available for rental again.

From 1931 to 1941, Martha edited *STORY* with her husband, Whit Burnett, from whom she was later divorced. During these years *STORY* published for the first time an extraordinary number of American writers, among them Norman Mailer, Erskine Caldwell, William Saroyan, Peter De Vries, J.D. Salinger, John Cheever, Richard Wright, James T. Farrell, Tennessee Williams, Emily Hahn, Frederick Prokosch, Jesse Stuart, Tess Slesinger, James Ramsey Ullman, Dorothy McCleary, Jerome Weidman, Carson McCullers, Elizabeth Janeway, Ludwig Bemelmans, and Nelson Algren.

She was ferociously proud that *STORY* magazine, from its first issue, mimeographed in Vienna, was "the only magazine devoted solely to the short story"; she was proud that, during the years she edited it, it was known as "the magazine of discovery," and that these years came to be called (by Edward J. O'Brien, the founder and editor for twenty-six years of the annual *Best Stories*) "the *STORY* decade." In issue after issue she would point to her discoveries, to the fact that at *STORY*, "unknown" writers were given the same reading that "established" writers were given, to the fact that *STORY* "had been the means of launching on their careers numerous important writers." She was proud too that

8

during these years *STORY* also published—for fees of twenty-five dollars—the stories of established authors, who were earning thousands per story from the "slicks", and that these stories were often their most original creations.

When, in 1934, *STORY* marked its first anniversary in America, she looked back on the previous year's stories and pointed out that "more than half [*STORY*'s] space is given to the work of new authors"; with equal pride she noted that writers such as Kay Boyle, Gertrude Stein, Erskine Caldwell, Sherwood Anderson, Conrad Aiken, John Peale Bishop, and William Faulkner "were represented by stories not identified with the type of work on which [these] authors have made their reputations." And she also, in this first American anniversary issue, reaffirmed *STORY*'s commitment to being a magazine of "short fiction which makes no compromise with outmoded formulas and commercial demands." Throughout her career she would continue to make these two distinctions—between the new writer and the established writer, and between formula fiction, associated usually with large-circulation magazines, and quality fiction, associated usually with the "little" magazines. "The editors have refrained from any narrow definition of the short story," *STORY* declared in 1935, in a "Restatement" of aims, "from saying, other than by the implication of the published examples, what a short story is or might be. They have no preconceived notions of its limits or its possibilities: they feel it can, perhaps, be better than we know." *STORY* was to be, always, "a magazine edited with scant respect for the formulas and taboos created in this century by the magazines of great circulation in their effort to publish a type of fiction that could never offend anyone—much."

Earlier, in April 1933—the first issue published in America—Martha and Whit had written that the editors "have no wild ambitions for *STORY;* they have no illusions that it will suddenly produce a new crop of Conrads or Chekhovs. But they believe deeply that it may easily open the pathway to one or two such, and that it is of infinite importance that a pathway be kept open. Little known as the magazine has been, they have already seen that the stories submitted to them—for honor, apparently, and little more—are more original and in general far superior to the run of those which editors of magazines of large circulation, with fixed notions about their readers, apparently seem to feel they should accept."

During the decade in which Martha edited *STORY,* the short story was not the waif it has since become. For most of this time, *STORY* was published monthly, ran to more than 100 pages, and included eight to ten stories per issue. For most of these years the magazine also ran other regular features—informal essays ("Notes" and "End-Pages") by Whit or Martha, best-seller lists, letters (often lengthy story-by-story critiques by readers of previous issues), book review excerpts, and literary essays by writers such as Thomas Mann, George Bernard Shaw, Van Wyck Brooks, Hendrik Willem Van Loon, Sherwood Anderson, Edward J. O'Brien, and Eugene Jolas. It also came to print poems, adaptations of plays, photo-essays, film criticism, and—all this without reducing the number of stories—more than forty novellas. It ran a readers' literary service and an annual college short story contest (James Laughlin, later the founder and publisher of New Directions books, was the first winner), produced a weekly radio program ("Tonight's Best Story"), sponsored a W.P.A. story contest (which discovered Richard Wright), and founded and ran the Story Press (in association, first, with Harper & Brothers, and later with Lippincott), a publishing company whose first book was Ignazio Silone's *Bread and Wine.* Its circulation, in the mid-1930s, was more than 20,000. (During these same years, the *Saturday Evening Post,* then a weekly with a circulation of more than 2 million, was publishing a half-dozen stories per issue, and literary magazines such as *Harper's, The Atlantic Monthly, The New Yorker,* and *Scribner's* were often publishing four stories an issue, and sometimes a short novel.)

From 1931 to 1941, *STORY* published, in addition to work by its "discoveries," stories by Kay Boyle, William Faulkner, William Carlos Williams, Alvah Bessie, Conrad Aiken, Gertrude Stein, Howard Fast, Katherine Anne Porter, Sherwood Anderson, Meyer Levin, Budd Schulberg, Albert Maltz, Elliott Arnold, Louis L'Amour, John Gunther, Warren Beck, Wallace Stegner, Irwin Shaw, Aldous Huxley, Dorothy Canfield Fisher, Carleton Coons, Hal Borland, Allan Seager, Zora Neale Hurston, Nancy Wilson Ross, Helen Hull, Edita Morris, Mari Sandoz, and hundreds of others whose work was, in varying degrees, already known or beginning to be known to readers of the American short story. *STORY* also published fiction by writers from abroad. *STORY* was the first magazine in America to publish the work of Robert Musil, Ignazio Silone, Peter Neagoe, Graham Greene, Malcolm Lowry, V.G. Calderon, H.E. Bates, Alfred H. Mendes, Manuel Komroff, Mikhail Zoshchenko, and Eric Knight, and they also published stories, often, for non-English authors, in their first English translations, by Anton Chekhov, Luigi Pirandello, Ivan Bunin, Stoyan Christowe, Isaac Bein, Abraham Raisin, Flann O'-Brien, Sean O'Faolain, Liam O'Flaherty, Morley Callaghan, A. Averchenko, Ralph Bates, I.A. Kuprin, Synnove Larsen Baasch, Romer Wilson, A.E. Coppard, Eric Jens Petersen, Oliver Gossman, and Padraic Fallon.

Many of the magazines that published fiction in the Thirties *(Scribner's, The American Mercury, Collier's, Vanity Fair, The Hound and the Horn)* have since vanished, and though there are now hundreds of quarterlies (most with very small circulation) that publish stories of literary excellence, there are, in 1980, less than a handful of magazines—and we can name them: *The Atlantic Monthly, Harper's, The New Yorker,* and *Esquire*— that have *both* a wide circulation and regularly publish what has come, alas, to be called "serious fiction." (Yet even *Esquire* and *Harper's* have recently published issues with no fiction.)

To list the writers Martha discovered and published, then, and to know the history of *STORY* magazine in the 1930s is to remind ourselves of how different times once were for the short story writer in America. When we read Martha's memoir and the notes she and Whit wrote for each issue of *STORY,* we learn of a time when an editor could still hope that a magazine "devoted solely to the short story" could join high culture to a wide audience. In recent times, only magazines of general interest—Norman Podhoretz's *Commentary* or Ted Solotaroff's *American Review*—have had such aspirations, and the amount of fiction (when printed at all—Martha canceled her subscription to *Commentary,* she told me, because it rarely published any stories) is greatly exceeded, always, by the amount of nonfiction.

As I read through Martha's memoir—through her drafts and notes and index cards and handwritten yellow sheets—and then through the notes and letters and biographical sketches in *STORY,* I kept thinking: How intimate it all was!—as if *STORY*'s editors and readers and writers were part of an extended family, a family in which the new and young writers were the admitted favorites. (Martha's only son, David, was born in 1931, the year of *STORY*'s birth.) It was as if Martha and Whit were running a kind of general store in which the prime merchandise was good fiction—a store onto which they kept adding (with radio programs, contests, best-seller lists, a publishing company), a store in which one could always find good literary shop talk, a store into which they kept introducing new goods, a store in which, with constant self-promotion ("If It Isn't The Best We Can't Afford to Print it!" . . . "Save all your copies of *STORY* . . . some of them may become valuable collectors' items . . .") and bargains (*"STORY*'s FIVE DOLLAR PLAN!" . . . "Anniversary Offer to Book Lovers" . . .), new and old writers, and their readers, were always welcome. For the short story, in those years, and especially at *STORY,* all good things seemed possible.

Not all the stories, of course, were good, or even literary in any way. Many, especially turgid "proletarian" stories of the Depression, now seem awkward and dated, almost quaint in their naïveté. Here, for example, is the opening paragraph of Peter DeVries's first published story, "Eine Kliene Nacht":

> With a sudden rush another of those waves of sick fear surged there under his stomach. It came when he swept his eyes from her face to her snugly belted abdomen. With it came a sharpening of the annoyance he had felt toward her the moment they had seated themselves in the parlor. It was exasperating the way she sat there on the couch, her legs doubled up under her, coolly and indifferently eating an apple. For days this had been going on, these surges of fear, this worry; but now, with that woman's body of hers curled up there before his eyes, it was terrific, unbearable. He was gnawed with suspense and could hardly wait another minute for the chance to ask her the question.*

And here, the opening paragraph from Nelson Algren's first published story, "So Help Me":

> Now perhaps you-all will think that I am just lying to you, and maybe you will even think that Luther really wanted to get rid of the Jew kid, so's we would oney have two ways to split instead of three, but you know, Mr. Breckenridge, guys like me can't never get away with bull like that to big-league lawyers like yourself, so you can just taken my word for it Fort didn't really mean to hurt the Jew kid a-tall, and that's the truth so help me.

---

* In a more familiar style, De Vries writes: "I can still relive the joy of plucking out of the mailbox the letter saying it was so. That orange diagonal logo in the upper left-hand corner sent you spinning. (Why did they not send the letter in the return envelope enclosed by the author with the manuscript?) I was at the time an editor of *Poetry* and of a flock of candy vending machines, when not picking up a few bucks as a radio actor. That was my day for servicing the vending machines. I could have had four flat tires, been riding on the rims, but I still would have floated on air through my rounds that day. That was how being accepted by *STORY* affected us in those bygone glamorous times." And he adds, "Of course *we* discovered writers too, those in the magazine, and though naturally I had by that time read some Faulkner, I can still recall my pleasure in reading 'Lo!' in *STORY*. A great humorist, he."

Introduction

To read through these stories and the notes about them is, also, to remind oneself of what Martha often said about "the test of time"—of the vagaries of literary styles and taste and the transience of literary reputation. Many authors whose names and works were considered well known ("Rachel Crothers is one of the most widely known American playwrights") both to *STORY*'s readers and to the general American public (Kressman Taylor, Mary O'Hara, Julia Davis, Helen Hull, Eric Knight, Robert Ayre) now seem unfamiliar. Martha was well aware, despite her penchant for list-making and her pride in her discoveries, of what time does to reputations. Writing in the foreword to the *Best Stories* of 1950, she noted, "Among the contributors to the first *Best American Short Stories* [1915], which was dedicated to Benjamin Rosenblatt for his story, 'Zelig,' were such writers as Maxwell Struthers Burt, Donn Byrne, Will Levington Comfort, Ben Hecht, Fannie Hurst, and Wilbur Daniel Steele. Their names are still known. But what has happened to such writers in that volume as James Francis Dwyer, Thomas Gregg, Arthur Johnson, Virgil Jordan, Harris Merton Lyon, Newbold Noyes, and others whose names are not? Apart from any who may have died, why did they not go on to fulfill the great promise they showed?"

As I read through Martha's memoir and the pages of *STORY*, I asked the same question concerning many of the writers first published there—writers who often, *STORY* felt, were among their great discoveries and who went on to have their stories widely anthologized, to have successful careers, and to publish several books. What, then, of the work of Villa Stiles, A.I. Bezzerides, E.A. Moll, Elizabeth Hall, Helen Thilenius, Meridel LeSeuer, Lewis Carliner, Eric White, Rebecca Merrick, Elsa Hertel, Harriett Hassell, William Negherbon, Elsie Plaut, Frank Brookhauser, Roma Rose, Ellis St. Joseph, Angelica Gibbs, Mary Medearis, Elisa Bialt, I.J. Kapstein, Carl Jacobs, Alan Marshall, George F. Meeter, Eluard Luchell McDaniel, and Francis Eisenberg?

Martha left *STORY* in 1941. From that year until her death in 1977, she edited the annual *Best American Short Stories* anthology for Houghton Mifflin. During these years she continued her singular dedication to the American short story by gathering "short stories of literary value" that might otherwise remain unknown and forgotten and giving them "permanent publication in book form."

In her annual anthologies as well as in the three special anthologies she edited *(The Best of the Best: Short Stories 1915 to 1950, Fifty Best American Short Stories, 1915–1965,* and *200 Years of Great American Short Stories),* she continued to make the distinctions she had often made while editing *STORY:* between unknown and established writers, and between the "little" magazines (our "richest source of fine short stories") and the large-circulation magazines. She was proud, while editing the *Best Stories,* to have recognized early on—long before they received wider acclaim—the talents of dozens of writers, including Saul Bellow, Bernard Malamud, Philip Roth, Stanley Elkin, Harvey Swados, Delmore Schwartz, Flannery O'Connor, W.II. Gass, Vladimir Nabokov, Peter Taylor, Eudora Welty, Joyce Carol Oates, J.F. Powers, Ray Bradbury, Lionel Trilling, Shirley Jackson, Isaac Rosenfeld, Jack Kerouac, James Agee, John Updike, Robert Coover, and Jean Stafford.

Whenever I would find an old *Best Stories* in a used-book shop, I loved to look through the biographical sketches—the material was sent in to Houghton Mifflin by the authors themselves—to see how these writers had regarded themselves. Thus, we learn of Saul Bellow (author of the story, "Notes of a Dangling Man"):

He was born in Lachine, Quebec, in 1915, but has spent most of his life in the United States and was educated in American schools. In 1937 he took a degree in anthropology at Northwestern University. Afterward, he became a teacher, devoting his spare time to writing. He worked on the staff of the Encyclopedia Britannica. He has published stories and reviews in *Partisan Review, The New Republic, The New York Times Book Review,* and in various little magazines, and has just published his first novel, *Dangling Man.* His home is Chicago.

And of Faulkner:

He grew up in Oxford, Mississippi, a descendant of a once wealthy family. His schooling was intermittent and he spent most of his youth loafing around his father's livery stable. He wrote poetry, strongly influenced by Omar Khayyam and Swinburne, but, he says, it was no good except as an aid to love-making. Jolted out of his lazy life by the First World War, he joined the Canadian Air Force. After the war he turned to earning a living at odd jobs such as housepainting, selling books in a department store, and shoveling coal into a factory furnace. He started writing fiction and suddenly, he explains, "I discovered that writing was a mighty fine thing. It enables you to make men stand on their hind legs and cast a shadow." Since then he has written many notable novels and short stories.

And year after year, perhaps Martha's most precious gift to writers, she printed the stories of hundreds of writers, sometimes less well known, who began to reach their more special audiences because of their inclusion in Martha's anthology: Tillie Olsen, Thomas Williams, Mary Lavin, Raymond Carver, William Wiser, Cynthia Ozick, Mary Deasy, Vardis Fisher, Josephine Johnson, Frank Butler, John Stewart Carter, Ann Petry, Niccolò Tucci, Barry Targan, Stephen Becker, William E. Wilson, Elizabeth Hardwick, Maureen Howard, Herbert Wilner, H.E. Francis, Berry Morgan, David Madden, Robert Stone, Robie Macauley, Russell Banks, William Eastlake, Abraham Rothberg, Evan S. Connell, Jr., Hal Bennett, Tim O'Brien, Leslie Epstein, Fred Busch, Stephen Minot, and Leslie Silko.

I first discovered many of my own favorite short story writers in volumes of the *Best Stories.* Loving their stories, I'd go to my local library in search of their books, and when I'd found and read more by each of them, and later on, when these writers would begin to receive wider recognition, I would luxuriate in the feeling of having known them and loved them and discovered them early on.

Several months after Martha's death I drove to Mystic, Connecticut, with Judy Stark to go through three dozen cartons that Martha had left in storage there in 1973. Martha was, by her own laughing admission, chaotic in the organization of her personal life. (Although she was in bad financial straits during her last years, she never filed for Social Security. After her death, the Social Security administration awarded more than $20,000 in back payments to her brother, Francis; we located him, a retired pharmaceutical salesman, living in a mobile home in East Wareham, Massachusetts. Separated before Martha was five, they'd grown up in different homes.) There, among jars of jam and cans of beans and boxes of chocolates—in her apartment we'd found eight boxes of Russell Stover hidden away in closets, in the bottoms of drawers, behind folders in her file cabinet—among old clothes and rags, letters, bills, lamps, dishes, pieces of a telephone, cameras, and photographs, we found several unpublished manuscripts: a novel (Martha had written many prizewinning and widely anthologized stories herself—five chosen by Edward O'-Brien for *Best Stories* volumes); a completed draft of a book on the craft of writing; and a selection of novellas for a proposed collection. We also found a good deal of material for this book—the memoir Martha had been working on during the last years of her life: *The Story of STORY,* a narrative of the founding of the magazine *STORY* in Vienna in 1931, and of its early years.

The cartons contained other things, among them books, photographs, and incomprehensible notes on matters occult left by her son David, who died in miserable circumstances, the results of drug addiction, in 1971; manuscripts of novels from former students, to whom she was almost religiously dedicated and stunningly frank; manuscripts from writers hoping to be chosen for the *Best Stories;* published books inscribed lovingly to her from writers, both well known and obscure, whom she had encouraged and helped; and letters of gratitude from writers chosen for inclusion in an annual *Best Stories.* I even, by chance, came across my own, from the spring of 1965.

Martha was a good friend to writers. She found good homes for thousands of good stories. She liked writers, even while she believed that we were, collectively, the stupidest group of people on the face of the earth; no other group would be dumb enough to let themselves be used as badly as writers let publishers use them. When you're not being ignored, she'd say, you're being insulted. Not by her, of course. She never tired of reading stories —hundreds per week—and of loving good ones. The cartons were filled with thousands of index cards, in three different colors —orange, blue, and white—on which she painstakingly wrote out brief comments for each of the several thousand stories (more than 8,000 in one year, when she kept count) she read a year. (She describes her method in detail, in the foreword to the 1950 volume.) Although Houghton Mifflin had reduced the annual number of stories to twenty (instead of the thirty reprinted in the 1940s and 1950s), she always wound up with at least 100 stories she wanted to use. "I put the 100 stories in a pile on a table and I suffer over them," she said. "I do the best I can, but I'd hate to argue a case against those I reject."

When students inquired as to how the annual anthology was edited—how *all* the stories in American magazines were read— she would smile and answer: "I edit it by myself. I read all the stories and I choose the ones I think are best. That's why it's called *The Best American Short Stories,* edited by Martha Foley."* In the

---

* Cf. the following from the April 1934 issue of *STORY* (at a time, when, for example, the annual *O. Henry* anthology had a staff of more than a dozen readers and judges): "At one time the editors were nearly 6000 manuscripts behind in their reading. . . . Instead of a mere 70 to 80 manuscripts a day, it is a rare day

1940s and 1950s she often had an assistant, but for the last twenty
years of her life the task of going through all the slicks and
quarterlies and periodicals and monthlies—through every story
that reached her—was largely (despite some help from David)
hers alone.*

Her taste was, of course, far from flawless. She had favorites.
Houghton Mifflin was—no secret—not always happy with her
selections. And she erred in other ways, as letters we found
showed. She was forgetful. Subscriptions to some magazines
lapsed and were not renewed. She listed American writers as
foreign, and therefore did not include their stories, and vice
versa. Still, her overall record seems, in retrospect, no less extraordinary than her labors.

By 1965, when I was twenty-seven years old, I'd written seven
unpublished books and more than a dozen stories. My most recent novel was making the rounds and getting encouraging rejections ("If it's any consolation to the author, this book was a

---

when 150 don't show up, and on Mondays—called *Blaue Montag* in Vienna, and
a lot bluer at 57th Street—it is not an exceptional Monday when numerous
mailmen stagger in with a total of as high as 270 to 350 stories. . . . Even with
glasses, the editors have only the usual number of eyes, and unless manuscripts
are to be shovelled back, which is not quite fair, a delay much longer than occurs
in the usual editorial office is inevitable. We ask STORY contributors to be
patient. Every manuscript is read by the editors themselves. There is no large staff
of readers. The bad manuscripts get short shrift; the better ones take longer; and
the best ones get into type—eventually. The editors really feel for the authors,
and particularly for the newer ones, and STORY has attempted to avoid any
machine-like and stereotyped consideration of what is offered here. Every inquiry
about a manuscript has been answered, but this is no fun, and benefits little. We
would like also to explain when asked, and do explain in hundreds of cases, why
a manuscript is unavailable—but this obviously is becoming less and less a possible
matter. At present many good stories which at another time would have been
printed are now going back (reluctantly, it is true) because of the proportionate
increase in the number of excellent manuscripts received."
* Cf. again, as with *STORY,* a 1978 issue of *Fiction* magazine—which contains
work by sixteen authors, is supported by one university and three foundations, and
has a staff of twenty-two assorted senior, managing, contributing, and associate
editors.

Introduction

near-miss. . . . ") I was, to say the least, as discouraged as I was persistent. One Saturday afternoon that spring, my wife, Betsey, and I were browsing in a bookstore on the upper West Side of Manhattan, near the Thalia, and I took a copy of *The Best American Short Stories 1964* off the shelf, leafed through it, and showed it to Betsey. Later, as we walked home along Broadway, I talked some more about my reactions to seeing and holding the copy of the latest *Best Stories,* about how much I would have given to have been chosen for it, about the grim state of my nonexistent literary career. I remember saying to Betsey—we smile now, at the way I qualified my vow; we didn't then—that perhaps, if I didn't have a book published by the time I was thirty, I would have to *begin* to think about giving up the idea of being a novelist.

That evening I received a call from Joe McCrindle, editor of the *Transatlantic Review,* asking me if I'd heard that a story of mine that *TR* had published in 1964 (it had been rejected, during a four-year period, by more than thirty magazines) had been selected by Martha Foley for her 1965 collection. Betsey and I stayed up almost all night, telephoning everyone we knew to share the good news. Within a year, when Martha's editor at Houghton Mifflin, Joyce Hartman, saw the story in galleys and wrote to ask if I had a book in the works (I'd just finished my eighth, *Big Man),* I had found an editor and a publisher.

When Martha moved to Northampton in 1973, Joyce mentioned this to me—mentioned how depressed Martha still was over David's death—and I called Martha. We got together every few months. Sometimes I'd bring my children to her apartment —she liked teasing them and serving them Sara Lee Pound Cake (which they still call "Martha Foley Cake") and Russell Stover chocolates—and we enjoyed each other's company. I remember two occasions with special fondness. The first time was when she came to dinner and met my mother and father, and talked with them for hours about her childhood ("In Boston, one never went to bed. Oh, no! One *retired* for the night.") and about her years

as a newspaperwoman and a fighter for women's rights during the
1920s and 1930s, of her years in Paris, Haiti, Vienna, Spain, and
Los Angeles. She was full of wonderful stories about Joyce, Hemingway, Stein, Jolas, Garbo, Chaplin, Dorothy Thompson, and
Hart Crane, most of which she set down permanently in this
memoir. "I suppose," she said, laughing, "you could say that I'm
in my anec-dotage."

The second occasion, in the spring of 1977, proved to be the
last one on which Martha ever met with and spoke to a group of
writers. At my request, she agreed to judge a fiction contest at the
University of Massachusetts for the annual Harvey Swados Memorial Prize. "I liked Harvey," she began. "He was a good man,
and he was a damned good writer." She smiled at the room of
young writers and pounded on the arm of her chair with her fist.
"And he was a socialist too!" She reminisced freely about writers
she'd known, some whom she'd hated ("Oh, Hemingway. Hemingway was such a mean bastard. He never did a nice thing for
anybody in his life."), and some whom she'd loved. She spoke of
Rex Stout, who'd died recently, and of the new copyright law
Congress had just passed, for which Stout had fought so long. She
told us that *STORY* was the first magazine that allowed individual
authors to retain rights to stories—and that she had been the first
editor to let authors chosen for a prize anthology share in royalties. "Until that point," she said, "they were supposed to be
happy with the honor."

She told the kinds of stories young writers love and need to
hear. About Stout and Dorothy Parker and Erskine Caldwell and
William Saroyan and Ludwig Bemelmans and Richard Wright.
She told her favorite Ray Bradbury story—of how she'd selected
a story of his for *Best Stories* and had received a telegram back
saying that under no circumstances would he ever allow a story
of his to be printed in her anthology. A week or so later she
mentioned this to an editor who knew Bradbury. A few days later
she received a second telegram from Bradbury, stating that he

had changed his mind, that it had been his great hope, for years and years, to have a story in Martha's collection. Later, Martha met Bradbury in New York and asked him what had happened to change his mind. He laughed and told her that he'd never changed his mind. He'd been on the outs with a girlfriend, it seemed, and the girlfriend, without Bradbury's knowledge, had taken to getting to his mailbox each day before Bradbury did. The young woman had read the letter from Martha and had sent the first telegram, in Bradbury's name.

Martha also told of another writer, suddenly famous, who, while in the New York office of a well-paying magazine, asked how they kept records on submissions. He wrote down the titles of a half-dozen or so stories of his own that the magazine had previously rejected, went home, changed the titles, resubmitted the stories, and sold them all. The moral—not really a happy one —was not lost on the group.

As we drove home from the warehouse in Connecticut, I kept thinking of the distance Martha had come, in the last forty years of her life—of the rich and wonderful literary life she'd been a part of and had helped to shape. Her influence on the American short story was enormous. She had been on intimate terms with the major writers of several generations. She had given many of them the breaks that they believed were crucial to their careers; and she had also, in her stubborn, cantankerous way, fought with many of them. At the time of her death she was corresponding with her old friend William Shirer, exchanging data and memories on the 1930s. She had been recalling the first successes of her friends Bill Saroyan, Tennessee Williams, Tess Slesinger, Erskine Caldwell. She wanted more than anything to be able to finish her memoir, and she worked at it daily, despite excruciating back pain, until the very morning she entered the hospital on the day before her death. A week or two before she had told me that, when she completed the memoir, she hoped to return to her first love: the writing of fiction. She had several short stories and two novels—all complete in her head—that she hoped to get to. She smiled at me. "All I ever really wanted to do," she said, "was write."

I kept thinking of how large, in my imagination, and that of other writers, those years were—of how the prose of those writers who were published early on in *STORY* and in *The Best American Short Stories*—Bellow, Faulkner, Saroyan, Boyle, Salinger, Cheever, Wright, Caldwell, O'Connor—had shaped the taste and hopes of so much that has come since. And then, of course, I thought of what Martha's life was like during her last years—of her constant pain, of her furnished apartment, of her awful financial situation, of her unpublished manuscripts, of her unfinished memoir, of her isolation. I had not known her well. Nor had Judy Stark or the two sisters who cleaned for her and drove her around town once a week I was astonished—sadly and angrily so—to realize that we were, during the last years of her life, in the place in which she lived, her only friends. The literary life indeed

A NOTE ON THE MANUSCRIPT

Martha submitted the memoir, chapter by chapter, to W.W. Norton, over a four-year period. George Brockway, chairman of Norton, had never forgotten being cheered by a personal rejection note Martha had sent him sometime in the Thirties on a short story he had submitted, and he encouraged Martha in the project. Martha did not live to make final revisions on her manuscript. I have added nothing of substance that was not in Martha's own words, but I have trimmed the memoir here and there where it seemed repetitious, and I have added to it, especially in the first and last chapters, from Martha's own notes and manuscript pages —material I found in her papers after her death. I have rearranged or added a small amount of material for purposes of

Introduction

continuity, and, where necessary, I have corrected spelling, punctuation, and dates. I have also added a new and final chapter to the book, to tell that part of the story of *STORY* that Martha did not live to tell.

Despite the grimness and partial isolation of Martha's last years, during which she worked on this memoir, the book remains, I believe, not only a splendid chronicle of an extraordinary era but, more important, a tribute to a woman whose dedication to stories and to the writers of stories was exceptional. No one, in the last half-century, has been more of a friend to the American short story. Her devotion, energy, and enthusiasm—her determination and spirited will—shine through these pages.

Jay Neugeboren
North Hadley, Massachusetts 1979

THE STORY OF

STORY

MAGAZINE

"Tell me about when you were young," a little boy named David, who was never to grow old, used to ask. He'd settle down in his bed, his yellow hair and dark blue eyes obscured by the enormous Stetson hat his grandfather had brought him from a Utah ranch. His gray kitten was cuddled in the crook of his arm, his black cocker spaniel couched at his feet. *"Tell me about when you were a newspaper reporter and went with my father to Vienna where I was born and you started a magazine people said was a crazy thing to do and to Spain where you wouldn't go to bullfights and came back to America when everybody was poor, and even some of the famous writers you knew were hungry and—"*

"Whoa, cowboy!" I would say. *"That's an awful lot of story for one bedtime. We'll have to continue it in our next and next and next and—"*

"All right, but please remember it all." He'd smile at me. *"And don't forget the funny parts, all right?"*

I am remembering now but I am remembering alone. Real loneliness, I feel today, is not when nobody loves you, but when you have nobody to love. The little boy grew up to be a handsome, talented young man who died too soon, and the story he loved has taken on a different meaning with the years. Still, though there will be only the silence of a grave for answer, I shall tell it here once more, not as if to the child David was, but as if to the man he would be today . . . and I promise not to forget *"the funny parts,"* because before trouble came there was great happiness along the way.

Martha Foley
Northampton, Massachusetts
1973–1977

ONE

⌒

BEGINNINGS

When I was a small girl my home was broken up by the illness of both my parents. With my brother, I was sent to stay for a time with people who either did not like or did not understand children. It was a harsh and brutal period in my life. Fortunately, my parents' library—the kind assembled by a former schoolteacher and a doctor—accompanied us.

All the old-fashioned, uniformly bound sets of the classics were there. Dickens and Thackeray, Hugo and de Maupassant, Shakespeare and Tolstoy, Jane Austen and George Eliot, along with Wordsworth and Tennyson and Keats. There were individual volumes of Melville, Hardy, and the Brontës, and many, many others.

Those books became home to me, the only home I was to know for a long time. Looking back across the years, I see myself lying on the Brussels-carpeted floor of a New England parlor, a book open before me; I am lost in such utter joy that it is of no importance at all that surely, some time during the day, I will be wrongly whipped for something I have not done. At night, before sleep came, I could lie thinking of the people in those books and know that I might be only a little girl who was very unhappy in many ways, but that there was another world beside the one in which I lived, to which I could always flee for refuge.

Somehow I recognized even then that the books that were giving me so much happiness were often made out of the unhappiness of their authors. That they too had once been children and that they knew what it was to be unhappy and helpless, not only when they were young but when they were older, and that they had had the great courage so to transform their own small lives that many people could share in their joys and agonies and find strength. And every time I edit a book, it is a little like paying back a bit of what the little girl who was myself once received.

My mother had been principal of the MacIntyre Academy, in Zanesville, Ohio, where Zane Grey was her student. She met my father, a Harvard Medical School alumnus, when she took literature courses at the Harvard Summer School. She was the author of a novel and of a book of verse—the latter being the first book ever dedicated to me. (The second was a volume on higher mathematics, by William James Sidis, the famous and tragic prodigy who was the first boy ever to pay court to me. Ready to enter Harvard at the age of nine, he was held back until eleven, became a university teacher at fifteen, pioneered discoveries in the fourth dimension, became the focus of international attention, and had his life blasted by notoriety.)

My mother was a teacher, my father wanted me to be a teacher, and I never expected to be a teacher. Always, I wanted to be a writer. My first short story was published in the Boston Girls' Latin School magazine, *The Jabberwock,* when I was eleven. But I had tried to write a novel before that, when I was seven and my parents were ill. Out of wish-fulfillment I wrote a novel about how wonderful it would be to be sent to a boarding school, and not to be living with the people I was living with, whom I disliked intensely.

During that same period, I used to wish I could be cast away on a desert island with all the books in the world, and nobody to say, "Go out and play." There was no bed light in my room, so

I saved my pennies and bought candles, and I would read by candlelight. If I heard a step near the door of my bedroom, I would blow the candle out and put it under the blankets. I learned to read fast. One of the great blows in my young life occurred was when I was about eight. I had read all of Dickens by then. My parents' library was stored in the attic of the house I was boarding in, and I had a wonderful time up in that attic. (The library included all my father's medical books, so I learned a lot about things I shouldn't have known at that age.) Then there came a very snowy winter day, and I thought, "How wonderful!" I'd been saving the very last story in the set of Dickens for just such a day. I started out so happily to read *The Mystery of Edwin Drood,* not knowing that Dickens had never finished it. It was one of the tragedies of my literary life.

My education—my *financial* education—was peculiar. I was required by my father to earn my allowance by memorizing poems. To me, a lot of those famous poems still have price tags on them. Shelley's "Ode to a Skylark"—fifty cents. "L'Allegro" and "Il Penseroso"—seventy-five cents each. . . . My father should have been a professor, rather than a doctor. He was never happy as a doctor and gave it up finally.

Little girls should not even know about drunken men, let alone be permitted to read or write about them. Thus saying, the author of *Alice in Wonderland,* Lewis Carroll, angrily ended his association with *The Jabberwock,* the Boston Girls' Latin School magazine, because an intoxicated man had been a character in a student's story it published. But that was in another century, long before my own first published story appeared in the magazine. The man in my story was sober. A wonderful teacher had been engaged to introduce for the first time, despite the embattled protests of long-entrenched Latin and Greek departments, courses in that upstart language English, and her classes were the liveliest in the school.

Euripides was still performed in the Assembly Hall, but Shakespeare came to be tolerated. Several of my classmates went on to become well-known writers, including, above all, Louise Bogan, a slender girl with a lovely face and lavender-blue eyes. Her writing already was so good that we all expected her to become editor of *The Jabberwock,* but the headmaster warned her mother to disabuse Louise of the idea. "An Irish girl can never be *The Jabberwock*'s editor!"

I decided I would go to Boston University because Louise went there. She was a year ahead of me at the Girls' Latin School, and she and I were friends. I was very fond of her, but the year after I got to Boston University, Louise left to get married, so that I never had the continuous association with her I had hoped for.

I never finished college and never received a degree (though I taught for more than twenty years at Columbia and gave seminars and courses at many colleges, including New York University, George Washington University, Emory University, University of Colorado, University of Utah, and the University of Missouri). I was too interested in other things—in writing and in politics. When I was twenty years old, I was arrested and thrown *out* of jail.

I was busy minding my own business, licking envelopes in the Socialist party headquarters, when a member of the Woman's party came in looking for somebody to go picket the State House in Boston. It was the day of Woodrow Wilson's return from the first League of Nations meeting, and there was to be a big parade in his honor. Hundreds of thousands of people were lined up all through Boston. There were twenty-two of us. Wilson was very opposed to woman's suffrage. We carried signs like EQUAL RIGHTS and TAXATION WITHOUT REPRESENTATION IS TYRANNY.

We lined up with our picket signs, and a police captain came along and said, "Unless you ladies move on within ten minutes, you'll be arrested for loitering and sauntering." The minutes passed and we didn't move on, so they called up the paddy wagons, and we were put in them and taken down to the Charles Street station house. From there we were taken to the Charles Street prison. We were treated very, very gingerly, because a number of the women in our demonstration were prominent. We were taken to the Tombs, which is under the courthouse, and given the freedom to walk around. Then one of the really posh men's clubs of Boston—I've forgotten which—sent over supper, and we dined luxuriously.

The next morning, Alice Paul, president of the Woman's party, came to us and said she had discovered that we were going to be tried separately and secretly, because there was such a mob outside the courthouse and they didn't want a riot. We were going to have what Alice called a Star Chamber proceeding, and we were to refuse to participate in it. We were to stay where we were. The court officers came down and called out somebody's name; when none of us stepped forward, they grabbed the first woman they could and lugged her up the winding iron stairs to where the courtroom was.

I followed instructions. When I was carried into the courtroom, I sat there, and when the judge said something, a court officer tapped me on the shoulder and said, "When his honor speaks to you, you shall stand up." I sat still and twiddled my thumbs and stared at a corner of the ceiling. Then the judge said that if I would only plead guilty or not guilty, he would release me. I kept mum. Then they called a policeman who testified that I had been loitering and sauntering, and the judge said, "Guilty! Five-dollar fine or eight days in jail." I didn't say anything, so I was carried out of the courtroom.

I felt sorry for the court officers, because with the winding iron stairs, it was not easy to manipulate us. So we were taken to the Charles Street prison, all of us, and put in the hospital section, which was supposed to be very considerate of them. That night we were serenaded by the women's clubs of Boston. They paraded around singing songs to cheer us up. We went on a hunger strike.

In the afternoon of the middle of the third day a prison guard came to my cell and said that the warden wanted to see me downstairs. I asked why, and he didn't know. The rest of the demonstrators were very curious. I was one of the two youngest members of the demonstration and had never even been a member before of the Woman's party. I was taken to the warden's office, and he put out his hand and said, "Well, good-bye, Miss Foley, I hope we meet under more pleasant circumstances in the future." And I said, "Why? What do you mean?" And he said, "Oh, we're sending you girls home now." And I said, "You can't do that. You put us in here legally, and now you're putting us out of here illegally." And he said, "Now look. You've caused enough trouble. Just go quietly, please." But I wouldn't. All my comrades were upstairs and I felt as if I were betraying them. So he said, "If you don't go quietly, we'll just have to see that you go," and he called a couple of guards who picked me up—by that time I was getting used to being carried around by strange men —and dumped me down on the sidewalk outside the prison. I didn't know what to do. Maybe, I thought, if I sat there, they'd arrest me again for loitering and sauntering.

Then I thought that I'd better let the people at party headquarters know what was going on. So I got a cab and went up to Park Street (almost next door to where my publisher's office—Houghton Mifflin—would later be). When I walked in, they were flabbergasted. How did you get out? they asked. "They're throwing us out," I replied. So they got busy on the telephone, calling up their lawyers, and they piled into cars and they went down and I went with them. We got there just as they were evicting Katherine Morey, daughter of the president of the Massachusetts branch of the Woman's party. Her mother, a very dainty little white-haired lady, shook a white kid-gloved fist at a prison guard, and kept shouting: "How dare you put my daughter out of jail! How dare you put my daughter out of jail!" We were all put out of jail, except for one woman, a lawyer's wife; her husband got an injunction to keep us *in* jail, but by the time the injunction was served, there was only one woman left, his wife, so he kept her in the entire eight days.

I always wanted to be a writer—that was why I went into newspaper work: because it was the nearest thing to writing that I could earn my living at. My father disapproved of all newspapers except the *Boston Transcript,* so that a part-time stint I obtained on the *Boston Herald* lasted only briefly. I decided to leave Boston University to go to New York and become a newspaperwoman in earnest. I turned down all jobs as society editor or club editor or woman's page editor. I got a job as copy editor—unusual for a girl then—and as a rewrite woman and a book reviewer. Those were colorful and exciting days—a time before radio had stolen the thrill of extra editions. Oh, to be roused at three in the morning and told to get the hell as quick as you can down to the shop, an extra had to be put out! I remember getting into an argument with a red-headed copyreader named Boyle (or Doyle) at the *New York Globe.* Like most newspapermen in those days, he was adamantly opposed to women in city rooms. "No woman can read copy anyway," he said. I bet him five dollars I could get a job on a copydesk. Which led to my quitting a perfectly good job as a reporter to join the staff of that fabulous newspaper of New Jersey, the *Newark Ledger.*

Getting a job on the *Ledger* was a simple business. All one had to do was walk in and ask. I could probably have been managing editor if I'd thought of it. The *Ledger* had the largest turnover of any paper in the country. It had had twenty-three managing editors in five years. The managing editor at the time I was there was out on parole as an alleged embezzler of the funds of an upstate town for which he had been treasurer, and he was released in the custody of the Salvation Army. The Army used to hold its meetings right outside our offices. Every time the band started tooting, the editor jumped to attention.

* * *

Although *STORY* magazine was not to be published until 1931, in Vienna, it had its genesis in 1925 while I was working on the *Los Angeles Daily News.* I arrived at that paper, a woebegone, bedraggled girl, looking, I was later told, "like something the cat dragged in." I had hitchhiked from San Francisco, where I'd been fired from the *Journal* when the publisher, who'd been out of town, returned to find me working on his copydesk. He was outraged to find that a female had sneaked there behind his back and was busy editing reporters' stories and composing headlines. "Get her out!" he ordered.

A single free-lance assignment was the only other newspaper work I'd been able to find in San Francisco, but it was an important one. Eugene V. Debs arrived to visit Tom Mooney in San Quentin prison, and with him came Otto Branstetter, national secretary of the Socialist party. I'd known Debs back East—I'd soapboxed in Scolley Square—and Otto was a good friend of mine. When they invited me to go with them to see Mooney, I hurried around to the *Record,* a liberal Scripps paper, and offered it the story. Debs himself only a short time before was in a prison cell where, in the 1920 election, he had received almost a million votes for president. Debs did oppose the war, but Mooney was innocent of the crime he was charged with—bombing a 1916 Preparedness Day parade. Despite prosecution witnesses' confessions of perjury and the perfect alibi—a newspaper photo, showing him watching the parade from a rooftop far away from the scene at the exact time of the explosion, as proved by a tower clock behind him—Mooney, a radical union organizer, was sentenced to death. (This sentence was commuted to life imprisonment, which he was to endure until 1939, when he received an unconditional pardon.)

The heart-wrenching meeting of Debs and Mooney took place in a large room just inside the prison entrance, with the warden and a guard present. I was standing next to Debs when a door opened, and I could see the joy on Mooney's face as, in his gray prison uniform, he rushed toward Debs and threw his arms around the tall old man. "Tom, Tom," Debs murmured, and patted Mooney's shoulders. Tears were in the eyes of two other reporters, as well as in mine. "It's been so long!" Mooney said. "I know," Debs said. "But now they've let me out, I'm going to get you out." They sat down at a long table to talk. When, an hour later, it came time to leave, they embraced one another again and then tore themselves apart. They knew it was their last meeting. Outside the high prison walls and their thousands of incarcerated men, Debs paused to gaze at the wide San Francisco bay and the misty violet hills beyond. "So much suffering where there's so much beauty!" he sighed. In silence we boarded the launch that was to take us back to the city.

Even though the *Record* printed my story prominently, with my byline, I still was not able to get a job in San Francisco. With five dollars left after settling my bills, I started walking south. It was my plan to stop at every place big enough to have a newspaper, and to ask for a job until I got one. Hitchhikers were not common then, and motorists were so generous with offers of lifts for long distances that I had difficulty keeping to my plan. Not until I reached Glendale, on the outskirts of Los Angeles, did I have any luck.

The *Glendale Evening News* hired me to do something of everything: reporting, rewrite, copy editing six days a week, and covering sermons on Sunday mornings. I was given a pep talk about Glendale being the fastest-growing, most admirable community in Southern California and was told to conduct myself so as to command respect for the *Glendale Evening News.* I failed and lost the job. Maybe it was because I was seen speeding through the town's main street on the rear end of a fire engine, scared to death, my eyes shut tight, my face buried in a coil of hose, and my skirts flying in the air. But it was not my fault. I'd been in the Burbank police station, interviewing the chief about a robbery, when a general alarm sounded in the firehouse next door. A general alarm meant a fire of disastrous proportions. The chief grabbed my hand, yelled, "Come on!" and pulled me with him through the doorway. Before I could stop him, he'd hauled me up on to the back of a fire truck and on to the scene of a tremendous forest fire.

After being fired from the *Evening News,* I resumed my travels. I had a letter of introduction to a woman doctor in Los Angeles, who, I hoped, might invite me to be her house guest. Walking along a strange street looking for the doctor's address, I met Dudley Burrows, a drama critic I knew in San Francisco who was a nephew of Frank Baum, author of *The Wonderful Wizard of Oz.* "Hello!" he said, "I thought you were in San Francisco. What are you doing in L.A.?" "Looking for a job," I replied. "The *Journal* fired me." "Go around and see the Vanderbilt paper. They're hiring."

Cornelius Vanderbilt, Jr., a tall, curly-headed young man in his middle twenties, had started the *Los Angeles Daily News* a few weeks before I arrived from Glendale. He conceived of it as a clean, unsensational tabloid, unlike the scandal-prizing tabloids then in existence. He was very young and very enthusiastic. The day the new paper started he'd had pictures taken of himself as publisher, assistant to the publisher, managing editor, city editor, reporter, proofreader, cameraman, linotyper, engraver, pressman, and as a newsboy out on the street in white canvas cap and apron, selling the paper. He was also photographed in the barbershop (to which he'd imported his favorite barber from New York), giving a reporter a haircut. All the pictures were published.

Vanderbilt—"Neely" to us—wanted to live down his grandfather's motto, "The Public Be Damned." On the masthead of his paper, he printed in bold, black italics, "The Public Be Served!" Vanderbilt himself wrote all the editorials for the *Daily News,* signing them "Your Publisher." Some were extraordinary. One celebrating his wedding anniversary caused much ribald comment. After recounting his day's activities, he concluded with, "And Your Publisher's wife? What was she doing on this important day? She was remaining quietly at home preparing a pleasant surprise for Your Publisher in the evening."

International repercussions resulted from another editorial. The British fleet was touring around the world. When it reached the Canadian West Coast, Vanderbilt was named official emissary, charged with inviting it to California. He was entertained aboard the admiral's flagship. On his return to Los Angeles, Vanderbilt wrote an editorial criticizing the British officers' table manners; he did not know that in England it is *comme il faut* to eat peas from the back of a knife blade and that the fork is never changed from hand to hand or put down until one is completely finished with it. A Washington apology persuaded the fleet not to withdraw acceptance of the invitation to visit California.

It is a pity Vanderbilt did not have more experience. He was in love with newspaper work and with newspaper people. He thought nothing was too good for them, and he was a wonderful man to work for. The generous salaries he paid were unprecedented in Southern California; other Southern California publishers were happy to take advantage of the many newspapermen who came from other parts of the country because the warm, sunny climate was then believed to heal tuberculosis, from which either they or someone in the family suffered.

Hired by the *News* as a feature writer, I was given a press card and a big, shiny nickel badge and sworn in as a deputy sheriff, a customary Los Angeles procedure for reporters. When I protested to "Mother" Kotterman, the lovable, roly-poly city editor, that I was a socialist and didn't want to be a sheriff, he said, "Sure you do. You can arrest a capitalist."

My duties were more routine. I accompanied a cameraman and wrote the daily "Inquiring Photographer" column; I interviewed visiting celebrities; and I assisted Mort Donoghue, the feature editor, with "Kiddie Kute Sayings," "My Most Embar-

rassing Moment," and letters for the "Voice of the People."
Many of the letters, when the mail slackened, I wrote myself. A
sure-fire device to bring in plenty of letters was to print one
signed by some such name as "Puzzled Male" (me), asking,
"Should a gentleman take off his hat when a lady enters an elevator in which he is riding?" The letter I remember most vividly was
a bona fide one, signed "A Blushing Citizen." "A decent woman
can no longer walk down the streets of Los Angeles without
blushing," the citizen wrote. "The men dressers in the store
windows do not draw the shades when they change the clothes
on the female dummies. I demand, in the name of this city's
outraged womanhood, that for every female dummy so exposed
a male dummy be likewise exposed."

The managing editor of the *News,* Douglas Turney, who'd
hired me, was a widely read man and a fiction writer. (He was
the most intellectual managing editor I ever worked for—a
strange, bitter man with a thwarted talent for writing, whose life
ended in suicide.) We became good friends and often discussed
books we both liked. Doug instituted a weekly book page on the
News and gave it to me to edit. It was called "Turning the Pages
with Martha Foley." The page not only provided me with a lot
of books but also involved me in correspondence with New York
publishers, whom I considered next to God in *literary* importance.
Boni and Liveright, well known for progressive publishing, was
the first firm I contacted. A Boni brother sent an encouraging
letter, promising an ad and books for review. He considered my
book page a valuable experiment, he said, because so little was
done to promote books on the West Coast. I received books from
other publishers, but Boni's was the only advertisement.

There was no shortage of good fiction writers in Los Angeles.
Since I hoped to become a successful fiction writer myself, I
sympathized with their despair over the dwindling market for
stories. The previous year H.L. Mencken and George Jean Nathan had abandoned editing the *Smart Set,* which was mainly

devoted to fiction by important writers, to found *The American Mercury*, where they would emphasize factual writing and "the sociological article." As a New Englander used to the staid, dull yellow of the old *Atlantic Monthly*, I had been repelled by the *Smart Set*'s tawdry covers, which I associated with a trashy pulp. I was surprised when told that *Smart Set* writers had included George Moore, D.H. Lawrence, James Joyce, Ford Madox Ford, and F. Scott Fitzgerald.

The immediate great success of *The American Mercury*, with its bright green cover, made other magazines prefer articles to stories. Quality magazines, like *The Atlantic Monthly, Harper's, Scribner's, Forum,* and *Century*, which had been printing as many as eight short stories in a single issue, began to reduce the number sharply. Smaller-circulation literary magazines, *The Southern Literary Messenger, Southern Review,* and *Sewanee Review*, devoted more space to critical than to creative writing. Some of the better "slicks," the *Saturday Evening Post* and *Collier's*, as well as some of the women's magazines, *Pictorial Review, Woman's Home Companion, McCall's, Ladies' Home Journal*, continued to print fiction, some of it distinguished, but not regularly. "Give me facts!" demanded Gradgrind, that "eminently practical man," in Dickens's *Hard Times*. "Give us facts!" echoed American magazine editors, pleasing the Babbitts and relegating fiction to the already obscure position of poetry.

Doug Turney had been a fiction contributor to the *Smart Set*. One afternoon during a lull in the city room, he bemoaned, as he had many times before, the withering away of fiction markets. I commiserated. Then I had a brainstorm. "Let's you and I start a serious fiction magazine!" I exclaimed.

Doug's face brightened for a moment, but then he shook his head and said slowly, "No-o-o . . . I can't. I've got 'Me and My Wife' to look after." ("Me and My Wife" was a witty dialogue between a husband and wife that he'd been writing for the *News* and hoped to get syndicated nationally.) We dropped the idea.

Just as the *Los Angeles Daily News* was beginning to break even financially, Vanderbilt, in his overwhelming eagerness to be an important newspaper publisher, started a second paper, the *Herald,* in San Francisco, and soon after, the *Tab* in Miami. Like the *News,* they were circumspect, unsensational tabloids. The expansion proved to be a mistake. The new papers drained the successful *News* and were eventually to wreck the entire Vanderbilt enterprise. "Well," Doug Turney would say to me, "we might as well make the best of this, Martha, for we'll never see another paper like this again."

Mort Donoghue was transferred to San Francisco to be feature editor of the new *Herald,* and I was promoted to his job. I was put in charge of all the pages that carried features (editorial, society, women's household, and comics), and of the people who worked on them. In addition, I still had my beloved weekly book page, for which I wrote many of the reviews. If it now seems as if a girl in her twenties was very young to have such responsibility, I should note that everyone on the *News,* from our twenty-seven-year-old publisher on down, was young. Only two men in the city room—the drama critic and one of the comic-strip artists—were over thirty.

We were a strange and unique staff. Eleanor Barnes, one of the best newspaperwomen I have ever known, was there, and Havemeyers and Marshall Fields floated around the city room, getting "a thrill out of the game." Their life was not made any too happy for them at times by a jolly round balloon of a man named Douglas Churchill (later Hollywood correspondent for the *New York Times*), who was Vanderbilt's assistant. One earnest young millionaire was ordered by Churchill to keep in touch with the city desk at all times, even if he just went around the corner or across the street. "A big story might break at any minute," Churchill said, "and they'd need you." The young millionaire complied.

Several of Vanderbilt's other Social Register friends had

joined him on the paper, and some were younger than he. One was Cappy Crawford, niece of Marshall Field of Chicago merchandising fame, who was my assistant. She offered to work for nothing, saying she didn't need the money. I protested that it was unfair to others who had to earn their living, and this time Deputy Sheriff Foley's socialist principles prevailed—Cappy was paid a standard salary. She was a pleasant, hardworking girl, and we became good friends. She had brought a lavish wardrobe from her uncle's Chicago store. The price of one of her hand-sewn, hand-embroidered slips would have paid for three of my dresses. Generously, she offered to share her things with me; for the first time in my life I went to parties garbed in elegant *haute couture.*

Contrary to the attitudes of newspapermen elsewhere, the men on the *News* were friendly toward the four women on the city room staff. When I happened to mention how I hated my blob of a nose, "Doc" Wilkinson, a rewrite man and medical student, eagerly offered to bob it for me free the very next day. It would give him a chance to practice the new science of plastic surgery, he urged. I was strongly tempted. I came across his obituary not long ago. There was no mention of plastic surgery. For years he had been publisher of the gossipy film paper, *The Hollywood Reporter.* I felt my nose with relief. It remains a blob, but it is still there.

No smog hung over California in 1925, and the brilliant blue of the Pacific Ocean reflected the clear, clean blue of the sky; blue too were the lupin blossoms sharing the hillsides with the sunbright golden poppies. At night the air was pure and sweet for young lovers, of whom I was one, unmolested and blissful in the shadowy canyons. I was happy, happier than I had ever been before in my life, and wanted no change. But change came.

One evening after work when I was about to leave—Ed Skinner, a copy editor from Texas, standing by to take me to dinner —the phone on my desk rang. "Hello," said a vaguely familiar voice. "This is Whit Burnett. Can you have dinner with me?" I was startled. And curious. The last time I had seen Whit Burnett he'd seemed to detest me. Like myself, he'd worked on the San Francisco copydesk. Quoting from H.L. Mencken's book, *In Defense of Women,* I had criticized Mencken for being antifeminist. "Hell!" said Whit, who sat directly across from me. "Mencken's damn good. He bought two stories from me for the *Smart Set.*"

I had studied Whit. Until that moment he had seemed an ordinary sort of good-looking, blond young man. Not the sort you would think had any special ability, literary or otherwise. He did, it was true, wear corduroy pants, which were unusual for a newspaperman. I associated them with painters. There *is* something odd about him, I told myself, but what it was I was unable to say. Whit evidently thought it was I who was odd. During one of our discussions, on every point of which we disagreed, he told me, "I've never met a girl like you." I felt as if he considered me a freak.

Now here he was in another city, suddenly calling me up and asking me to dinner. "It's Whit Burnett, a boy I knew in San Francisco," I said to Ed. "He wants to take me to dinner. Do you mind?" Ed didn't mind. He never really minded anything I said or did.

Later that evening, when I met Whit in the small, cheap restaurant he suggested, I was shocked. He was seriously ill. His face was flushed with fever, his eyes watered, and his hand trembled as he put it out to shake mine. He told me he had worked his way from Salt Lake City on a cattle train and had had no sleep for several nights. As the freight cars swerved around curves, the cattle would fall down on one another, and it had been his job to keep them upright. He was broke and looking for work. He remembered a telegram I had once sent to a man he knew in Salt Lake City, offering a job, and he now asked if I could give him a job. But he was in no condition to work. I asked where he was staying. It was in a fifty-cent a night rooming house in the Mexican quarter.

I called Ed Skinner and told him about Whit. He came in his car to the restaurant, and we took Whit to Ed's apartment and called a doctor. Whit had the flu, and the doctor told him to stay in bed for at least a week. That night he and Ed shared the bedroom and I slept on a couch in the living room, to help in case Whit's condition got worse.

When I returned to the *News*, I tried to tell Doug Turney how sick Whit was, but I never got a chance. "Whit Burnett's in town and looking for a job—" I started, but Doug cut me off with, "Whit Burnett will never get a job on this paper while I'm here!" and turned and walked away from me. He did not speak to me for several days, except in connection with work. Then one afternoon he came across the city room and half-sat on a corner of my desk. "Burnett's no good," he declared abruptly. "His father is a good man, but his son—what he did—" Again Doug broke off what he was about to say and walked away.

I asked Whit what the trouble was between him and Doug. He was as evasive as Doug had been. "Nothing to write home about," he said. "I worked on the *Salt Lake Tribune* when he was editor there. We didn't get along."

"But surely from the way Doug sounds there must have been something wrong," I said.

"No, just different temperaments."

That was that. I never did find out, although I did hear a secondhand, disjointed rumor to the effect that Doug had helped Whit with his fiction writing and that Whit had reciprocated by making Doug a homosexual in a story. The suggestion was silly.

After a couple of weeks in Ed's apartment, Whit was better, and he made the rounds of other Los Angeles papers looking for work. There were no openings. He decided to hitchhike to San Francisco. I asked how much money he had, and he told me twelve dollars. I suggested that if he didn't get on a San Francisco paper, he should try the East Coast, where there were a great many more papers, eleven in New York City alone, and I offered to lend him the fare.

A San Francisco paper did hire him as a temporary replacement for a man on vacation but then let him go. He came back south to Los Angeles, and I lent him a hundred dollars for fare on a freighter bound for New York, through the Panama Canal. It must have been a pretty rugged trip, for he sent me a postcard from the canal and mentioned that rats had eaten a pair of his shoes. In New York he landed a job as copyreader on the *Times* and wrote that he almost lost it the first day because he thought someone on the *Times* was pulling his leg. He'd thrown away a piece of copy because he didn't believe there could be in Maine, or anywhere else, a place called Kennebunkport.

It had been a long time since I'd seen my family in Boston, and I asked for a month's leave of absence to visit them. Doug Turney told me the paper would continue my pay while I was gone, and that I would find it waiting for me when I returned. I stopped in New York to change trains, and Whit met me in the station. "I think I'm falling in love with you," he said. I did not go on to Boston or back to Los Angeles.

TWO

∽

WHIT AND THE
NEW YORK TABLOIDS

In the days when I worked on tabloids in New York City, Phil
Payne, the managing editor who was the genius of tabloid
journalism—called Mr. Tabloid—was still alive. Every girl en-
meshed in scandal really was beautiful to him, and every rich man
was a multimillionaire. Phil was a happy little man, who, as befit-
ted a genius of sensational journalism, married Miss New York.

The papers Phil edited went to press to the rhythm of "Yessir,
She's My Baby!" It was the only tune that Phil, who was half-deaf,
knew; and he hummed it over and over again, from the moment
he got to the office till the time he left. "A young lady copyreader!
What next?" Payne teased, but he hired me as a caption writer,
and was undoubtedly the only managing editor in the city at the
time who would have done so. A *New York Times Book Review*
writer noted that I was the first woman newspaper copyreader in
New York, and a historian of the *Paris Herald* said "Miss Foley
. . . was the only girl in the history of the *Paris Herald* who could
sit down at a desk and hold up her end at reading copy." Malcolm
Cowley's lament that, with the new freedom of expression in
literature, women were learning "men's private language," gave
me a clue to the widespread prejudice against women copyread-

ers. Sitting around the big table called a "desk," with mugs of coffee or spiked prohibition "near beer," making ribald comments as they edited the day's news, male copyreaders enjoyed a grand, uninhibited stag party.

Caption writing differed from copyreading (whose function is clearer from the title given it in England, where it is called "subediting") since it required no editing; still, as a caption writer, besides composing headlines, I had to write an account, in a limited number of words, of each news event that was illustrated by a picture. Carbon copies of all news stories were channeled to me for that purpose. The makeup editor sent me layouts of the picture pages, including front and back pages and the "double truck" or centerfold. On these pages were drawn the size and position where the photographs would be placed, and beside the outlines were numbers. If the number were a generous forty or sixty I was happy. If it were a stingy twenty or thirty, I shuddered. Those figures stipulated the number of words I was allowed to use in a caption. And, as in headline writing, an *m* or a *w* counted as a word and a half, whereas an *i* or an *l* measured half a word. More difficult, the rule on the *News* was that readers needed only the picture pages to know what was going on in the world, so that the captions had, perforce, to be digests of the news events. Skill under pressure was imperative. Weekly prizes were awarded for the best news story, photograph, and so on. One week I won ten dollars for the best headline, and my prize-winning caption gives an idea of the literary heights to which the *News* sometimes soared. Over a picture of a cow standing near a burning barn, my headline, in big type, read, "THIS BOSSY ALMOST ROAST BEEF."

Part of a caption writer's duty was to stand before the printer's "stone," the table on which page forms of type are composed, and indicate where photoengraving cuts of the various pictures should go. Union rules allowed me only to point and never to touch either the cuts or type. With the type to be read mirror-fashion and the picture also in reverse, mistakes were easy. The previous winter, I heard, an unfortunate caption writer had written the kind of caption that delighted Payne's heart. "Oh, Boys and Girls! Look who's come to town! Santa Claus with a big sack of Toys!" Above the caption was no picture of a department store Santa Claus. Instead it showed, in full ecclesiastical regalia, Cardinal Spellman. The caption writer's job was saved only because a rival morning paper had a sports caption that read, "If good old John L. Sullivan had been in the ring last night, this is the mighty punch he would have thrown." Instead of showing John L. throwing a "mighty punch," there stood the pope with hands upraised in a papal blessing.

When Payne hired me and explained my duties, he mentioned that I would be doing captions for all the pictures, including sports. The entire back page of the *News* was devoted to sports pictures. I told Payne that I didn't know anything about sports. "Don't worry," he reassured me. "Just ask Paul and Peg. They'll take care of you." "Paul" was Paul Gallico (not yet the well-known popular writer), and "Peg" was Westbrook Pegler (whose love/hate obsession with Eleanor Roosevelt, which he pursued in a widely syndicated column, also lay in the future).

My debut in the *Daily News* sports department was not auspicious. Never having watched any baseball game, I badly needed information for a caption about that day's event. "Jesus! A dame!" said Paul to Peg, or maybe it was Peg to Paul. "Payne is nuts!" Their mutterings and moans when they discovered how ignorant I was made me more confused. Somehow, though, my caption passed muster when printed. All I remember of it is that it expressed profound admiration for "artists of the diamond." Paul's and Peg's act was repeated every time I went, with fear and trembling, into their den. (How I yearned for friendly, easygoing Bob Cronin, the sports editor of the *Los Angeles Daily News!*) Those daily verbal assaults in the sports department were not the only reason for my looking back longingly at the sunny Los Angeles city room three thousand miles away, where I'd held the best job I had ever known. The New York job was turning out to be the worst in every respect. But Whit and I had signed a lease for an apartment in Greenwich Village, and it was too late to turn back.

The modestly priced apartment on a quiet side street was expensively furnished in excellent taste. The young woman who owned it belonged to a rich Philadelphia family and was leaving for six months in Europe. She was terribly worried about her ashtrays. Apologetically, she asked it it would be all right if she took them with her, she treasured them so. I looked around at the lovely paintings on the walls, the fine furniture and rugs, and consented.

The apartment also had two bedrooms, and Whit and I considered this of extreme importance. Fannie Hurst, whose early short stories were so superior to her later best-selling works, had caused a sensation by announcing she was married, and that she and her musician-husband had separate residences. "In this way," she declared, "we'll never get bored with each other. Our marriage will never go stale." Whit and I decided we would improve upon Fannie's idea by not getting married at all. Two apartments, however, were beyond our means. We were sharing expenses fifty-fifty, and one apartment with two bedrooms seemed the next best thing.

Our arrangement worked out well, and Whit was pleased with my cooking. It was an orderly existence, with Whit each day going uptown to his job on the *Times* and I going in the opposite direction to Park Row and the *News*. Whit's job paid less than mine because salaries on the dignified *Times* were much lower than on the raffish *News*. At first, Whit did no writing, which was a disappointment to me. An attraction of the two-bedroom plan had been my vision of each of us writing in quiet seclusion. But neither did I do much writing. I kept house and cooked and hostessed parties for newspaper friends and paid half of the expenses. "Going Dutch" was not the common custom it is today, and I was told that I was destroying Whit's incentive.

I once heard a man say of a friend's relationship with a woman, "She has him by the balls." I never heard it said of a woman's relationship with a man, "He has her by the womb." But there are many situations, it seems to me, where a man has captured a woman's maternal instinct, not by giving her a child but by presenting himself for mothering. I was two years older than Whit, far too young to be his mother, but his need to be cared for was so desperate that I abandoned Ed Skinner, who adored me but who, I felt, was self-sufficient, to answer Whit's need. Did I destroy Whit's incentive? How do you not destroy the incentive of one who comes to you sick and broke off a cattle train? By letting him die?

Did a woman destroy James Joyce's incentive? Every copy of *Ulysses* and *Finnegan's Wake* could be labeled "Thanks to Harriet Weaver." A rich Englishwoman and a communist, she not only financed Joyce's writing but also endowed his family so that he might be completely free from money worries. Joyce got a lot of mothering. There was Nora, the patient woman who tolerated his temperamental ways, living with him for many years and bearing him two children, before she and Joyce were married; and among other women who helped him, the most important was, of course, Sylvia Beach, the owner of the bookshop Shakespeare & Company, who published Joyce when no commercial publisher would. Was Joyce weakened because he accepted the help of women?

Poor Whit did not have Joyce's luck. If only he could have laughed, I often thought, life would have been so much pleasanter for him! But laughter, even a quiet chuckle, was impossible for him, and he never smiled. Much of his talk that antagonized people would not have seemed harsh if had it been softened with a smile. I still wonder why there was always that somber look on his face. Didn't his mother smile at him when he was a baby, and didn't he smile back? (His mother loved him. She died while

Whit was in the hospital for an appendicitis operation; her very last words were, "Do you think Whit is comfortable now?") Or was Whit's mournful expression due to his blaming himself for his younger brother's death, and feeling, perhaps unconsciously, that he had no right to look happy? Theirs was a normal sibling rivalry, except that the brother died after Whit, a little boy jealous because he had scarlet fever and his brother didn't, rubbed his rash-inflamed hands over his brother's face and body. I've often imagined a scene where Whit's brother died and his mother broke down. "Look!" people must have told her, "Look, you still have a wonderful boy. You have Whit!" And maybe, in her uncontrollable grief, she cried out, "I don't want Whit! I want Quentin!" And maybe Whit heard.

But that is my own private imagining, and not the scene as it was written in Whit's finest short story, "Sherril." There the story is movingly told from the point of view of a small boy. The child, overcome by feelings of guilt, promises God he will live the kind of splendid life his brother would have lived if he had not murdered him.

Many times Whit's face, though still unsmiling, did have a look of utter bliss; this was when he played one of the many musical instruments he collected—violins, violas, bassoons, guitars, even two pianos, an upright and a grand. We went to surprisingly few concerts. Whit wasn't interested in listening to music; he wanted to play it. If his hand hadn't been maimed in childhood, when he thrust it between the rollers of his mother's washing machine, he told me, he would have become a musician. My own musical education had been neglected. I could no more read a musical score than Whit could read the classical Greek and Latin texts I'd studied at the Boston Girls' Latin School. Music was vital to Whit—it was an essential part of his life that he was unable to share with me.

On the other hand, I could not interest Whit in socialism, pacifism, equal rights for blacks and women, the then crying need for a child labor law, or any social injustice. Not even the Sacco-Vanzetti case, which was arousing the fury of most of our leading writers and inspiring poems, plays, and short stories, moved him. He listened patiently to me, though, until one day I told him I thought I might use a pseudonym. Then his attitude became plain. He said, "Make it Martha Quixote."

Whit's lack of social conscience was due, partly, to the incredibly narrow provincialism of life in Utah in the early part of this century. "When I was a kid I thought Jews had horns," he shocked me by saying once, after I'd introduced him to Mike Gold, whom I'd known when he was a reporter on the *Boston Herald*. "That's what everybody around me in Salt Lake believed."

"And Negroes? What did they have, tails?"

"You guessed it. That's why they were forbidden to become Mormons."

While most of Whit's relatives remained Mormons, Whit's immediate family became apostates—Jack Mormons—after his grandmother chased a Mormon bishop who had ordered her husband to marry a second time out of the house with a broomstick, screaming at him, "I'll have no second wife in my home!"

As the year wore on into a record-breaking hot summer, I found that I could no longer endure the *News.* I wondered, while I wrote my captions for the ever-lurid pictures, how a man who had once felt so strongly about good for all people could stoop to corrupting them with sensationalized sex and crime. (Joseph Medill Patterson, founder of the *News,* had once been an ardently active socialist, a socialist member of the Illinois legislature and the Chicago commissioner of public works; he had written socialist propaganda novels and plays.) Still, sensational as those pictures and news accounts then seemed, they were mild compared with those now printed and shown on television (fragmented corpses, policemen shooting helpless prisoners, napalm-drenched children). Our loss of empathy might be suggested by the large number of indignant letters the *News* received when it printed a photograph of a sand pit in which a child had been buried alive, the child's small hand sticking out from under the avalanche of sand. "No more gruesome pix" was the order immediately given news cameramen.

I toiled in misery. Paul and Peg became more and more insulting; there was a general lack of kindness throughout the organization; the strain of writing captions under pressure for two editions, and the incessant worry that I had made mistakes—all this left me, when I reached our apartment late in the evening, too exhausted to eat dinner, too exhausted to sleep. When I did sleep my sleep was an endless series of nightmares. At the end of my first month I called up the paper and resigned. They asked me to reconsider, so I tried again for a while, but things were no better.

On Whit's day off from the *Times,* we hiked out into the country, with no special destination. At a place called Wappingers Falls—a name that amused me as much as Kennebunkport had amused Whit—I sent a telegram, resigning for a second time from the *New York Daily News.* This time it was final.

The end of that summer, then, found me without a job and with my savings gone. Hearst, who had been eyeing the success of the *News,* started his own New York tabloid, the *Mirror,* and bought Payne away from the *News.* I went to Payne and told him I needed a job. Before I could explain that I wanted to do reporting, Payne said, "Swell. I need a caption writer." Damn! I thought, but didn't say. Economic determinism prevailed.

As soon as I was introduced (on my first day) to Dan Parker, the sports editor, and saw his smile and felt his warm handshake, I knew that things on the *Mirror* were going to be all right. And they were. I heard laughter (which had been nonexistent in the other city room), and staff people, both men and women, came to my desk to make me feel welcome. The printers, with whom

I worked on only one edition, fit my image of printers exactly—
they were the friendliest of men.

Payne's singing "Yessir, She's My Baby!" guided the *Mirror*
to press just as it had the *News.* There was a difference, though.
The baby herself, Miss New York, was often in the *Mirror* city
room, perched on a desk, chatting with reporters and rewrite
men. It was a measure of the paper's relaxed atmosphere. A more
intoxicating reason for the city room's geniality was the proximity
of a popular speakeasy. A fire escape at the rear of the city room
adjoined a fire escape at the rear of the speakeasy. Many men on
the *Mirror* never came or left the paper by any other route. One
of them, George Buchanan, once returned from an assignment on
the day's biggest story, went straight to his typewriter, and started
pounding away. After it appeared that quite a few words had been
written, George McDonald, the city editor, ordered a copyboy,
"Get a take from Buck!" The boy came back emptyhanded and
bewildered. "Sorry, sir," he told George, "Mr. Buchanan doesn't
have any paper in his typewriter."

Payne's was not the only love life that titillated the *Mirror*
staff. We kept close track of our publisher William Randolph
Hearst's great romance with Marion Davies. As long as new
photographs of the actress kept coming to us regularly from California, we knew there was rapture in the castle at San Simeon. If
no new picture arrived and we were ordered not to use old ones,
then we knew there had been a quarrel. If orders came to feature
pictures of some other actress, we knew the trouble was serious.

George McDonald, the city editor, showed a fatherly protec-
tiveness toward me. "You are too young," he would tell me when
I asked why I hadn't received dupes of some such story as the fight
of the Rhinelander family to annul the marriage of a son to a black
girl. George did not know how thin was the wall between my
desk and the art department's darkroom, where the men liked to
gather. Until then I had not known how important mathematics
was to sex. What I heard mostly from the other side of the wall

was the question, "How many times?" If the number went up from "two" or "three"—there didn't seem to be any "one"—to "eight" or "ten" there were gasps of awe. Over and over again. It was not shocking—it was a bore.

Arthur Brisbane, whose editorials millions devoured daily, was the most popular editorial writer of the period and the man closest to the owner of the vast Hearst newspaper chain. The newspaper grapevine reported that he was furious over Payne's growing popularity with Hearst. Brisbane's jealousy was so extreme that some blamed it for Payne's eventual death. An incident that occurred one Saturday, when the editorial office was closed, did nothing to lessen Brisbane's enmity. One of the older copyboys was left in charge. He occupied himself by playing editor, leaning back in George McDonald's big swivel chair with his feet on the city desk, and answering telephone calls in an authoritative voice. A messenger arrived with Brisbane's batch of editorials for the week ahead. "What are these, manuscripts?" the office boy demanded. Told yes, the office boy scrawled across the top one, "*The Daily Mirror* does not accept unsolicited manuscripts," and ordered the messenger, "Take them back!"

One day I noticed a pallid wisp of a teen-aged girl cowering on a chair in a corner. I paid no attention, thinking her a timid visitor appalled by the pandemonium of a newspaper city room. When she was there the next day I asked who she was. She was the daughter of Mrs. Mills, the choir singer who had been found murdered in New Jersey along with the Reverend Doctor Hall, an Episcopalian minister. The *Mirror* was keeping her in its custody because Payne lived in New Jersey and had learned of new evidence. He was reopening the case and needed her help. Sad, scared child, it was she who needed help.

When the *Mirror* exploded onto the streets with the new evidence it declared proved that the minister's rich widow and other members of her socially prominent family were guilty of the murders, the intense excitement sold thousands of extra copies. They were arrested and held for trial.

The Hall-Mills case is my favorite murder mystery. It is far and away a greater American tragedy than that which is the basis for Dreiser's popular novel. Its psychological, social, and economic dimensions are tremendous. Its cast of characters is Dickensian: the romance-starved housewife who is a choir singer and the equally romance-missing rich dowager; the meek little janitor husband who shovels coal into a basement furnace while over his head an adulterous minister preaches sermons from an elevated pulpit; the dowager's half-witted brother who is the town character (with a passion for jelly beans); the old "Pig Woman" who patrols her small farm at midnight to fend off poachers from stealing her swine; the dowager's lady's maid who provided her mistress with an alibi for the murder night; and the lady's maid's estranged husband, who startles the judge at their divorce trial by declaring that the alibi was perjury—thus breaking open the murder case. Not to mention the array of corporation executives, Wall Street brokers, and assorted Social Registerites, also involved as relatives or witnesses. And shocked parishioners, some weeping, of Dr. Hall's church.

Like something out of Hawthorne was the setting—the typical puritanical small town, placid by day but with strange doings at night. Too many of its respected citizens were out in De Russey's Lane, the scene of the murder, on that fated bloodstained night when they should have been in their beds. All seemed to have been in illicit pairs of one kind or another. (An incestuous father and his daughter were the first suspects arrested, but they were soon freed. Other pairs included a church deacon and a married woman, several locally prominent businessmen with women not their wives, and one with a male lover.) Virtue was also in the neighborhood of the lane, represented by none other than members of the Ku Klux Klan, out on a morals crusade.

A chilling, tantalizing aspect of the murders was that, while Mrs. Mills, like Dr. Hall, had been shot to death, her throat had been slashed and the vocal organs mutilated. Someone made sure that she would never sing a love song for the minister again.

Popular opinion decided it was the cruelty of a woman, on fire with jealousy. The police, who had seen bodies of rape victims mutilated by their male attackers, did not jump to the conclusion that only a woman would so avenge herself. They were equally suspicious of Mrs. Hall and Mr. Mills, the singer's husband, and the latter was held for long investigation.

Whoever did it wanted the body of the minister quickly identified, for his calling card was propped against his feet. Love letters written by the two were also scattered on the ground about them. The letters told, ecstatically, of plans for a flight to Japan. They made sad reading. Sad, too, was the thought of what that flight would mean to those left behind: a cuckolded husband left to care for two young children; the children themselves, their lives broken in half; and a proud woman, not without a heart (as was proved by the tender lifelong care she gave her retarded brother), abandoned to the realization that her sanctimonious husband had loved not her but her money. (A beautiful short story by Robert McLaughlin has the nearest thing to a universal title I know, for it applied, as here, to every human situation: "Poor Everybody.")

I wrote hundreds of captions about the murders. The *Mirror,* proud of its scoop in being the first to publish the doubts about Mrs. Hall's alibi, ran many extra picture pages in addition to the usual tabloid practice of front, back, and two centerfold ones.

"Wait 'til Willie gets on the stand! He'll spill the beans!" Everyone anticipated, with glee, the day Willie would be cross-examined. Smiling his perpetual, good-natured smile, waving a pudgy hand at people he knew in the court, Willie settled his soft, fat body, well-nourished by the jelly beans sent to him in jail, in the witness chair, and beamed at the prosecuting attorney. He never faltered in the answers he gave, in the friendliest of voices, and he tried to help the flustered prosecutor when the latter mixed up dates. Willie was the star of the trial. Not even the deathbed testimony of the old Pig Woman, dying of cancer (she was brought in on a stretcher to swear she had seen the defendants at the crime scene while she was defending her pigs), overcame Willie's.

Thanks to him, Mrs. Hall, her cousin, and Willie himself were acquitted. The family immediately brought suit for libel against the *Mirror* and Hearst. Over the years since there have been many theories (the latest one accusing the Klan of the murders), but the mystery has never been solved. Ten years later, Henry Paynter, a *Mirror* writer who had caused a sensation of his own during the investigation, told me he was thinking of writing a book about the case. Like everybody else, Henry had been sure that Willie could be induced to reveal incriminating facts about the murders. Henry had gone unshaven for several days, put on ragged old clothes, stuffed the pockets with jelly beans, and, waving an empty whiskey bottle in each hand, raced yelling down the town's main street, scaring dogs and old ladies. He was arrested as he planned but was put in a distant cell, far from Willie's, and had to eat the jelly beans himself.

Later, Henry and I drove out to New Jersey on a Sunday morning. After visiting De Russey's Lane, no longer a rustic rendezvous for lovers, we went to Dr. Hall's Episcopal church, arriving in time for the morning service. We took seats in the rear. The choir filed into their places, and the organist sounded the opening chords of a hymn; then the door opened, and a tall, regal woman, richly dressed, swept in. Henry nudged me. It was Mrs. Hall, and the way she made her entrance was a definite challenge—"I defy you to think I murdered them!" With her was a maid, who (as they sat down in a pew), gave Mrs. Hall one of two prayer books she carried.

Had Phil Payne been downcast by the acquittal and libel suit? Not he! He was already deep in the newest tabloid sensation, a clean one for a change, but one that would lead eventually to his tabloid-style death—the record-breaking historic airplane flights of that era. "The Flying Fool! Call Him the Flying Fool!" Payne went from city desk to copydesk, to the row of reporters' and rewrite men's desks, to the sports department and to the society and drama departments, to the picture desk and to my caption desk, giving the order. "It's going to be a big, a big, big head, Martha," he told me. "No type. Art department job." That meant that a hand-drawn headline would take up a good part of the front page. "Flying Fool" was the most sensational name he could think of for Charles Lindbergh, who had arrived in New York and was flying out immediately and alone for Europe.

Lindbergh inspired Payne to emulate him. He would be the first man to fly from New York to Rome, where, as a Catholic, he would bring greetings from the president to the pope. Two well-known pilots and a navigator were to accompany him.

The takeoff was splendidly smooth, watched by a large crowd. But a few hours later came the S.O.S. The plane was down off the Newfoundland coast. Frenzied arguments ensued at the *Mirror* and over the Hearst telephone network to California. Henry Paynter, who had piloting experience, wanted to charter a fishing vessel to go to the position given by the plane. Others insisted it was hopeless, that the plane would be sunk in the rough waters by the time a boat could reach it. Brisbane was undecided. After hours of bitter discussion, Henry Paynter chartered a boat of his own. Its crew found the plane. They were too late. The men were gone. The disaster was on page one of every paper in the country. If he had to die to do it, Phil Payne, a brave man, still made sensational news.

THREE

⟳

PARIS
IN THE TWENTIES

W hen I taught at Columbia, I had an oversimplified definition of what a short story writer does, and this was the way
I put it: "I'm telling you about some interesting people I have
known, how they became what they were, what they did, what
happened to them when they did it, and how they felt about what
happened to them." And that, I suppose, is what I'm doing here,
in telling the story of *STORY*.

Sometime in 1927, the *Times* gave Whit two weeks' notice. It
was being comparatively kind; many papers in those pre-Newspa-
per Guild days gave no notice when they fired a man. The loss
of Whit's job coincided with the termination of our lease, and
instead of renting another apartment, we decided that since Whit
had not been writing—and since Paris sounded both wonderful
and cheap—he should go to Europe and do nothing but write, for
as long as his money lasted. A few months later, I received a leave
of absence from the *Mirror* and went over to visit him.

The night before I was to sail, I had a nightmare in which I
stood before a high, dark wall on the other side of which was a
terrible place called Europe, full of horrors. So frightening was

the dream that I almost changed my mind. But Whit was waiting for me, so I went. Had Whit not lost his job, had our lease not expired, had he not been writing, had the *Mirror* not granted me a leave of absence, had Paris not been so inviting—the story of *STORY* might never have come to pass.

The boat stopped on its way to France in the English harbor of Portsmouth. It was five o'clock in the morning on a fair day, and I stood on the deck for my first sight of Europe. The beauty of the small harbor, the endearing quaintness of the low buildings along the waterfront, the gray old castle on the greenest of hills, the calling seagulls and the soft English air, the gentle ambience of it all, made me feel that I had come home.

Whit met me at Boulogne. "Late as usual," he said, with his solemn expression.

"I'm going right back!" I answered, trying to be as serious as he looked, and I actually turned to go back up the gangplank.

"Hey!" He grabbed me then, twisted me around, and kissed me. We spent the night in Boulogne. I did not know what the sounds were I heard during the night in the street outside the hotel until Whit told me they were *sabots*—the clatter of wooden shoes on cobblestones; and that, for me, was further enchantment.

In the morning we took the train for Paris. Paris! What can I say, what can anyone say, though thousands have tried, that will do that beautiful city justice? Like everyone, I have known much pain in my life, some terrible things have befallen me; but when I remember that, when I was young, I was blessed with three glorious years in Paris, I rejoice.

Whit had written a couple of short stories that he had not been able to sell, and his money was gone. I had a letter of introduction to Jay Allen, the Paris *Chicago Tribune* correspondent, who suggested I try for a job on the *Paris Herald.* I went to see the people there. All they could offer me, they said, was a couple of weeks' work on a travel supplement. Maybe later. . . . But when the two weeks of work were up, we didn't have enough money to wait for "later." I still had my job at the *Mirror,* so we returned to America. That is, Whit may have come back. I didn't—not all of me. My heart stayed in Paris. Saving to return, I begrudged spending a single penny of my earnings. Because the Great Depression in the 1930s was so much worse, it is forgotten that there was also a depression in the mid-1920s. The only job Whit could find was a bleak wire-service position with the Associated Press. Except for their foreign correspondents and feature writers, most of their employees loathed the belt-line routine of the big press services. Whit became assistant city editor.

The minute I counted my savings and found they finally had reached five hundred dollars—enough at the then unbelievably favorable rate to live comfortably for five months in Paris—I did not wait for Whit to come home to our furnished room. I startled him by phoning him at the Associated Press office to tell him I was leaving for Paris on the next boat. He was dazed when, the following day, he saw me off on an old Cunard liner.

I had planned exactly what I was going to do in Paris as soon as I got settled in a hotel room, and I did it. First I went to the Shakespeare & Company bookshop (more like a charming living room than a store—with the open fire on its hearth) to let its owner, Sylvia Beach, with whom I had become friends on my first trip, know that I was back, and to buy a copy of *Ulysses.* Sylvia was a gentle, unbusinesslike woman, not the kind you would picture running a successful store. That is probably why she, when no "businesslike" publisher would touch it, undertook the heroic task of publishing Joyce's *Ulysses.* As a student I'd first become enthralled with Joyce when I came across his writing in *The Little Review,* a magazine burned several times by the United States Post Office, a fact I did not know at the time. *Ulysses* had been banned by the United States Customs from importation. So were any alcoholic beverages. Literary and spirituous smuggling, then, became as respectable crimes as moonshining in the South. Returning from my first European trip, I sneaked past the New York

"Revenooers" my copy of *Ulysses* and a bottle of cognac, each wrapped in a nightgown. The cognac vanished at our first Village party; the copy of *Ulysses* I left with Whit. In picking up a replacement in Sylvia's shop, I bought the first issue of a new magazine called *transition*. The table of contents was headed: "JAMES JOYCE: Opening Pages of a Work in Progress."

At four o'clock, the time I knew both the publisher and the managing editor would be at the *Paris Herald,* I crossed the Seine to Les Halles, the ancient marketplace of Paris. I walked along narrow streets jammed with disputatious farmers and their carts, the sidewalks a dumping ground for vegetables, dairy products, haunches of meat, and live poultry, to where, in the midst of the odorous uproar, the *Herald*'s editorial office was located in a rickety building. I asked for a permanent job and was hired.

As the only woman in the city room, I became a maid-of-all-work. I reported (making sure I personally got to interview every book publisher who came to town, hoping some day they might want to publish me); I went through the French papers looking for items of interest to Paris Americans; I rewrote local, telegraph, and cable reports; I read copy and sometimes substituted briefly at the city desk—and I censored Ezra Pound's mail. Daily the *Herald* received from Pound a letter or postcard, and some days both, laden with maledictions, obscene and scatological, upon persons and events reported in the paper, as well as upon the paper itself. I was instructed, if I found nothing printable, to toss them in the wastebasket, which I did with the great majority of his angry scrawls.

Like most people at the time, I thought of the Nazis as a gang of street-corner hoodlums, headed by a clown with a Charlie Chaplin mustache, who tried to start a revolution in a beer hall. I was startled, then, to see names of prominent American and British financiers and corporations mixed in with mention of the National Socialist Workers' party (the formal title of the Nazis' organization). The reason for their interest was Hitler's opposition to Marxists and trade unions. They expected the Nazis to be a bulwark against the Soviets. History was to prove again the fallacy of assuming that because someone is an enemy of your enemy he is your friend. "Between 1924 and 1930," according to William Shirer in *The Rise and Fall of the Third Reich,* "German borrowing amounted to seven billion dollars and most of it came from American investors, who gave little thought to how the Germans might make eventual repayment. The Germans gave even less thought to it." Much of the money was used by the German Republican government for legitimate purposes, but my reading the Sunday night Berlin reports showed that a lot went to the Nazis. (It was my job to rewrite the weekly German financial dispatch, for printing in the Monday morning *Herald* and *N.Y. Herald-Tribune.* German telegraph operators garbled its English, and were followed by the French, who added their own wonderful financial flourishes. My job required not only rewriting but deciphering.) What I learned was to stand me in good stead when later I went to Hitler's native land, Austria, as a foreign correspondent.

Going routinely through *l'Intransigeant* one afternoon, I was stopped by an account of an "Englishman" arrested for beating up a couple of *flics* (slang for Paris policemen) outside the Café Select. Whoever he was, I thought, he was in serious trouble, poor fellow, and headed for Devil's Island. I gave the name a second look. The spelling was garbled and did not seem quite English. Madame Select was notorious for abuse of her American customers, so I passed a clipping on to the city editor. Eugene Rossetti, the reporter covering the Police Prefecture, was ordered to investigate. The prisoner was Hart Crane.

I got on the phone and begged Rossetti to impress upon the police that Hart Crane was our greatest poet, which, in literature-loving France (with its more than 2,000 literary prizes), would mean much more than it would have to American officials. "Tell them," I said, "we love his poems so much that if they don't let him out of prison this minute not another single American tourist will ever come to France again!"

It was a lie, of course. Of the thousands of American tourists who visited Paris that summer, how many would have recognized Crane's name? (Now, if it had been Edgar Guest!) The strategy worked. Clutching a piece of stale bread left over from his prison diet, Crane was released, free to finish his famous long poem "The Bridge." (Once, later on, in Paris, I saw laborers rushing to help a man whose life was in danger, shouting to one another, "He's a poet! He's a poet!")

The *Herald* had a record-breaking year. We doubled the number of the pages, and a number of men, and two women, were added to the city room staff. I cabled Whit, who'd been sending me almost daily love letters, that there was a job for him, and he came at once and joined the *Herald* staff. He worked as a copyreader, and then was made city editor. His sarcastic way of speaking when he was giving assignments again caused him trouble. There were complaints from the staff, and Whit was transferred to feature writing. I wish I had been more straightforward then when he mourned, "I guess I don't know how to talk to people." He was so miserable I wanted only to console him, so I said, "At least you're honest." What I should have said and what might have helped him more was, "You keep forgetting that everyone is as thin-skinned as you yourself."

Eric Hawkins, managing editor of the *Paris Herald* while we were there, didn't like Whit. In his autobiography, he wrote, "Burnett was born with a jaundiced eye." Whit was, to be sure, a withdrawn introvert; still, as a socialist, I believed that character traits were determined by one's environment. Whit frequently went to the American Hospital in Neuilly, either for a brief examination of symptoms bothering him, or to stay for a few days. I was waiting for him in the office of the superintendent of nurses one afternoon and saw a record of Whit's visits in an open file drawer. Next to each entry on his card was written "phobia." Whit, I thought, could be likened to an injured animal, which, terrified lest it be hurt more, bites those who only mean it well. That "jaundiced eye" would overflow at a sad movie, and its owner was forever bringing home stray cats and dogs. . . .

The *Herald* was then a fuddy-duddy Republican paper which read as if it were being published for the Victorian readers of 1887 (the year it was founded by James Gordon Bennett). The staff was neither fuddy-duddy nor Republican, as we proved when we staged the first editorial strike in history on an American newspaper. Our salaries were in French francs, which were being inflated at a rapid rate, while our pay was stationary. Our discontent turned to anger when we learned that the publisher of the home paper in New York, the *Herald-Tribune,* had exclaimed, when asked to contribute to the funeral expenses of a reporter, "What! You mean he died insolvent!"

I asked everyone to write a list of expenses (shoe shines, cigarettes, haircuts, food, clothing, shelter, etc.). We averaged the lists and presented that sum, which was far higher than the salaries any of us was getting, to Laurence Hills, the publisher, as our minimum salary demand. He made no reply. Instead he went to the bars, cafés, and other American haunts, seeking would-be newspapermen to take our places. He also called me into his office and offered me a big raise. "What about the others?" I demanded. "What do you care about them?" he wanted to know.

We set a deadline for strike action at six o'clock on a certain day. We cleared our desk drawers of personal possessions and waited nervously as the clock hands turned. We knew that Hills was in his office, but he never came out. So must those embattled farmers have waited on that bridge at Concord, I thought at the time, and, by God, just before six o'clock, a shot *was* fired! Not by us. The head of the printing department came into the city room and said, "We've taken a vote downstairs and we have voted not to cross your picket line."

Thanks to those wonderful printers, the first American newspaper editorial strike was won. The *Herald* could get plenty of barflies to scab, but where would they find French printers who knew English?

In my teens, reading *Roderick Random,* I had been puzzled as to why the admiral, surrounded by young male attendants, should be so effeminate. I was twenty-two years old before I knew there was such a thing as homosexuality. I was still naïve about such matters in 1927 when the *Paris Herald* sent me to interview Gertrude Stein. Alice B. ("Pussy") Toklas, swarthy, spiderlike, and with wispy black mustache, let me in and hovered close to the mountain of flesh that was the mannish Miss Stein. I did not enjoy Miss Stein's arrogant, rude way of answering my questions, and Pussy's constant interjection of her own comments confused me. Thinking I might get a better interview if Pussy were absent, I whispered to Miss Stein, "I would like to see you alone sometime." I had heard the expression "bum's rush." Pussy made its meaning clear. I was out of there, the street door slammed behind me, before I could say good-bye.

Richard Wright told me he had been visiting his small daughter, who had had a tonsil operation, in the American Hospital in Neuilly the night Gertrude Stein died there in 1946. The next morning he had tea with Sylvia Beach and was worried as to how he could break the news of Gertrude's death without saddening her. "Did you hear about Gertrude?" he asked Sylvia as she was bringing him a cup of tea. "No. What?" "I'm sorry to tell you she died last night." Sylvia dropped the cup and saucer she was carrying. "Thank God!" she cried, Wright told me. "Thank God so much evil has been removed from this earth!"

Gertrude Stein hated Joyce. "Joyce is a third-rate Irish politician," she told Eugene Jolas, the editor of *transition.* "The greatest living writer of the age is Gertrude Stein." Sylvia had been Joyce's publisher, and I thought that was why she was delighted at Miss Stein's death. No, Wright told me, it wasn't the reason. Like Ezra Pound, but not so publicly active as he, Gertrude Stein, he said, had been a Nazi collaborator. When the Nazis and the Italian Fascists occupied France, everyone opposed to them had to flee for their lives. Joyce was publicly denounced as "decadent" by the Nazis, and copies of his writings were burned in a bonfire. He got his family and himself out at the cost of leaving his manuscripts behind. They were rescued for him by a friend, who, as a Jew, would have been shot if caught. Like Anne Frank, Sylvia hid in a French friend's attic, never venturing out into the streets. Miss Stein and Miss Toklas, with the protection of Vichy government officials, stayed safe and comfortable in France. If Gertrude Stein had not died, according to Wright, she would have been arrested by the American military authorities who were investigating her.

I sometimes wonder, if she had not been rich enough to afford idiosyncracies, how much of Gertrude Stein's writing would have been taken seriously. I know Sherwood Anderson, whose own writing I think was more seminal than Stein's, expressed a literary debt to her, saying she had revivified the English language for him, and I know that she was credited with influencing Hemingway (which infuriated him: he inscribed a book to her with a circle of words—"a bitch is a bitch is a bitch is a bitch"). Of those of her works I have read I prefer her two early books, *Three Lives* and *The Making of Americans;* also the play, *Four Saints in Three Acts,* which owed much of its effectiveness to the black actors and Virgil Thomson's music. The depth of Miss Stein's sincerity can be measured by her calling P.G. Wodehouse her favorite author. Perhaps she felt kinship with Wodehouse because, like herself, he too stayed safe behind enemy lines.*

---

* Discussion of Miss Stein's homosexuality always brings mention of Sappho, who was revered by her contemporaries with the same reverence we give the literary genius of Shakespeare. According to my reading of Greek history, Sappho was left a widow with a small daughter to support. She founded a school for girls,

Maria Jolas was a more important figure in the Paris literary world than Gertrude Stein. And a nicer person. A beautiful, fair-haired, and warmhearted woman from Kentucky, she devoted her small private income to financing *transition,* and, with her husband, Eugene Jolas, was its publisher and co-editor. I loved them both. Among my dearest memories of France are of their tiny Paris office, where for a brief period I did some clerical work for *transition* mornings before going to my afternoon and evening job on the *Herald;* of long, long talks with them about writers and writing over wine in sidewalk cafés and meals in gourmet restaurants, and weekend visits to the "Boisserie," the ancient hunting lodge they rented in Colombey-les-Deux-Eglises. (The lodge became famous after the Second World War as the residence of General Charles de Gaulle.) Colombey-les-Deux-Eglises was the only place where I heard a town crier. The resonance of his voice as he called out the hour and news was music as romantic to me as had been the clatter of those wooden shoes on the Boulogne cobblestones.

Gene Jolas and I had the *New York Daily News* in common. He'd worked on it a few years before my time there and, like me, had walked out on it in disgust. We had a wonderful time telling one another how much we hated it. We both knew where we were too. In Paris. (Not like the managing editor of the *New York*

---

much like our Wellesley or Smith College, to which prosperous families around the Aegean sent their daughters to be educated. Many of her poems were epithalamiums, lyric odes sung at weddings alternately by a male chorus to the bride and a feminine chorus to the bridegroom. They were passionate poetry, and, like any competent author of today, Sappho could express the emotions of either sex. She fell in love with a political radical, Phaon, who jilted her. In her grief Sappho leaped to her death off the white cliffs of Leucas.

Aristophanes, the most Rabelasian of ancient Greek dramatists, is famous for his lampooning of notables of classical times, beginning with Socrates. He lived three centuries later than Sappho and never knew her. With humorous ribaldry (and perhaps because he was a male chauvinist), he depicted Sappho as masculine. Ecclesiastical authorities in Rome ordered all her works destroyed; we are left with only a few manuscript scraps of the poetry her contemporaries called magnificent. In their writings there is no suggestion that Sappho was homosexual.

Times. Whit asked him at a carefree Anglo-American Press Association party in a nightclub on the Champs-Elysées, "Do you remember me, Mr. Birchall?" "Of course, you are the young man on the *Times* who always wanted to go to Paris and never got there." Whit retorted, "Where do you think you are now, Mr. Birchall?")

"Man from Babel," Gene called himself. He was born in New Jersey in 1894. His mother was German and his father French. When he was four years old they returned with him to Forbach in Lorraine, the province over which, along with Alsace, France and Germany have warred for centuries. There he lived until he was sixteen, when he again went to the United States. He again returned to France, where he succeeded Ford Madox Ford as literary editor of the Paris edition of the *Chicago Tribune.* His growing years were like those of Henry James. On one of his many shuttling trips between America and Europe, James said to himself, "The nostalgic poison had been distilled for him, and the future presented to him as a single intense question: was he to spend it in brooding exile, or might he somehow come into his own?"

The problem of which James complained was minor compared with the three-cornered cultural conflict that tormented Gene. He described it as "frontier anguish." Equally skilled in English, French, and German, he agonized over which language to write. Sometimes he chose one of the three, sometimes he combined two, and sometimes all three. Jolas had studied for the priesthood but had left the church. Literature was the altar at which he worshipped.

Transition was not, as many thought, a surrealist magazine. The magazine did publish many French surrealists, such as André Breton and Philippe Soupault; Jolas had close friends among them and was sympathetic with their views—but he himself took an independent course. His intimate knowledge of the three important languages gave him the unique editorial ability to introduce English readers to significant authors and literary developments of three cultures. One example of his achievement was serial publication of Franz Kafka's masterpiece, "Metamorphosis." (The list of his ground-breaking successes and discoveries is too long to print here but can be found in Douglas MacMillan's fine documentation, transition *1927–38.*)

The Jolases introduced us to James Joyce. Our acquaintance was limited to sitting with other friends on a café terrace, listening to Joyce talk and watching his handsome face, the almost blind eyes hidden behind glasses. The only clear recollection I have of his words is his saying, in regard to the "Work in Progress" (which was to be entitled *Finnegan's Wake* and would appear serially in *transition*), that he planned it as "a mighty synthesis." Nora, his wife, was always with him. When her husband's writing was praised, it was said that she complained, "Ah! but you should have heard him sing! Better the voice on him than John MacCormack's!" Nora was certain that Joyce had wasted his life by writing.

Elliot Paul, a strange man, was one of the original three persons who started *transition.* He was hired as an editor by the Jolases, but their association ended abruptly under distressing circumstances within a year. I got to know Elliot well because he was a member of the *Herald* city room staff. I had reviewed an early novel by him, *Impromptu,* for the *Los Angeles Daily News,* so I was especially interested to meet him. Stocky, with a heavy black beard in a day when beards were rare, Elliot seemed to me to take a mischievous delight in obfuscation.

At my urging, Whit had started a novel about the Mormons he knew so well. I knew nothing about Mormons until I met Whit and through him discovered their fascinating history, which was like something out of the Old Testament. There seemed an epic sweep to their migration across America, and what first fired my imagination about them was hearing how, after they had finally settled in Utah and had planted their first year's crops, a plague of locusts had descended upon the heartbroken people, devouring their harvest. Out of the West came a strange sight in a land-bound region. Thousands of seagulls swooped down upon the locusts. They came from the Great Salt Lake, which the Mormons were yet to discover.

Elliot was interested in Whit's novel, and we spent many hours in the "Barrel House" (Elliot's favorite drinking spot—a wholesale wine dealer's establishment around the corner from the *Herald*) discussing it. Elliot disparaged Whit's plan of a long novel. "Keep it short," he urged. "Understatement is more effective. The impact is more concentrated." He alternated his sipping with emphatic repetitions of "Understate! Understate! Understate!" Gone was my vision of a dramatic epic. I yielded in silence to what I considered Elliot's superior knowledge. (He was the author of *published* novels.) An old girlfriend of Whit's once told me, "I can always tell to whom Whit has been talking." Whit tore up many pages of hard work and tried to rewrite his book as a novella. But, after the punishing criticism Elliot gave the manuscript, Whit became too disheartened ever to reassemble the fragments.

Elliot gave Whit a copy of the manuscript of a novel he had written. Whit took it home to our apartment to read. I had just finished the English translation of *In the Ravine,* by Chekhov, which Elliot's wife, Camille Haynes, had lent me, when Whit gave me Elliot's manuscript. I read a few pages and screamed. "What's the matter?" Whit asked. "Oh, no! It can't be! I don't believe it!" I told him. "Elliot has plagiarized Chekhov!"

Except for the careful changing of Russian customs and foods to Down East ways, Elliot had copied Chekhov's story word for word, moving it to Maine, and giving it the title of *Low Run Tide.* Caviar became baked beans and borscht became clam chowder. The next day Whit asked Elliot, "Have you ever read *In the Ravine* by Chekhov?" Elliot looked thoughtful, as if searching his memory, and answered, "I think I did. A long time ago in a French translation." *Low Run Tide* was published in New York in 1929. As far as I know there were no references to Chekhov in the reviews.

When I spoke with Gene Jolas about Elliot and Whit's novel, he explained why he forced Elliot to resign from *transition*. One of the French surrealists gave Elliot a manuscript to translate into English from the French. The French writer soon came raging to Gene. Elliot had published the piece in *transition* under his own name. In Spain I later visited the island of Ibiza and saw Elliot, who was living there. Whatever his literary sins, he redeemed them in *Life and Death of a Spanish Town,* written during the Spanish civil war. It is a moving, honest accout of the sufferings of the Spanish people under Franco.

I have found it almost impossible to explain to Americans the epicurean French devotion to exquisite food. Americans confuse it with gluttony. A French gourmet is never a greedy glutton. The French have a separate word for glutton—*gourmand.* Their leisurely meals may have many courses, but each portion of food is small and the soup, fish, meat, vegetable, and salad are each a separate course, as are the dessert and cheese with fruit courses. The French way of eating is not fattening. So exceptional was a fat Frenchman that I interviewed for the *Herald* a man who was organizing an exclusive club whose membership was limited to men weighing 200 pounds or more.

Eugene Rossetti, renegade Rumanian aristocrat become communist, and a political reporter for the *Paris Herald,* was both *gourmet* and *gourmand.* It was Rossetti's working acquaintance with government officials that enabled him to help extricate Hart Crane from police clutches. Rossetti did more than rescue poets; he taught Americans on the *Herald* how to eat.*

---

* In his history of the *Herald—The Paris Herald, The Incredible Newspaper*—Al Laney, who knew Rossetti long before I did and long after, commemorates him thus: "Rossetti was a large, ponderous and bald man with a red face that could

"Another visiting fireman!" I thought when I received a letter from Forrest Bailey, director of the American Civil Liberties Union, saying a friend of his named Rex Stout was coming to Paris and would we please show him a good time. I liked Forrest and admired the work of the Civil Liberties Union, so when Rex Stout telephoned, I invited him to have dinner with Rossetti and ourselves at Pharamond's.

Rex Stout had lively brown eyes, a small beard, and the lithe physique of a man in his forties who exercised. His manner was more engaging than that of the usual businessman, and we felt it would be safe to take him to Pharamond's. The *Herald* staff conspired to protect Pharamond's from becoming like the much-touted Maxim's, where the food was inferior, the prices exorbitant, and the customers all tourists. Pharamond's was never mentioned in the *Herald.* It was a simple, pleasant place of medium size presided over by the Norman owner, Monsieur Pharamond, assisted by Monsieur Émile, a friendly headwaiter. I think we of the *Herald* and our friends were the only non-French ever seen there.

Rex and Rossetti were delighted with one another—Rossetti because Rex was an interested, brand-new audience for his gusta-

---

somehow manage to express at the same time both cunning and stupidity. He always wore a derby hat and dark shiny suit, and he might have been cast as a flat-foot American detective in the silent movies. His speech, however, was on the grandiose, measured side, and he would deliver an oration on the slightest pretext. He liked, it seemed, to give the impression of stupidity and, although one knew perfectly well that he could not be as stupid as he pretended at times, one could never draw the line anywhere. He could work himself up into the most magnificent rages, apparently turning them on at will, like a water spigot.

". . . He was an enormous eater and drinker, a gourmand and gourmet in one and he knew the eating places of Paris as well as any man. It is to his eternal credit that, throughout the . . . years, he introduced many a *Herald* man to the joys of dining out in Paris and especially to Pharamond's, that sublime eating place tucked away in a tiny street only a few hundred yards from the office.

"All around the world today, there are men who are ready, as the saying goes, at the drop of a martini, to run up a *salade sauce Albert* according to the recipe which Rossetti worked out with the headwaiter at Pharamond's. For this alone, Rossetti's memory will remain green."

tory orations, and Rex because he was studying Rossetti as an extraordinary character. "Barbarians! You Americans are all barbarians!" Rossetti declared. The noble proportions of Rossetti's bald head, like that on the busts of the Roman emperors who once ruled his native land, gave his words the force of imperial decrees. "You should be civilized! Learn how to eat! Stop anesthetizing your palates with cocktails! Stop smoking at the table! Fill your mouths full and give all the taste buds a chance! Put your meat and vegetables on separate plates! Not all in a mess on one plate! Throw all your Coca-Cola in the ocean and learn to appreciate wine!"

I forget what we had for dinner that evening. It probably was one of Rossetti's favorite menus: *tripes à la mode de Caen,* served bubbling over a brazier of glowing coals; *tournedos,* a thick steak, with *pommes soufflées;* a salad of crisp watercress with fresh tarragon; *soufflé* Marie Brizard; Pont l'Évêque cheese with a ripe pear; black coffee and the native Normandy brandy, Calvados, served in large snifters to enhance its aroma of apple blossoms. And, throughout the meal, bottles of red macon.

"Bier vor Wein mach Man Schwein/ Wein vor Bier mach Man Stier!" Rossetti pronounced at the end of the meal. "Beer before wine makes man a swine/ Wine before beer makes man a bull!" "Shall we be bulls?" "Yes! Yes!" "Then we shall go to Lippe's. The only place in Paris where the beer is good."

So across the Seine we went and to the Boulevard Saint-Germain on the Left Bank where Lippe's, a German establishment, was located. On the way we passed café terraces where friends were sitting. They joined us. By the time we reached Lippe's we numbered fourteen. Tables were drawn together to accommodate us, and we ordered beer. We were so busy talking, or rather listening to Rossetti talk, with Rex asking questions, that when it grew late and was time to leave, there were only twenty-eight saucers on the table to tally the number of our drinks.

"Cinquante!" said the waiter.

"Oh, no!" *Vingt-huit!* Count them!"

"Quarante!" said the waiter.

"What's the matter?"

"Your waiter is crazy. He's charging us for a lot more drinks than we had."

The manager blew a whistle. It was a signal. Everyone in the restaurant rose up, descended on us, and, bundling us together, rushed us out of the place and on to the sidewalk outside. It was a chilly night and we gathered around the bucket of charcoal a newsstand dealer burned for heat. We were excited and confused. We had no idea why we had been so forcibly ejected. Will Barber (a *Herald* reporter who was awarded the Pulitzer prize posthumously for his correspondence during the Italian-Ethiopian war), kept throwing his hat angrily down on the sidewalk, running in a circle around it, picking the hat up, and throwing it down again. I noticed that Rossetti did not have his overcoat. I went back into Lippe's to get it. This time I was picked up bodily, carried out, and set down on the sidewalk. A couple of *flics* came sauntering along. We appealed to them. "Always trouble there!" they told us. Then each took Rossetti by an arm and led him away, but not before he bowed to us and said, "Wait here for me. I shall return."

We wanted to get to the *Herald* office quickly to get help for Rossetti. We hailed a cab for Rex. He told the driver "Hotel Maurice." I was shocked. It was the most expensive hotel in Paris. "Oh! You're being robbed!" I protested. "There are so many good, cheap hotels in Paris. Call me tomorrow and I'll help you find one."

We burst into the city room with our tale of woe. "Don't you know what kind of joint Lippe's is?" demanded Don Donaldson, the night editor. We looked blank. "It's the headquarters of the *Camelots du Roi*—the bully boys of the Royalist movement! You went in there with Rossetti! The communist who was meant to be a prince! You are goddamned lucky to be alive."

Rossetti himself showed up at the *Herald* office while we were calling the Prefecture. "I told you to wait for me!" he complained. "I went back and you weren't there."

"We came here to get help for you."

"*Pouf!* That was all a make-believe, their taking me. To calm the Camelot bastards."

Rex called me up the next day and I told him about the Royalists. "You mean, for the sake of a glass of beer he risked his own life and our lives? Good God!"

When I learned who he was and why he was in Paris, I did not help Rex find a cheap hotel. The Anglo-American Press Association was having a stag affair, so Rex invited me to have dinner with him. He told me he was a banker and also vice-president of the Vanguard Press. But he was not in Paris either as a banker or a publisher, but to keep a promise he had made to himself twenty years before, when he was twenty-two years old. He wanted to be a writer, a good writer, but he needed money, and the only stories he could sell were tawdry contrivances for pulp magazines. He stopped writing those stories with a vow that for twenty years he would make lots of money so that he could forever after write what he really wanted to write: important literature of permanent value.

He went into banking and, through a saving account system he organized for school children, he made enough money on which to retire. Now here he was in Paris, free of financial worries and ready to write. His plan was first to write a play. After dinner we went to a café, where, over coffee and liqueurs, Rex outlined the play he planned. Not only outlined, but described it scene by scene and act by act. We discussed it in detail until two o'clock in the morning. When Rex left me at my door he said contentedly, "Our talk was a big help. The play is all done now except for the typing."

When I saw him a few days later, I asked how the play was going. Rex told me, "I have decided to write a novel."

"What about the play?"

"I lost interest in it."

He stayed in Paris for several more months, going frequently to Pharamond's, where he and Rossetti became friends. I did not ask him about the novel, nor did he mention it to me. After he left Paris I did not see him again until my return to the United States in 1933. Called *How Like a God,* the novel was published, received excellent reviews from literary critics. Two more serious novels by Rex followed; then came *The League of Frightened Men,* the first of the long series about the gourmet detective named Nero Wolfe who solved murders without leaving his desk. It didn't take many pages before I wanted to call out, "Hi Rossetti! It's swell seeing you again. But when did you take up orchid raising? I don't remember you doing that in Paris. And that secretary of yours, Archie Goodwin. Could his real name be Rex Stout? He's made you a Montenegrin. But he kept you in the Balkans. Hmm. Montenegro is in Yugoslavia right next door to your native Rumania, which used to be called 'Romania,' an extension of ancient Rome, whose founder was raised by a wolf. Well. You are hardly serious literature of permanent value but you are fun and the plans of writers do 'gang aft agley.' . . ."

While he was in Paris, Rex told us he had the manuscript of a new novel by D.H. Lawrence which no one wanted to publish because of its sexual frankness. The few passages he quoted to us shocked Whit, who himself used plenty of profanity. I don't know whether he ever read *Ulysses,* but I had, so I felt *Lady Chatterley's Lover* would not corrupt me, and I said I would like to read it. Whit ordered Rex not to let me see it, and Rex obeyed. Not until it was published in the United States did I have a chance to read it. (While Rex was deliberating over whether to take a chance at publishing it, someone in Florence, Italy, obtained a copy and printed it).

Whit's conservative literary tastes were not limited to sexual frankness in writing but embraced all forms of literary experimentalism. "It's interesting, isn't it?" I asked him after I had showed him a copy of *transition.* "No," he said. But after the Jolases became our friends, Whit did try his hand at experiment. Five of his stories, two realistic, two fantasies, and one wholly experimental, were published in *transition.* I also contributed a brief short story (in obsolete English, using words that had fallen by the wayside, such as *agamist* and *airling**) to the magazine. In a hurry one evening, we both signed the "Revolution of the Word Manifesto." I wish I had had more time to discuss it with Gene and Maria, but neither Whit nor I realized what widespread attention it would attract, or how many would be the arguments for years after in which it would involve us. The rise of the Nazis made Gene himself question some of the clauses such as "The writer expresses, he does not communicate" and "The plain reader be damned." The Nazis had denounced James Joyce as decadent and burned a copy of *transition* in a public ceremony in Munich. Jolas changed his attitude, saying that "the poet had not the right to remain entirely aloof."

William Bird, the publisher with Robert McAlmon of the Three Mountains Press, which published Hemingway's first book, *Three Stories and Ten Poems,* in 1923, was the European manager of the Consolidated Press. He had seen Whit's work in *transition* and liked the feature stories Whit was writing for the *Herald.* He offered Whit a job in Vienna at twice the salary the *Herald* was paying him.

I had sold a couple of free-lance stories to the "chamber-maid section," the Hearst Sunday supplement with the screaming headlines and lurid illustrations, so I wrote to William Hillman, head of the Universal Service in Europe, who had bought my pieces, asking about a job in Vienna, and I was assigned to one. In the month of December 1929, when everybody was laughing at the

---

* *agamist*— a man who doesn't believe in marriage; *airling*— an airplane pilot.

way *Variety,* the Broadway theatrical weekly, headlined the gigantic stock market crash ("Wall Street Lays an Egg!"), we prepared to go to Vienna.*

---

* Elsewhere, in an outline she once prepared for the memoir, Martha wrote: "Those years in the late Twenties were crammed with excitement and there is too much material to detail here. There was the wonderful Ezra Pound-sponsored concert of George Antheil's *Ballet Mecanique.* There was meeting Isadora Duncan, who kept a vigil with lighted candle outside the American Embassay the night Sacco and Vanzetti were executed. Later I was to cover her funeral. The next night I saw thousands of *Gardes Républicains* and Parisians battle, and I saw men so angry they were able to rip up with their bare hands cobblestones solidly implanted in the pavement. Hemingway was in Paris but I did not meet him. He hung out at Montparnasse cafés and we who prided ourselves as being 'serious' looked down on Montparnasse *habitués* as tourists and remittance men. I was to meet him in New York when I became involved in his hair-on-the-chest battle with Max Eastman. [Eastman had written something about Hemingway trying to write "as if his prose had hair on its chest." When the two men met at Scribner's, with Martha present, Hemingway reached across the table, tore open Eastman's shirt, and laughed, declaring that he only wanted to see if Eastman had hair on his chest.]

"My sojourn in Paris was interrupted for a few weeks when I went to Moscow to cover the Second All Soviet Writers' Congress. My most vivid recollection of that event is of the harried little man who saw me off at the station with a bunch of wilted cornflowers. He was translating Joyce's *Ulysses* into Russian."—ED.

FOUR

∽

TALES FROM
THE VIENNA WOODS

S omewhere in my childhood I had read that coal was called
black diamonds. In Vienna, in February 1930, I learned why;
if you wanted to keep warm during the severe Austrian winter,
a ton of coal was more important than a ton of diamonds. After
the recent dismemberment of the Austro-Hungarian Empire (by
the Treaty of Saint-Germain), all coal, Austria's principal heating
fuel, had to be imported and guarded from theft. You had to
watch it when it was weighed in at the depot, and you had to
follow the wagon to your home. When Viennese friends first gave
Whit and me this advice, I laughed; but when I realized that they
were serious, I gained a notion of how desperate their economic
situation was. The Viennese middle and upper classes, with their
worship of ceremony, titles, and etiquette, were the proudest
people I'd ever met, so that their obsession with appearances
made it hard to picture them at the grubby task of protecting coal
from theft.

After being stranded for six weeks in a gloomy mausoleum of
an apartment (all done up in faded dark reds and browns and
chipped gilt), around the corner from Sigmund Freud's home in
downtown Vienna, Whit and I found a delightful small house for

rent on the edge of the Vienna Woods. It was on a cobblestoned street in a village with a fairy-tale name—Pötzleinsdorf, Little Bear Village. Until our friends warned us otherwise, we'd thought buying coal for our furnace would be a simple matter of telephoning in an order.

"I'll be goddamned if I'll walk for miles behind a coal wagon watching a horse drop you-know-what," Whit snorted. Because I liked horses well enough so that their natural functions didn't upset me, I volunteered to be the escort. The driver, Herr Wagner, was sooty-faced and friendly, the horse was old and slow-paced, and it was easy for me on the sidewalk to keep up with him. I had brought along an apple for him. *"Yawohl!"* Herr Wagner agreed in a hearty peasant voice when I asked if I could give his horse the apple. As I held up the apple to the horse, who eyed it with interest, his driver touched my arm. "Excuse me, *gnädige Frau*," he said to me; then to the horse, *"Sag bitte,* Franz Josef!" The horse pawed the ground with one hoof, tossed his head, and whinnied. Herr Wagner looked at me proudly. "Franz Josef said please." When the apple disappeared, the driver coaxed, "Franz Josef?" The head-tossing, ground-pawing, and whinny were repeated. "He said, 'Thank you very much,' " Herr Wagner translated. "You are very welcome, Franz Josef," I said politely to the horse, and Herr Wagner was delighted. Herr Wagner invited me to share the wagon with him, and from my perch I got to see parts of Vienna that were new to me. In a few hours, the three of us arrived safely at Number 16 Pötzleinsdorferstrasse, and not a lump of coal was missing.

Resi welcomed us. Resi-Frau Therese Sommerer! What a deprivation it would have been not to have known her. When friends recommended her, and her age—sixty—was mentioned, I was horrified. I wanted no housekeeper so ancient. My friends persisted, declaring I did not understand what a marvelous opportunity I was passing up, that the city of Vienna had awarded her a gold medal for her prowess in cooking and that her last employment had been with well-known people, the Quallas, who kept her for twenty-seven years and let her go only when Herr Qualla died. I said I would take her on trial for a month. After two days life in Vienna without Resi became unthinkable.

She was a plump, bustling, and cheerful little woman, who in a best black dress with white lace collar, cameo pin, and a black hat on which a bright pink rose bobbed, went to early mass every morning. The rest of her day, after she changed into a print dress and crisply starched white apron, was punctuated by her favorite profanity, "Jesu, Maria und Josef!" Herr Qualla, for whom she had cooked so many years, was a businessman and a gourmet whose interests took him to many countries. She told us that from each trip he brought back new recipes for her, with the result that she had become a great cosmopolitan cook. From our kitchen, where she scorned the modern gas range in favor of an old wood and coal stove, she produced Lucullan dishes which kept us exclaiming "Rossetti should be here!"

Resi had worked most of her life under the old Austro-Hungarian aristocratic régime, and she was a traditionalist. The first time I paid her, I stopped her from kissing my hand by commanding sharply, "Never do that again!" It was more difficult to convince her that, much as we admired her cooking, we did not want all those meals she tried to serve us. For those few Viennese who could afford them, and they were far fewer than when Resi had been young, there were five meals a day, beginning with *Frühstück,* early morning breakfast served in bed. Resi was puzzled. "But you can afford it," she protested. (Like most Europeans at that time, she thought all Americans were millionaires.) She wanted to stock our attic with provisions against a war and was so upset when I first refused, telling me how during the First World War and the later rioting she had walked for miles into the Austrian countryside or across the border into Czechoslovakia to bring back, hidden under her skirts, butter, or a ham or some vegetables, that I yielded. On our attic third floor were stocked, for a war that did come, as Resi prophesied, but not until after we were gone from Vienna, sacks of flour and sugar and salt, tins of lard, dried fruits and vegetables, coffee, tea, and candles.

We completed our domestic arrangements by hiring a *Bedienerin,* a strong young woman to help a couple of days a week with the heavy work and with entertaining. And we acquired a cat. Viennese, seeing a live cat in our house, were startled. The only time cats were seen in Vienna during those years was when their skins were displayed in pharmacy windows, for sale as winter chest protectors. Resi again proved how unusual a person she was because, although an Austrian, she loved Friederich (whose name she shortened to Fritz, and finally to the Austrian endearment, Fritzl).

Beyond our long, walled garden, with its tall blue spruces and espaliered apple and pear trees, ran the Sommerheidenweg, or Summer Heather Way, a lane in the Vienna Woods, scene of Arthur Schnitzler's beautiful short stories. Schnitzler himself lived on our street, a few houses away. As soon as I heard he did, I wanted, of course, to interview him. I couldn't, I was told, because he refused to see any American correspondents. He was angry that so many of his early books had been published in pirated editions in the United States, where they had no copyright protection.*

---

* Gustav Meyrinck, whose novel, *The Golem,* I admired, took the same stand and for the same reason. I could have told them American authors also suffered from a bad copyright law. The United States copyright situation is and has been for many years a mess. Part of the fault lies with those members of an authors' society who, in 1909, were asked by the printers' union to help it frame an adequate copyright law covering all their interests. The authors, stupid fools, refused, saying they were writers and the printers were laborers and they had nothing in common. It was below their professional dignity, they explained, to be associated with a union. The printers had been prompted in the first place to seek a strong copyright law because so much printing was being sent overseas to be done by cheap labor. Their first requirement was that writing to be copyrighted must be printed in the United States. Another requirement, and this was meant to ensure continued employment for them, was that a copyright must be renewed every twenty-eight years.

> Souls of Poets dead and gone
> What Elysium have ye known
> Happy field or mossy cavern
> Choicer than the Mermaid Tavern?

The Elizabethans had the Mermaid, the *New Yorker* writers the Algonquin Round Table, and we Americans of the early Thirties living in Vienna had the Café Louvre Stammtisch. The nucleus of the group that gathered nightly around the tables pushed together in a semicircular booth at one end of the Café Louvre were foreign correspondents. In spite of its French name, the Louvre was a typical Vienna coffeehouse where one was served two glasses of water upon sitting down at a table, and, for the price of a cup of coffee, was then welcome to remain for hours reading newspapers in a dozen languages. Novelists, playwrights, poets, and actors joined us at the Stammtisch, along with visiting publishers and columnists. William Bullitt, who rented an apartment in Vienna as a lookout post on Europe for Franklin D. Roosevelt (not yet president), was often there. Spies came too, for in such a lively, talkative cosmospolitan assembly, valuable bits of intelligence could unwittingly be dropped.

The affection the correspondents had for each other sustained the Stammtisch. We were young because Vienna did not rank in importance with London, Berlin, or Paris, where news bureaus were headed by older, more established journalists. But we didn't care. We looked beyond newspaper work to more important writing. We did not plan to spend our lives at ephemeral day-by-day reporting. We wanted to produce literature.

Outside our coffeehouse lay a dark, bereft city, its wide avenues deserted except for an occasional automobile, its street and building lights ghostly in the dimness of low-wattage, power-saving electricity, and the nine nations it once ruled as an empire now forbidden lands to it. Ruined by defeat in the First World War in 1919, Vienna in 1930 was not the waltzing city of song and story. Nor was it yet at peace.

On the day of our first visit to the Stammtisch, the *Heimwehr* marched through Vienna. Who or what was the *Heimwehr? Heim,* we knew, meant "home," but *Wehr* has a variety of meanings, ranging from "show fight" to "protection." Newspaper accounts named a Prince Starhemberg as leader of the march, but they did not give his politics. We were still trying to disentangle in our minds the alignments of the various political groups: We knew Vienna, with its largely working-class population, was controlled by the Social Democrats, who were socialists. In the rural sections of Austria there was a strong Christian Socialist party of peasants led by priests. The Catholic Church strongly opposed all forms of Marxism, yet the great majority of Vienna's socialists were loyal Catholics. There was also the Austrian National Socialist party, backed by Hitler's German National Socialists, who were Nazis.

Our befuddlement ended that evening when we sat beside M.W. Fodor, the round-faced, bespectacled *Manchester Guardian* correspondent, who drank *Kaffee Ohne,* coffee without the ubiquitous Viennese whipped cream. In accented but meticulously correct English, Fodor told us, "Starhemberg is Austria's great patriotic name, like Washington's in your country. The first Starhemberg, in 1683, with only a small garrison of troops at his command, held back an enormous army of Turkish invaders who were besieging Vienna until the armies of Poland and Sweden could reach him with help. Not only did he save Vienna. He saved the whole of Europe from incorporation into the Ottoman Empire. It is one of the great turning points in history. But this Starhemberg today! Pfui! Perhaps it is good you Washington had no descendants to spoil the name for you."

Fodor smiled and went on to explain patiently to Whit and me, as novices in Central European politics, the modern Starhemberg's history. In the notorious Munich beer hall putsch, he had been an Austrian monarchist accomplice of Hitler; afterward they quarreled. Now he was eager to be the fuehrer of Austria. The *Heimwehr* was a Fascistic militia he had developed as the private army of the Christian Socialists. The real socialists, the Social

Democrats, also had a private army, called the *Schutzbund* (for the republic). Fodor showed no boredom in telling us, in great detail, what was such an old story to him. It was our introduction to the kindness with which Fodor always shared his expertise. Not for him any "scoops" at the expense of his colleagues. Many a correspondent might have lost his job if Fodor had not kept him informed of important news developments and their significance.

Fodor was the only real intellectual among us. He had been a professional scientist in his early career. During the First World War he worked in the Vickers munition works in England. There he invented a sensational device that accelerated a gun's fire. In the excitement over the invention, his Austro-Hungarian origin was revealed. What was an enemy alien doing in the very heart of the British munitions industry? The question was raised in Parliament. Fodor was sent to an internment camp, where Ramsay MacDonald, the future socialist prime minister of Great Britain, was a prisoner. The two men became friends, and, at the war's end, the liberal *Manchester Guardian* made him its Vienna correspondent. Fodor also wrote histories. Because his books—for example, *South of Hitler* and *Plot in Central Europe*— were written with a scientist's cautious precision instead of journalistic audacity, Fodor never received the recognition he deserved in America.

"Where's Best?" asked Martha Fodor, who was sitting at the Stammtisch beside her husband. Martha had the slender dark beauty of the Hungarian women who, with their very black hair and dancing eyes, were such an intriguing foil to the softly rounded beauty of the Austrian women, with their golden hair and gentle, brown eyes.

"He went out of town," came a reply. A roar of laughter burst from the Stammtisch group.

Again we looked to Fodor for an explanation. He, too, was laughing. "It's a joke. We all know that not once, since he arrived in Vienna, has Bob Best put a foot outside the city."

When a stout young man in his early thirties joined us a little later, we met Robert Best, the man who was to become notorious during the Second World War as "the American Lord Haw-Haw" for his Nazi broadcasts, and, less lucky than Ezra Pound, to die for treason in an American prison. But all we saw that evening was a slow-spoken colleague with a southern drawl who smiled sheepishly when he was greeted.

As correspondent for the United Press, the second biggest American news service, Bob Best was one of the most important newspapermen in Central Europe. Although his territory, like ours, stretched over the thousands of miles from Czechoslovakia to Turkey, requiring frequent trips to spots where news happened, Bob Best stayed anchored to the Café Louvre Stammtisch all day and half the night. He left only to go home to the "Countess," whom he called "my fiancée." She was a much older woman, who dressed in gaudy, outmoded finery. Resi insisted to me that she was no countess but had, in fact, once been known on the streets of Vienna as "the whore of Constantinople."

It wasn't only Bob's sedentariness that set him apart from the typical newspaperman. He did not swear, smoke, or drink. Every other newspaperman I knew did all three. Surely, I thought, he must have some indulgence. He had an eerie habit of frequently rolling his eyes upward during conversations. Drugs were not the common problem in America they are today, and all I knew about them then was what I'd read in DeQuincey's "Confessions of an English Opium Eater." I couldn't remember anything about rolling eyeballs in that book, but I had heard that drugs were easy to get in Vienna.

"I think I know why Bob Best never goes out of Vienna," I told Whit. "He's a drug addict and afraid to leave the source of his supply."

Whit looked thoughtful. "I wouldn't be surprised if you're right," he said.

When, during the Second World War, Best broadcast Nazi

propaganda to the United States, I thought that, yes, I was right. Best's drug habit had given the Nazis a hold on him.*

The *Heimwehr* faded as a topic of conversation at the Stammtisch when "customs union" between Austria and Germany was mentioned. This was to be an arrangement between the two countries eliminating customs restrictions on goods exchanged between them and adopting a uniform tariff policy toward other countries.

"The Treaty of Saint-Germain—" someone began, but he was interrupted by someone else saying, "A customs union would lead to an Anschluss!" "The Treaty of Saint-Germain will never allow it!" said the first speaker. It seemed to me I had been hearing about the Treaty of Versailles all my life, but this was the first I had heard about the Treaty of Saint-Germain, imposed upon Austria at the end of the First World War, parallel to the Versailles document.†

---

* I was wrong. I am sure now I know the real reason for Best's championship of the Nazis, and I discovered it only a few years ago when I was having dinner with George Britt and his wife. George and I have been friends ever since he treated me, a delighted, wide-eyed girl newly arrived in the big city, to lunch in the restaurant of the old *New York World.* "The old *New York World!*" What an affecting depth of emotion is in the voices of elderly newspapermen when they say those words! It was the brightest, liveliest, most liberal, and most sophisticated and literary newspaper of the time. Its columnists, Heywood Broun, F.P.A., and others, were famous. Britt and Broun had collaborated on a book about anti-Semitism, *Christians Only.* It was Broun's sad fate to put an end to the *World's* glory. When President Lowell of Harvard University advocated the execution of Sacco and Vanzetti, Broun, a Harvard alumnus himself, called Harvard "Hangman's House." He was fired, and the *World* no longer seemed so splendid a paper.

But that was long ago, and it was more recently at the dinner with the Britts that I heard George say, "I have only one regret in life. I was born too late to fight for the Confederacy." *Best!* I thought. That explains Best. I had heard Best speak the very same words, not once but a number of times. Best was from the South, and his usually slow drawl would vanish when Roosevelt was mentioned; his voice vibrating with fury, he would refer to him as *"your* Yankee president." Best, poor fellow, was merely a hallucinated, unreconstructed Rebel, under the delusion that he was fighting for the Stars and Bars alongside the Nazis, whom he mistook for allies, in a war against the hated Union.

† According to *The Columbia Encyclopaedia,* "The Treaty of Saint-Germain (1919) forbade as did the Treaty of Versailles any political or economic union

During the First World War I was an adolescent who had a favorite retreat. It was a spot in the woods halfway up the side of Big Blue, the highest of the hills in the Blue Hills Reservation in Milton, Massachusetts. I loved to sit there, sometimes reading a book, but more often just daydreaming and gazing out over the green countryside at a distant river. As the war progressed and there were reports of bloody fighting, sunken ships, and devastated cities, I would close my eyes and try to imagine how it would feel to be on a battlefield. When I opened them again, I would feel that I had no right to enjoy the peace of the beautiful scene before me. The first adult organization I ever joined as a member was pacifist, the Fellowship of Reconciliation.

So I knew at the Stammtisch that I was for the Anschluss. I wanted a union, and still do, not of just those two countries joined in peace but of all the nations in the world. Sentimental? Perhaps. But it is generally agreed today that if the Social Democrats of Germany and the Social Democrats of Austria had been allowed to join, as so many of their people wished, in a peaceful union of their two republics, Hitler might never have come to power. It was such a logical arrangement. Both were German in race and language. They had been associated until Bismarck, the Iron Chancellor, in 1866, excluded Austria from the North German Confederation. In 1919, as a symbol of its peaceful, cultural character, the new German Republic had chosen Weimar as its capital because of that city's association with Goethe and Schiller. Music and medicine were the achievements, also cultural, of which Austria was proudest. On the practical side, the economic advantages would have been enormous.

---

with Germany. This left Austria, a small country, with some 6,000,000 inhabitants, more than one-third of whom lived in a single large city (Vienna) that had been geared to be the financial and industrial hub of a large state. The Dual Monarchy had been virtually self-sufficient economically. Its breakup and the consequent erection of tariff walls deprived Austria of raw materials, food and markets. Reorientation was balked by the insistence of France, Italy, and Czechoslovakia on the Treaty clauses against Union."

The Story of STORY Magazine

Except when we took trips, Whit and I fell into a daily routine. After breakfast in bed, a continental custom to which we had become habituated in Paris, we went to the room we shared as an office on the second floor of the Pötzleinsdorf house. There we were joined by Frau Schwartzwald, the secretary we also shared. Once she had been the rich mistress of a big, upper-class home. Now she was living in a three-room apartment with her husband, daughter, and the two maids who had been with her for many years. She and her husband shared a bedroom, her daughter slept on a living room couch, and the maids slept on folding cots, one in the kitchen and the other in the bathroom. She was an intelligent, well-educated, and well-traveled woman who was a valuable assistant.

Frau Schwartzwald read and marked the Vienna newspapers for us and later took dictation. We went through our mail, much of it written reports from our string men in the various capitals, and received or made telephone calls to and from them and to our main offices in Paris and Berlin. We also sent cables to New York. (The transatlantic telephone was new, and cabling was still customary for dispatch of intercontinental news.) At one o'clock Frau Schwartzwald went home, and we went downstairs to the wonderful *Mittagessen,* the big midday dinner Resi prepared. Usually we would find one or more guests there standing at the kitchen door enjoying the good cooking smells while being entertained with *Blautchen,* Resi's word for chatting with people. (*"Blautchen"* is the nearest I can guess at its spelling, since no German dictionary has it and no Viennese seems to know it as slang.) Resi had changed a lot from her hand-kissing days. She embraced our democratic ways with zest and treated our friends as her own, which they loved.

Most Viennese men went home for the midday meal, and the hour after it was spent as a siesta. It was not the slothful practice Americans believe; waking up refreshed, Europeans found they had a second day. (Whit and I fully appreciated its efficiency only after we'd returned to the whirligig of frenzied activity in the United States—a frenzy that is too often mistaken for "work.") Whit spent the siesta hour in his room, and I would listen to the strains of a violin or viola or bassoon. I left to walk in the Vienna Woods—a big, beautiful forest with ancient trees, vistas of distant mountains, and the company of deer and other wild creatures, who were fearless because the woods were a sanctuary.

At three o'clock Vienna woke up from its siesta and Whit and I went out on the town to cover news events and seek interviews. At five o'clock, hour of the *Jause,* Viennese for teatime, we stopped at the Stammtisch for a conference with other correspondents on the day's developments. Under socialist control, many changes were being made, and reactions to them were varied and made interesting copy.*

The Inner City of Vienna is replete with magnificent baroque palaces, churches, museums, theaters, and statuary. After three years in France admiring French Gothic, which even at its most ornate has an exquisitely soaring, defined grace, it took me some time to appreciate the downward melting curves of baroque. Its testimony to past opulence was a damning commentary on the ancient slums that co-existed. The most ambitious municipal project of the new socialist city government when I was there was to move workers from the dark medieval alleys into sunlit modern housing. I wrote my first feature story from Vienna about the

---

* Among the reforms were separation of church and state, secularization of the schools, and legalization of nonchurch marriages. But one thing the socialists could not change—Viennese infatuation with titles. Hereditary princes and counts were still around, and every Viennese, down to those of the lowliest birth, had a title by which to be formally addressed. Presidents of the 18,000 clubs in the city were each *Herr Präsident* and the wives, according to custom, were Frau Präsident. There were all the *obers, ober* meaning "superior." There were *Oberkellner,* a headwaiter, although I never met a plain *Kellner; Oberleutnant,* a colonel; and *Obersteuer-kommissar,* like the tax collector who fined me fourteen schillings for not having a dog because I left blank the line on a tax form where it said *Hund.* Whit was *Herr Doktor* and I was *Frau Doktor* (not so impressive when you knew that it was used to address anyone who could read and write).

Karl Marx Hof, the first of these houses to be built.

It was not a cheerless, high-rise biscuit box, like so many of our own American housing projects, but a long structure of six stories. At intervals, archways gave access through the building front to rear and at the same time gave an impression of airiness. Wide green lawns with trees and shrubbery surrounded it, and flowers bloomed on balconies. The apartments into which I was welcomed by smiling women, proud of their new homes, were bright and sunny and shiningly clean. Women who were working mothers were paid a salary by the city to stay home and breast-feed their children. All babies born in Vienna received a layette from the city, along with the greeting, "Welcome, new citizen!" On the project's ground floor were nurseries, kindergartens, and day-care centers filled with healthy, clear-eyed youngsters. It was a happy place and the first place bombed by Hitler in 1938 when he invaded Vienna.

Of the exploratory trips Whit and I first took into our Central European territory, I liked best those to Budapest and Prague. The Danube, unlike its disappointing brown muddiness in Vienna, was a lovely shining sapphire, flowing between the twin cities of Buda and Pest. The first café I entered had walls lined with mirrors. When a party was exceptionally successful, I was told, mirrors were often broken by exuberant guests, who hurled glasses at them, damages for which they gladly paid. I thought it the wildest extravagance of which I had ever heard until I was told it was a traditional gesture of defiance, first to the Hapsburg emperor and now to Admiral Horthy's dictatorship. Then I remembered a gleeful ditty, forbidden to Boston children, but which we sang anyway in the early days of July each year.

> The night before the Fourth!
> The night before the Fourth!
> We won't go home 'til morning

The night before the Fourth!
We'll smash the dishes and glasses
We'll kick the British asses
We won't go home 'til morning
The night before the Fourth!

The gaiety in Budapest masked great bitterness. Although
Hungary protested that it had not gone into the First World War
of its own free will but had been forced into it as a part of the
Austro-Hungarian Empire, the Treaty of Trianon took away one-
third of its territory. Transylvania was given to Rumania and
Slovakia to Czechoslovakia. To this day, the 3 million Magyars
thus transferred protest. Its seacoast was also stripped from Hungary. A communist government, headed by Béla Kun, was sup-
pressed, and a monarchy proclaimed. There was no king, so
Admiral Horthy was made regent. Hungary Irredenta—Hungary
Unredeemed—the people called it, to advertise their determination to regain the lost territory. In the Thirties when I was there
Hungary was an anomaly, a kingdom without a king, governed
by an admiral without a navy.

Until I went to Central Europe I had the impression most
Americans had that the then new nation of Czechoslovakia was a
happy, progressive country with liberal policies. Instead, its
southern and eastern sections were in frequent revolt. And
Benes, first foreign minister (later president, succeeding Masaryk), tried to censor American news dispatches. Fodor was bitter
about Benes' interference with his reports.

Prague, the capital, fascinated me because it was a journey
into the Dark Ages and because it was Franz Kafka's birthplace.
Every time I read one of the many learned "explications" of
Kafka's writings in academic journals, I want to take the author
across the Moldau River on Prague's main bridge. A statue of
Christ once stood on the bridge, and passing Jews were required
by law to kiss its feet. I would show him the ghetto's tiny ceme-

tery, which, for more than a thousand years, was the only place Jews, digging deeper and deeper, were allowed to bury their dead. Next to the cemetery I would show him the world's only Gothic synagogue, where a fifth beam was added to the traditional cross-shaped arch to make a Star of David.

Finally, I would show the scholar from an American academy thousands of miles away (spinning gauzy abstractions about an author's life *not* influencing his work), the great, ugly, royal castle squatting on a high hill and dominating the city of Prague, and, weirdest of all, the Street of the Wizards, which hugs the stone wall surrounding the base of the hill. This unbelievable street is lined with diminutive houses, none more than a few feet high, painted in vivid pastel colors, and with minute windows, gables, and balconies. The doorways look almost too small for a dog's house. Grown men once squirmed through them. They were the wizards. In these absurd houses they dwelt, weaving spells and chanting incantations as they brewed their magic potions. "Now," I would say to my "New Critic," "tell me that a writer's life has nothing to do with the novels and short stories he writes!" This is Prague, where the Jew Franz Kafka was born and grew up, and where, to quote an anonymous biographer, he found "a world which is at once real and dreamlike and in which modern man, burdened with guilt, isolation and anxiety, makes a futile search for personal salvation."

"Save some coal for the icemen," Resi told me in the morning of an early spring day I was always to remember. Nowhere is spring lovelier than in Austria's Little Bear Village. Coal? Icemen? I looked out at our sunlit garden. Against one stone wall the espaliered apple and pear trees were in pink and white blossom. Across a smooth green lawn, along the opposite wall, lilacs were pale lavender and deep purple. Resi's words didn't make sense. "Why?" I asked. She made me understand that our coal supply was getting low and that she was worried about the chilly days which often come in the middle of June. These days were the "icemen"—what New England pioneers called "squaw winter."

A little later the phone rang. A voice that combined a broad British accent with the flat one of my native Boston said, "This is Edward O'Brien. May I speak to Mr. Burnett, please?" When Whit answered he sounded first surprised, then pleased. He invited the caller to lunch. "Do you know who that was?" Whit asked me.

"Somebody named O'Brien."

"He's somebody all right. He's editor of *The Best American Short Stories.*"

"Oh! *That* O'Brien!" That O'Brien was the Saint Peter guarding the gates to a short story writer's heaven.

I rushed to the kitchen to alert Resi to prepare a most *wunderbar Mittagessen* because a very important *Herr Doktor Besucher* was coming. The solemn tone of my voice impressed her. Other male visitors continued to be *Herr Doktor* but forever after O'Brien was *Herr Doktor Besucher* to Resi.

As I write of the awe I felt at meeting O'Brien because he edited *The Best American Short Stories,* and consider how I feel about myself now that I have edited the book for many years, I cannot connect the two. Perhaps, if I had founded the anthology as had Edward, instead of only succeeding to its editorship, I, too, would feel the importance I gave to him.* I felt more important as a feature writer on the *Los Angeles Daily News* editing "Kiddie

---

*   In a 1976 interview with William G. Jaspersohn, a small portion of which was published in *Harper's Bookletter* (June 7, 1976), Martha said, "Once, when I was staying with the O'Briens in London . . . I said, 'What'll ever happen to the *Best American* in case something happens to you?' And he said, "Oh, you'll be here to take care of it.' But it was just, you know, casual. That was all. And then, when he died, both Whit and I were asked by his publisher to edit the *Best American.* And Whit said he didn't want to read all those damned magazines. He wasn't interested, didn't want to do it. A good deal like not wanting to start *STORY.* either. So, I did it alone. And then, I think Whit was sorry afterwards."—ED.

Kute" sayings and "Inquiring Photographer" interviews than I have ever felt since. But why didn't I feel important about the more demanding jobs on the more important New York and Paris newspapers or when I was editor of a magazine I founded? Why had I changed? What difference was there in my life? Whit! After he came into my life I never felt important again. Whether it was a good thing or bad, I shall never know, but only Whit was important.

Yet, even if there never had been a Whit, the word "Best" is intimidating. No one knows what is best. One has only to think of the long list of writers who were really the best of their generation and who were not recognized until after they were dead. When I realized how presumptuous is the use of the word, I reason that at least I am offering writers praise and not critical damnation. With those writers who may feel aggrieved because they are excluded, I have empathy. I am of their company. I, too, am a short story writer. Five of my stories were reprinted by O'Brien, and when I accepted editorship of the book, I made it impossible for my own writing to appear in the collection. If I do or do not reprint an author, I hope I make no writer feel as did a young poet, who collapsed under savage criticisms of his poems and died when he was only twenty-six years old. He wrote the epitaph he wanted on his tombstone. To this day it can be read in a cemetery in Rome. It should be engraved also on the mind of every literary critic. "Here lies one whose name was writ in water." The name was John Keats.*

Toward noon, Whit went out to get a bottle of good wine. He returned, breathless, to report, "O'Brien is almost here. I saw him

---

* In the same Jaspersohn interview, when asked what was the hardest part of editing an anthology, Martha replied, "That's an easy one to answer. It breaks my heart because I have to leave out so many stories I love." When asked what advice she would give to a person compiling an anthology of stories, she replied, "Pay no attention to the author's names. Thank only of the story itself. Because too many anthologies collect author's names, and my own publisher, Houghton Mifflin, would like them too, because they do sell books. But you have to bend over backwards not to be influenced by an author's reputation."—ED.

on the street outside, a big man with a black beard." The man who soon rang the doorbell and was shown into our living room by Resi most definitely was not big, blackbearded, and fearsome. He was a smiling man of medium height, about forty, with light brown hair, blue eyes, and a small mustache. He spoke a fluent German to Resi, petted our cat, and chatted with us as friends, not tense young writers eager to impress him, as he knew only too well. He told Whit he had read his *transition* contributions and liked them. (He did not mention my obsolete-word masterpiece. He probably did not read it. I doubt if anybody ever read it. I myself can't read it now.) Perhaps he had not known Whit and I were living together and came unprepared to meet two of us. He did ask if I were writing, and when I told him *Harper's Magazine* had just rejected one of my stories, he offered to read it. It was called "One with Shakespeare." He advised me to send it to *Forum,* a quality magazine now defunct, and to say that he recommended it. I didn't and why I do not know. Perhaps the iciness of the *Harper* rejection slip scared me. Or maybe I was self-conscious about using such an important name, even with its owner's permission.

O'Brien's visit lasted about two hours. In answer to our questions, he gave us glimpses of his life in Oxford and what the American Rhodes Scholars were like who visited him. Because I came from Boston, I asked him, as he was leaving, why he made his permanent home in England. "In Boston," he answered, "I am below the salt with the Beacon Hill Yankees and above the salt with the South Boston Irish. There's no place for me." I knew what he meant.

He told us he had come to Vienna from Italy, was leaving for Switzerland the next day, and planned to visit France and Germany before returning to his home in England. What he did not tell us was that he was a lonely man wandering around Europe trying to ease grief over his wife's death. We learned that sad fact only much later when we were told his wife was Romer Wilson, the brilliant English author who had the unique distinction of winning both the British Hawthornden Prize and the French Prix Femina for her novel, *Martin Schuler.* (She was also the author of many stories, including "Who Killed Cock Robin?") If I had known, I would have urged him to stay as our house guest.

Edward J. O'Brien was a young poet in his twenties, a few years out of Harvard and working on the *Boston Transcript,* when he founded *The Best American Short Stories* in 1915. There were some excellent magazines then, *The Atlantic Monthly, Harper's Magazine, Scribner's, The Century,* and others, which printed good fiction. Compared with the enormous circulations of the so-called slicks, pulps, and women's magazines, their circulation was small. The importance of the short stories they printed, many of which have become classics, was overwhelmed by the amount of trash in the popular magazines. There was a plethora of shoddy crime and adventure stories in the pulps; the boy-meets-girl-boy-loses-girl-boy-gets-girl-back-and-job-in-the-bank formula in the slicks, and the Patient Griselda type in the women's magazines, where the heroine finds that happiness is to be found in a domestic purdah. To rescue from the welter of print those stories that might be of permanent value, O'Brien founded *The Best American Short Stories.* The collection was both a critical success and a best seller and the first of a long annual series.

After O'Brien's visit it was hard for me to think of anything but all the short stories I wanted to write. I was shocked back into the reality of daily newspaper work by a letter from a friend in New York. Infuriated would be a better word. He wrote that he couldn't understand why I was *for* an Anschluss in my letters to him but *against* it in my newspaper dispatches. I cabled him to send a clipping. There it was, datelined Vienna and signed with my name, a long article attacking in vitriolic terms any union of the Republic of Austria with the Weimar Republic and citing as sacrosanct those shortsighted documents, the Versailles treaty and the Treaty of Saint-Germain. I quit the Universal service.

FIVE

∽

STORY!

I joined Whit in working for the Consolidated Press, and Pembroke Stevens, the Englishman who was correspondent for the *London Daily Express,* asked me to be his substitute when he was away from Vienna. The *Express* job was fun. I had been brought up on all the English classics and I had a lovely time mining them for images in my *Express* dispatches. "Micawber" of course was an apt title for any number of Austrian politicians; unfortunately, I could use it only once. I hit gold, though, when the Express quoted my quotation from *Tom Brown's School Days.* A headline over my account of Crown Prince Carol being exiled from Rumania read, "Crown Prince Carol Sent to Coventry!"

"Christ!" said John Gunther to Whit and me the next day. "I didn't know Pembroke Stevens could write such tripe!" I told him I was the tripe's author, which I was sure he already knew. He did not apologize. Along with Gallico and Pegler, he belonged to the old guard of male newspapermen who detested newspaperwomen. He called Dorothy Thompson "the horse-faced woman." When she wasn't around, that is. When he wrote a blurb for one of her books he called her "a blue-eyed tornado." I heard him refer to her as "horse-faced" so many times I was surprised when I met her to find that she had a pleasant, round face—not pretty, but definitely not equine.

John Gunther was the only one of the Stammtisch regulars we knew before coming to Vienna, having met him at a circus performance in Paris. I was complaining to Whit about cruelty I suspected in a trained animal act there when a young woman seated in front of us turned and spoke to me. We had known each other in Los Angeles when I worked on the *News.* After the show we had drinks with her and her companion, a large, blond young man with whom she was having an affair. He was John Gunther, who was in Paris for the *Chicago Daily News,* and like Whit, was scheduled for assignment in Vienna. We saw them several times after that and once the two young men went out on an all-night binge, an unusual escapade for Whit, who was a moderate drinker.

We were the first to arrive in Vienna. I was surprised when John, writing to us the date of his arrival, said he was bringing his wife and newborn son. In Paris, watching him with the Los Angeles girl, I had been sure he was a typical, freewheeling young bachelor. I had not the slightest inkling that he had a wife in the hospital at the time, giving birth to a baby.

The Gunthers were an interesting contrast. Both were fair-haired and blue-eyed, but there resemblance ended. Frances, like myself, was five feet tall and slender. Beside her John was monumental. She was Jewish and usually taken for Gentile, while John, of Bulgarian ancestry, was often thought Jewish. John was popular—hail-fellow-well-met with everyone. Frances, on first meeting people, studied them with the candid, questioning gaze of a child, and she was considered cold. Appearances were deceiving.

We became such close, lifelong friends with the Gunthers that we seemed at times almost like one family. Whenever we were in the same country we celebrated Thanksgivings and Christmases together. Their son, Johnny, often stayed with us when they took trips, and our problems, professional or domestic, we discussed in common. But it was never really a four-way friendship. The relationship developed because Whit and John liked each other, as did Frances and myself.

John had written a novel, *The Red Pavilion,* published in 1927, and he was at work on a second novel, furious when important news interfered. By chance I had our radio on when the Nazis invaded the German Reichstag. The uproar was horrible. Whit was out of town, and I called John to ask if he had his radio on. He let out a wail. "No, I don't! I'm trying to finish a chapter! Now this crap! Why did you have to tell me? And I've got the 'phone'!" (John never learned German, and "phone" was the way he pronounced *Föhn,* the terrible wind we all hated; periodically, with deadening effect, it came down from the Alps, stupefying people and animals alike.)

Years later Whit and I were with John in America the evening he agreed to write *Inside Europe,* the first of his "Inside" series, sociopolitical surveys of various parts of the world. Drew Pearson's *Washington Merry-Go-Round* had been a tremendous success, and the publishing company of Harper and Brothers approached John to do a European *Merry-Go-Round.* He told us about it at dinner the night before sailing for Europe and said he had refused. He was going to write more fiction.

After dinner we sat out in the garden back of the Hotel Chatham until late, talking and drinking. We went up to his room to help him pack, and Cass Canfield, Harper's president and one of the most likable publishers I know, arrived to reopen discussion about the book. John had had a lot to drink, but he was a big man and happy, not drunk. He flung himself on the bed and lay back grinning at us. "Two thousand," said Cass, which was much more money as an advance then than now. "No," said John.

"Three."

"No."

"Four."

"No."

"Five."

"Yes." Thus began the series that was to make John famous, prosperous, and unhappy.*

John was never at peace with himself. He was the only one of us being psychoanalyzed, and happy people do not consult analysts. His analyst was Wilhelm Stekel, a colleague whom Freud accused of lying. Frances did not like Stekel. John, it seemed, was not very virile and Stekel told her so, urging her to give him more encouragement. "That isn't an ethical thing for a doctor to do, is it, to violate a patient's confidence?" she asked me. "He's made me self-conscious."

Schadenfreude is a strong German word for which there is no English equivalent. It means, to quote my dictionary, "malicious enjoyment of other people's misfortunes" (and not "hatred of Freud"). The word comes to my mind as I think of George's comment and of John and Hedy Gossman. Hedy was the pathetic star of a sensational British literary scandal. While she was writing the German translation of his *Outline of History,* she and H.G. Wells became lovers. A foreign girl, unaware what a notorious philanderer Wells was, Hedy took their intimacy seriously. She thought she was proving her devotion to him when he asked her,

---

* George Weller, the journalist and fiction writer who has been stationed as a foreign correspondent in Rome, recently came to see me. He is writing his memoirs and, because we both had been in Vienna in the early Thirties, wanted to talk with me about those days. John Gunther was one of our Vienna group we discussed. I mentioned that his *New York Times* obituary had quoted John's declaration that he would rather have written one good short story than all his "Inside" books.

George commented, "Gunther was a good, energetic journalist who could never write fiction because he was too objective. He had no interest in people and no compassion for them." George urged me to read John's last novel, *The Lost City,* which is laid in Vienna and is a *roman à clef* if ever there was one. As I read it, George's observation made me see John more clearly than I ever did when he was alive. The main character in the novel, easily identified as John himself, is a humorless, self-important correspondent who plays with women like toys, with no conception of them as people. He loves things as *things.* The most emotional writing in the book are the lyrical passages describing how he adored the elegance of the luxurious suburban villa in which the Gunthers actually lived.

as a favor, to teach German to a small boy he knew. She was horrified to discover that the child was Wells's son by Rebecca West, whose long affair with Wells was public knowledge in England. Her shock was too great, and she tried to kill herself.

Attempting suicide was a crime in England. Hedy was arrested. Wells's prominence made her suicide attempt in his home front-page news. Lady Astor, an American woman married to a peer and active in English politics, felt sorry for the girl. She invited Hedy to stay at Cliveden, the historic Astor estate, and intervened to save her from prison, arranging instead that she be deported to her native Austria.

At this point, Oliver Gossman, a writer, who was one of our closest friends in Vienna, asked Hedy to marry him. She did, and they journeyed together to Vienna, where they lived not far from our Pötzleinsdorf home. Oliver was a gentle, whimsical Scotsman from Glasgow who spoke with a delightful burr. He had a private income and treated his work as correspondent for a Glasgow paper in a desultory way. Sadly, he was also desultory about writing his charming short stories of simple Scottish folk, stories that were like ballads by Robert Burns. They were published in the *Manchester Guardian,* and several were reprinted by Edward O'Brien in *The Best British Short Stories.* But they were few and far between, and his readers, publishers, and friends constantly beseeched him for more.

When I met Hedy in Vienna, scars from knife slashes were still to be seen on her throat and chest. In spite of those scars, Hedy, with her beautiful brown eyes and good features, would have been an attractive woman if she had not been so extremely nervous. The Wells affair obsessed her. She talked of it incessantly, even to strangers. Hedy's worst scars were not on her body but on her mind.

John Gunther decided that Hedy was the reason Oliver did not write. A misogynist, John blamed every wife for a husband's problems. In the Gossmans' situation, however, we thought he had a point. A writer must have peace to work. The Gunthers had rented a vacation place in the mountains near Semmering, the famous Austrian ski resort, where John joined Frances and their baby on weekends. He persuaded Hedy to spend a month with them there. This would give Oliver a chance to write. Oliver did not write. Soon after breakfast every day he came to our house. While we worked upstairs, he sat in the living room downstairs, reading, playing with the cat, and *blautchening* with Resi. After *Mittagessen* with us, he went with me for a walk in the Woods, and later he sometimes joined us in our trips around the city for news. Around *Jause* time, five o'clock, he vanished, only to return the next morning. In the meantime, Frances was reporting to me that Hedy was frantically upset, constantly worrying about Oliver. At the end of a week they were back together again.

On a trip to London John asked H.G. Wells about Hedy, and Wells burst into a rage. "That woman ruined my best carpet with her damned blood!" he shouted. John laughed as he told us. So much for two cold men and a brokenhearted woman.

Both as a man and as a writer, William L. Shirer made John Gunther seem frivolous. John realized this and was jealous of Bill. I was once at a party where Bennett Cerf asked John what he thought of *Berlin Diary,* Bill's first book, which was than having a tremendous success. "You know where you can stick it," John said, and Bennett laughed. Soon after, Bill arrived and John exclaimed, "Oh, Bill, how wonderful! *Berlin Diary* has made the best-seller list! Congratulations!" Although I have not seen him since our Vienna days, when he was a *Chicago Tribune* correspondent, I remember Shirer as an utterly real person, one to be trusted as a friend.* His books on Hitler's Germany are solid achieve-

---

* Martha visited Shirer at his home in Lenox, Massachusetts, during the summer of 1977, shortly before her death. Shirer was, in fact, in the act of writing a letter to her, in answer to one from her, when he saw the news of her death in the *New York Times.*—ED.

ments, and his monumental *Rise and Fall of the Third Reich* is a classic. Like most of us at the Café Louvre Stammtisch, Bill's ambition was to write fiction, and he published novels and short stories. The popularity of his books about Germany has always overshadowed them. (Fiction, though, often has a way of outlasting factual writing; this may well prove true of Bill's stories.)

With Fodor, Best, and me, Bill Shirer was a stowaway on the fabled Orient Express, then the world's most luxurious railroad train, chariot of kings and nabobs. We stole the ride to interview a queen, Marie of Rumania. No matter how grim things became in the rest of Europe, little Rumania could always be counted upon for comic relief. Its ruling family belonged in a Gilbert and Sullivan operetta, not on a twentieth-century throne. Silly crisis followed silly crisis in their lives. Palace intrigues, elopements, morganatic marriages, divorces, and decrees of banishment, directed at one royal family member or another, followed one another in rapid succession. This time it was a power struggle which developed between Queen Marie and her son, Crown Prince Carol. Each in turn banished the other from Rumania. When it was her turn to be banished, the queen took refuge in Munich.

"Come Home, Mother, All Is Forgiven!" was the way the newspapers headlined Carol's invitation to his mother. We got word that the queen would pass through Vienna (aboard the Orient Express) on her way back to Bucharest, and that she would be aboard that heavily guarded train in Vienna for at least two hours. This was the time it would take the Orient to circle around the city, first stopping at the West Station to drop off passengers and stopping again at the East Station, on the other side of the city, to pick up passengers bound for the Balkans and Middle East.

I had a bright idea. In Austria, as in many European countries, people wishing to greet or say good-bye to train passengers buy platform tickets. These tiny cardboards they must show on entering and leaving the platform. My suggestion was to buy East

Station platform tickets and then to go to the West Station, to buy *its* platform tickets and to wait for the queen's train to arrive. We could thereby ride around the city with her and have plenty of time for an interview, and when we debarked at the East Station, the platform tickets we bought earlier would enable us to pass the guards unmolested.

There was always a big to-do when the Orient Express, that "monarch of the rails" as it was called, came into a station, its steam whistle giving a long, boastful blast. This time there was a greater than usual hubbub, with extra police to protect Her Majesty and the station jammed with excited Rumanians. In the confusion it was easy for us to board the royal coach.

We found the queen as regal and beautiful as her pictures, graciously extending her hand to be kissed by a bevy of obsequious courtiers, among whom Fodor recognized Rumania's ambassador to Austria. Vienna's Socialist Democratic mayor was conspicuous by his absence. Elegantly gowned ladies curtseyed. True to her reputation, Her Royal Majesty loved publicity and didn't at all mind our jostling her loyal subjects to ask personal questions about her quarrel with the crown prince.

Suddenly Fodor grabbed my arm. "We're in trouble," he whispered. "Look!" He held up an East Station platform ticket together with one he had just used in the West Station. "Our East Station tickets aren't punched!" It was true. Only the West Station tickets had a cryptic series of little holes, made by a guard. In our rush to reach the queen, his action had not registered on us. "How the hell are we going to get out of the other station?"

The train kept on its way, carrying us to our expected doom. We lost interest in Her Majesty. If it had been only an Austrian train it would have been all right. All newspaper correspondents in Vienna were provided with passes. But we had stolen a trip on the *Orient Express!* The great international train was under the protection of a number of governments and was the most expensive, most luxurious, most heavily guarded, and most sacrosanct train in the whole world.

The minute the train stopped in the East Station, we fell over one another in our hurry to get out and away. We found ourselves walking on a strip of red carpet extended across the platform. Station attendants bowed and beamed at us. We were ushered into the palatial gold-and-crimson waiting room of the Hapsburg emperors. The attendants may have taken our rudeness to them for haughty aristocratic disdain. We didn't wait to find out. We dashed onto the street and into a taxicab. A glance behind us showed workmen rolling up the strip of red carpet. His Excellency the Rumanian ambassador, as well as all the other dignitaries and their elegantly gowned ladies, were going to have to walk on a plain, uncarpeted floor.

Nostalgic for Paris when we first arrived in Vienna, Whit and I had collaborated on an article about the *Paris Herald,* titled "Your Home Town Paper: Paris." I suggested it because I thought H.L. Mencken, as a newspaperman himself, might buy it for *The American Mercury,* and I was right. He wrote me asking for some more Vienna articles. Knowing that another interest of Mencken's was medical matters, I thought of him immediately when Dr. Noah Fabricant, a young doctor fresh from medical school and newly arrived from Chicago, approached me at a party to ask if I would help him write an article for some magazine about American doctors in Vienna. He was appalled by the situation existing in postgraduate medical studies for foreign doctors, mainly American, and wanted to expose it. I, too, was shocked when he described a gigantic diploma mill.

From the early 1800s Vienna had been famous as the medical capital of the world. Sick people from many countries made pilgrimages there to be treated by Viennese physicians. Desire for consultations with the eminent specialists also brought countless doctors, many themselves well known in their own countries. By 1930 all that had changed. Since the founding of the American Medical Association of Vienna on Thanksgiving day 1903, no fewer than eight thousand doctors had arrived in Vienna as mere M.D.s and had left the association's pink-curtained coffeehouse headquarters as high-powered specialists.

The American Medical Association of Vienna was not to be confused with the mighty American Medical Association of the United States, which had repudiated any connection with it. The Vienna outfit had also been damned by the New York Academy of Medicine. Their enmity was based on opposition to the *Zeugnis,* the elegantly engraved certificate, bearing the name of the University of Vienna, which rewarded any doctor who went to Vienna to study, whether he spent four unsupervised months in clinical sessions or only in the company of a soft-eyed *fraulein.* Back in the States this *Zeugnis* could be prominently displayed in the doctor's office. The impressed patient then told friends, "My doctor, Dr. Hoopla, is wonderful because he is a Vienna specialist!"

Section I, clause A of the Vienna Association's bylaws proclaimed, "All applicants for membership shall have their credentials and their qualifications passed upon by a member of the executive committee appointed by the president, before they shall be granted full membership in this associciation." To test the law, I myself applied, stating I was a graduate of the Harvard University Medical School, and I was accepted for membership and made welcome.

The University of Vienna, whose name the association exploited, was an honorable institution acting in good faith. The swindle the association imposed upon both the university and American doctors arose out of the big difference between American and European educational systems. On the Continent the student was left to acquire knowledge on his own responsibility. In the United States he was ushered and managed from class to class to exam. Fine courses were provided by the University of Vienna, but the association, apart from announcements of courses plastered all over its walls like so many "For Sale" signs, gave no guidance to its members, who were unaccustomed to foreign education methods. And the university, following the rules that its own students knew how to follow, took it for granted that the Americans did the same.

Mencken published our article in the November 1931 issue of *The American Mercury,* and it caused wide comment. The *Journal of the American Medical Association* reprinted it, many other magazines quoted extracts from it, and newspapers used the article as a springboard for editorials on medical ethics. There were repercussions from as far away as Australia. Someone brought Dr. Sippey, president of the Medical Association of Vienna, and his wife to our Pötzleinsdorf house while I was having a party. I was petrified until I was called "Mrs. Burnett" in the introduction, so that he did not recognize me as the author of the *Mercury* article. The real challenge to my poise came when I in turn had to introduce Dr. Sippey and his wife to my guests. She was, of course, Mississippi.

There was another group of doctors who had no connection with the American Medical Association of Vienna. These were the many psychiatrists who came to Vienna because it was the fount of psychoanalysis. Freud, suffering from cancer of the jaw, saw a limited number of them. He gave no newspaper interviews while I was there. One of the few laypersons he saw was William Bullitt, with whom he collaborated on a psychohistory of Franklin D. Roosevelt. But even if Freud had been accessible, American papers had little interest in psychoanalysis. It seemed vaguely immoral somehow. I forget how great has been the revolution in sexual attitudes until I look back at the Thirties in Vienna. There we all were, in the birthplace of psychoanalysis, the home of Sigmund Freud himself, and we wrote little about the science. Not even during the World Sex Congress, when delegates who were internationally renowned analysts came to our Stammtisch, and we knew they wanted publicity, did we pay much attention.

I did interview Alfred Adler, "father of the inferiority complex." An inferiority complex sounded more respectable then the love life of poor Oedipus, I suppose. I liked Dr. Adler. He was a kind man who, busy as he was, gave me several hours of his time. It interested me to observe that he himself had an inferiority complex. "I would appreciate it, Fraulein," he told me, "if you will write in your interview corrections of two false reports about me. One is that I hear in New York they are saying I am in disfavor with the University of Vienna when I am actually giving courses there at this very moment. Also, if you please, Fraulein, be so good as to write—here, I shall show you a letter—that what people in Vienna say about Columbia University dismissing me is also not true. This I show you is a letter from Columbia giving the schedule of the hours they wish me to lecture next term." I promised him I would and I did.

The Jolases visited Austria, and we joined them for a weekend in Feldkirch, a small ancient city on the Swiss border. It was a joy to see Maria and Gene again, and to talk of writers and books with them as we had so many times in Paris. The most *avant* of the literary *avant-garde,* they made me realize how much I missed the excitement of knowing about important new writing. There was plenty of intelligent literary conversation at the Stammtisch, of course, but it lacked the challenge, the adventure of what went on in the *transition* group. Discussions with the Jolases were more intoxicating than the Gösserbrau (which is the world's finest beer, superior even to the more famous Pilsen, but can be drunk only inside Austria because it does not stand shipping). I have known many writers and many editors but none who could speak so rapturously about literature as Eugene Jolas. He was a man transported.

Now, in the intensity of his devotion to experimental writing,

he was probing deeper into literary exploration of what he called
"the night mind." *Transition* had published much stream-of-consciousness writing, but this, as Jolas described it, was different. It
stressed the visionary and the magical. It was a kind of metaphysi-
cal romanticism, a dialectic of the rational and irrational. Gene
used such words as "orphic" and "third eye" and "mantic" while
explaining his theory. "Orphic" I remembered from my school
days as referring to Orpheus, classical god of song and poetry,
whom the Greeks celebrated in the Orphic Mysteries. The "third
eye" I had read about as a mystifying gland in the brain, also
called "the pineal eye," whose function scientists have never
determined, but which has inspired many speculations. Some
have theorized that it is vestigial, dating from an earlier evolution-
ary stage in primitive man. The more imaginative of this group
have theorized that it gave primitive man magical powers of
foresight and telepathy. An opposing group, Gene among them,
thought that it was the start of a new organ that will have these
powers and eventually replace the "big brain." ("Mantic" I had
to look up in a dictionary, and I found that it meant having the
power of divination.)*

Jolas had, by this time, supplanted "The Revolution of the
Word Manifesto," with a new document, "Poetry Is Vertical."
Two of the statements in it were: "Esthetic will is not the first law.
It is in the immediacy of the ecstatic revelation, in the a-logical
movement of the psyche, in the organic rhythm of the vision that

---

* As a foe of New Criticism who does not believe that interpreting a literary
work must be strictly limited to the actual words on a page (while ignoring an
author's life), I think Gene represents a wonderful confirmation of my stand. It
is easy to see the source of his theories when one considers that he was swimming
all his life in an ocean of words fed by the rivers of three languages—German,
French, and English—and was given a mystical, monastic education for the priesthood in Catholicism, with that religion's belief in miracles. This is in no way meant
to denigrate his importance in modern literature, because he occupies a foremost
place in history. I am proud that I knew him and his wife and fellow editor, Maria
Jolas, as friends. The translator of Sarraute, Mrs. Jolas has continued contributing
to experimental fiction.

the creative act occurs"; and "The reality of depth can be conquered by a voluntary mediumistic conjuration, by a stupor which proceeds from the irrational to a world beyond a world." The best known, to Americans, of the new manifesto's signers was Samuel Beckett.*

After telling us about his plans, Gene suddenly announced that *transition* would publish no more fiction. "No short stories?" I asked.

"No," he replied. "No short stories."

Déja vu! It was not 1930 but 1925, and I was back in California listening to the unhappiness of writers disoriented by the *Smart Set's* sale and Mencken's and Nathan's emphasis on articles in their new publication, *The American Mercury.* Like the old *Smart Set, transition* had been publishing such splendid short story writers! The list was long and included, among others, Kay Boyle, Robert Coates, Laura Riding, Kenneth Fearing, Ernest Hemingway, Dawn Powell, Djuna Barnes, Peter Neagoe, John Hermann, Katherine Anne Porter, Paul Bowles, Edgar Calmer, Josephine Herbst, Erskine Caldwell—and more. Nor does the list include the many European short story writers, then unknown but now internationally recognized, whose work was furthered by Jolas in *transition.* Then, too, there were Whit and myself, out in the cold. After his original disdain for *transition,* Whit, encouraged by Jolas, had become an enthusiastic contributor. And I, myself, who had been writing short stories off and on since I was a child, still hoped to appear again in its pages. Although our weekend with our beloved friends was exhilarating, when we left Feldkirch we were subdued and depressed.

Soon after our return to Vienna, Whit was instructed to make what we correspondents called "a swing around the Balkans."

---

* Douglas MacMillan, in his book transition, *1927–38* (Braziller), has done a brilliant analysis, and I suggest that readers who are interested will find there a more detailed explanation than I have been able to give in a brief space.

This was a tour of our territory to explore personally develop-ments in the various countries, confer with the "stringers," and write firsthand interpretive reports. Whit's trip encompassed Yu-goslavia, Rumania, Bulgaria, Albania, Greece, and Turkey. There was no regular air service then, and he was to travel by train and boat and to be gone for close to two months. I remained behind to handle the Vienna Bureau.

Those summer months of 1930 were a comparatively calm period for Austria. It might be called not a calm before the storm but a calm between storms, that of the chancellorship of Monsi-gnor Seipel, the *Heimwehr* leader of the Christian Socialist party who attacked parliamentary democracy, and the fascist adminis-tration of Chancellor Dollfuss, who was to proclaim a dictatorship and be assassinated. Although I had been his guest at social func-tions, I couldn't remember the name of the intermediate chancel-lor. My history of modern Europe made no reference to the man who had occupied a difficult position between two villains who were accorded long biographies. (He exemplified the title of Flannery O'Connor's frightening short story, "A Good Man Is Hard to Find.") Finally the name, Johann Schober, came back to me and I looked him up in an encyclopedia. There, in a brief paragraph, he was described as "a respected civil servant who, more liberal than his predecessor, Monsignor Seipel, instituted constitutional reforms and advocated a customs union with the Weimar Republic of Germany." My invitation from Chancellor Schober read "reception," but it was unlike any official reception I had attended elsewhere. It did begin with the usual bore of a formal receiving line in the ornate, baroque ballroom. Afterward the government officials, diplomats, and various celebrities stood around in sedate groups, talking and listening to an orchestra. A murmur was heard among us. *"Das Bier! Das Bier!"* Attendants were wheeling in a long table laden with foaming steins. A gallant gentleman took my arm and hurried me along with the other guests rushing pell-mell, New York subway-style toward the table. It was, of course, the splendid Gösserbrau. When it arrived, the orchestra played the "Blue Danube," and a lively party, no longer formal, began.

If the Austrian people were being allowed a little peace during that placid summer of 1930, I was having almost too much excitement. A letter for Whit arrived from 118 Banbury Road, Oxford, England. "Dear Sir: I ask your formal permission to reprint 'Two Men Free' in *The Best American Short Stories of 1930.* Faithfully yours, Edward J. O'Brien."

I let out a whoop and headed for the kitchen and Resi. The poor woman had no idea what I was trying to tell her in a jumble of English and German, but she knew, whatever the commotion was about, that it made me happy. She simply kept smiling and repeating, *"Gott sei dank! Gott sei dank!"*

Next I called my closest friend in Vienna, Frances Gunther, who did understand and was properly impressed. "What did Whit say?" she asked. "Oh, my God! I haven't told him!" I hung up on her and put in a call for the Balkan town where I thought Whit might be. He wasn't there, and I had to struggle with telephone operators of various nationalities while I traced him. By the time I reached him, the full impact of the O'Brien letter had hit me and I was crying. "What's wrong?" He was alarmed. "What's the matter?"

"Nothing. I—" My voice choked up.

"Why are you crying"

"I'm happy."

"That's a hell of a way to be happy!"

I managed to read him the letter. "Gosh!" That was his only comment. It was typical of Whit.*

---

* "Whit will be so well known he will be able to sell every story he writes!" I thought jubilantly, remembering what I had heard in Paris about O'Brien and Hemingway. All of the many short stories Hemingway wrote had been rejected. He made little money from sporadic correspondence for a Canadian paper, and it was his wife Hadley's small income that was keeping him, her, and their baby son alive. When a suitcase containing all his manuscripts, except two stories on which he was working, was stolen in a railway station, he was so disheartened he

"Now Whit will only have to send his story to an editor to have it accepted . . ." my thoughts raced on. What editor? Where? Reality intruded like the dash of cold water I needed. Not to *transition* where "Two Men Free," the story O'Brien would reprint, was published. Gene Jolas had just told me he would take no more stories. Not to Mencken who had bought two of Whit's stories years ago. He, too, no longer wanted short stories. The other quality magazines in the States now had a puny limit of one or two stories an issue. Goddamn it! Short stories are an important part of literature, I said to myself. Why isn't there one good fiction magazine?

Why, indeed! And then it came to me. Whit and I would start one. But money! We would need money. I didn't know how much Whit had in the bank. My own account totaled sixty-five dollars. I thought briefly about my grandfather's money, which had been left to me in a trust fund, and forced myself to forget it. Dickens's case of Jarndyce and Jarndyce in *Bleak House,* with its years-long tangle of litigations, family fights, and constantly disappointed expectations of wealth, could have been a history of the Foley estate. Ours was microscopic compared with the fortune Dickens wrote about, but it had, like the Jarndyce money, brought misery and ruin to my family. I was sure that it would end with all the money swallowed up in court costs.

I also thought of Rex Stout. He had been in banking, had retired with money, and, as vice-president of the Vanguard Press, had publishing experience. But I abandoned the idea. Rex's letters from Brewster, New York, where he himself was building the new, ultramodern house he had designed, expressed so much

---

decided to abandon writing and try to earn a living at something else. In Switzerland he met O'Brien and told him his tale of woe. O'Brien asked to see the two stories Hemingway had left. One of them was "My Old Man." O'Brien reprinted it in *The Best American Short Stories of 1923* and dedicated the book to its author. Hemingway (then spelled Hemenway) was notorious for his meanness to the people who helped him, particularly Sherwood Anderson, but he never failed to acknowledge the help O'Brien had given him.

delight with his new life that I was sure he would not be interested in a magazine. He described how every morning he wrote a thousand words of his new novel and every afternoon worked at being carpenter, mason, and all the other jobs building a house require. No, I decided, his life was too full.

I tried to get through to Whit again. Resi was distressed that I would not eat *Mittagessen,* but I was too nervous. The hours went by and no call came from Whit in response to my urgent message. I guessed he might be on a train between cities. Resi asked what I would like for *Jause,* but I was too restless to stay in the house, and I told her I would have it at the Stammtisch. On the way to the coffeehouse I stopped in at the Journalistenzimmer, nearby, to see who might be there. I was bursting with my news about Whit and wanted to broadcast it. Only one man, operating a mimeograph machine, was in the room. He was Bill Shirer's Austrian assistant. I waited for him to finish before speaking to him. And as I stood watching him turn the inky roller, I knew how Whit and I could publish a magazine. We would mimeograph it on this machine!

Delighted with the discovery, I went to the Stammtisch, where I had *Kaffee Mit.* That meant coffee was heaped with baroque mountains of sugared whipped cream, which was no sweeter to me than my plans. Fodor and Best were at the Stammtisch, discussing the day's news, but they stopped to listen with interest to my report of Whit's success and to send him their congratulations. My exhilaration at discovering the mimeograph as a printing solution vanished as soon as another financial problem occurred to me: the authors would have to be paid.

The next morning, after a night so restless that Fritzl, who always slept at the foot of my bed, left it to seek serenity elsewhere, I had an idea. Our magazine would be a sales catalogue. Every story in it would be for sale. We would call it "a proof book," because it would be a proof of what splendid short stories authors were writing. Once editors and publishers had a chance to see them, they would be delighted to buy them, and we could give the authors the money. Go ahead and laugh! Years later I was having lunch with Eleanor Stierhem, fiction editor of *Collier's Magazine,* and she said, "You know, it's funny. I'll reject a story, but often, when I see it in print somewhere else it looks so good to me, I wonder what was the matter with my judgment." My idea may have been naïve, but it was not altogether mad.

By the time Whit was due to return, I had just about decided that if he took the same attitude as Doug Turney, I myself would go ahead with the magazine. The more I thought about it, the more I became convinced that disregard for the short story—for a literary art form equal in importance to poetry, novels, and essays—was plain stupid. The Bible was full of short stories, I told myself, as were the classics, such as *Aesop's Fables* and the *Satyricon. The Arabian Nights* has been traced far back in Persia. The Middle Ages produced the *Gesta Romanorum* and the *Decameron* and Chaucer's *Tales.* And in America! Good God, beginning with Irving and Poe, who are still read with delight, the number of beautiful American short stories was almost endless. They were still being written. So I raged on to my young self, forty-five years ago; and today my older self agrees.

Whit got back from his long Balkan tour, and before he had his hat and coat off, I handed him the O'Brien letter. He read it, said "Gosh!" again, put it in his pocket, and went upstairs to bathe and change. When he came down, I said, "If you say 'Gosh!' one more time, I won't be responsible for my actions!"

"How about a drink, then?"

We had the drink, and a couple more, and Whit maddened me by going into interminable details about his trip. How he had seen so many beautiful small rugs in Turkey and could afford to buy only two; how the Greeks and the Turks said the same insulting thing about each other—"If you shake hands with one, count your fingers!"; how in Albania, the family feuds were even worse than those of the Hatfields and McCoys in America, because, if all the men in a family were killed, their women relatives were expected to start shooting.

"I want to start a magazine." I declared, stopping his travelogue cold.

"Now that's a fine, cockeyed idea! How'd you get it?"

"Worrying about your short stories. Where you're going to get them published."

"Listen here! Start a magazine all by yourself? You can't!"

"I thought we might do it together."

"God Almighty! I've come home to a crazy woman!"

We were off. Into days of argument. Whit agreed that there was no literary short story magazine and that one was needed. He agreed that the chances against a short story, no matter how good, being published in those magazines that still used a few of them were astronomical. He agreed that mimeographing might be a feasible substitute for printing, but only after I reminded him that he once had risked going to jail for underground publishing via mimeograph. (When I first knew him he told me how he broke the law, as a cub reporter, by mimeographing a birth-control leaflet containing contraceptive information. And he'd done it surreptitiously on a mimeograph machine in the Utah State Capitol building in the very heart of Mormon Country, where polygamy had been promoted to increase the birthrate of Latter Day Saints.) He agreed with me about everything but that we should ourselves publish a short story magazine. I could see, though, that he was weakening.

"Let's ask John what he thinks," he said one evening at dinner, where Resi's fine food had grown cold while we argued. John, of course, was John Gunther. I was delighted. With his primary interest in his own fiction writing, I figured, John would approve. It was a short trip to Dollinergasse in Döbling, the suburb where the Gunthers rented the second floor of a mansion owned by a war-impoverished family. John was that legendary thin-man-inside-a-fat-man, screaming to get out, and was always trying new reducing diets. This time it was something called "the

Hollywood diet." It consisted only of grapefruit, which he ate all day long: but then all evening he drank calorie-rich beer. He was drinking beer when we arrived at his apartment.

"Martha wants to start a short story magazine," Whit told him.

John choked on his beer, sputtered, "That's the funniest thing I ever heard!" and roared with laughter.

In the cab going back home we were quiet. Whit tried to be consoling. "It was a nice idea, I appreciate your wanting to help me," he said. "But you can see how impractical it is."

More than once I have been called stubborn, and I guess I am. I went ahead with my plans for my as yet nameless magazine. I made out a list of titles, but none seemed right. In letters to friends in Paris and New York I said I was planning a short story magazine. Friends in Austria, Hungary, and Czechoslovakia with whom I talked were enthusiastic. Soon our postman was delivering manuscripts from short story authors, some well known, starved for a publisher. If you want to get a lot of mail, start a magazine!

Whit remained aloof, but it was impossible not to talk with him about what was consuming so much of my time and interest. His attitude was "wait and see." I read him my list of proposed titles, *Short Story Parade, Modern Tales, Fiction Journal,* and more, all inane. I asked which he preferred. Keeping to his stand that I was to be indulged but not encouraged, he answered, "They're all OK, I guess."

"Damn you! I hope you never get published again!" I said, and I took my list and marched out of the room. A few days later we were hanging to straps in a crowded streetcar on our way back to Pötzieinsdorf from the city, when Whit looked down at me and asked, "Why don't we call it 'Story'?"

It was the perfect title, and Whit had said "We"!

Whoosh! "Fritzl!" Whoosh! "For Christ's sake, somebody get this damn animal out of here! Resi!" Whit yelled down to the kitchen. Fritzl loved our starting a magazine. There were so many nice stacks of paper everywhere to whoosh through and send flying in all directions. Resi came, picked up the cat, patted his head, and carried him away with her, all with a long-suffering look on her face. Domestic perfectionist that she was, she hated the magazine that had brought untidiness into her orderly housekeeping.

Away off in New York, word of the magazine bothered other people. What were their Central European correspondents doing, the bosses at the Consolidated Press main office wanted to know —publishing fiction in a magazine or reporting facts in news dispatches? We were lucky the wonderful William Bird was our European boss. As I mentioned earlier, Bird had his own small "Three Mountains Press," which published important new writing, including Hemingway's first book, *Three Stories and Ten Poems.* He reassured the New York office in such a way that it left us in peace.

It was slow going, starting *STORY* as a mimeographed publication. I had learned my typing in a newspaper city room. There speed was more urgent than appearance, and mistakes were x-ed out instead of erased. But a lot of x's speckling a page would not be tolerated in a magazine. I had never cut stencils before, and I ruined many sheets. Shirer's assistant showed me how to operate the *Journalistenzimmer* machine, which was turned by hand. Oliver Gossman promised to help me, but after an hour at the chore, he vanished not to return for several days. He had no further interest in mimeographing. Nor was Whit interested. I knew better than to ask him, for I remembered how, years before in New York, when I was complaining about washing dishes late at night after a dinner party, Whit had said to me, "Get a woman in and pay her fifty cents to do them."

The plan to start a literary short story magazine was mine, but once it was aroused, Whit's enthusiasm was a driving force. We complemented each other in many ways. His conservatism and my radicalism struck a balance. He was neat with a desk bare of papers. Somewhere else there was a volcano that spewed paper instead of lava, and the eruption landed on my desk. I was impulsive, Whit was deliberate. I had most of the ideas, Whit saw to their execution. He had temper tantrums. I tried to laugh my way through crises. Ours, contrary to what might have been expected, was for a long time an ideal editorial combination.

STORY's first issue was delayed also because the newspaper work that was our livelihood had to come first. Important history was made by the events we reported that fall and winter; how important we were not to know until they exploded into the Second World War. The campaign for an Anschluss between Austria and Germany intensified. Leading Socialist Democrats, quoted in their party's paper the *Arbeiter-Zeitung,* made frantic pleas for union with the Weimar Republic. Nazi Germans, who loathed the democratic Weimar Republic, increased their Austrian propaganda. Hitler, too, wanted Anschluss with Austria, but with the kind of Austria the *Heimwehr* Fascists controlled.

I saw my first swastika on my way back from a peaceful walk in the Vienna woods. Its ugliness was splashed with white paint across the cobblestones of Neugasse, a narrow street near our house. I told Resi. *"Schweinerei und Schlumperei!"* she declared. Swinishness and Sluttishness! A week later I saw a *Heimwehr* mob attack a group of Jewish students at the University of Vienna.

Sometimes I think history is a record of the children's game —"Tag, you're it"—only played by adults with guns. A scapegoat had to be found for misled people, impoverished and humiliated by defeat in the First World War. The Jews were it. Until that time I was not conscious of anti-Semitism in Austria. I was blind. I should have seen that the very name of the political party that controlled the country's national government was an anti-Semitic affront—*Christian Socialist.* No Jews wanted. But I was so interested in studying the operations of the first socialist government I had ever seen in action, the Social-Democratic city government, I forgot that it was limited to Vienna.

The evening of the last day of October, I went into the kitchen before dinner to speak to Resi. Lighted candles were on the kitchen table. It was All Souls' Eve, Resi explained. "We call it Halloween in America," I told her. I wanted to explain that we, too, lighted candles and that we put them inside hollowed-out pumpkins and called them Jack o' Lanterns, but my German vocabulary was too sparse. Resi pointed to a group of candles bunched together. They were in memory of her father and mother and other relatives. She pointed to two candles set to one side. They were for the memory of her beloved former employers, Herr and Frau Qualla. The next day, All Souls' Day, she took flowers to her parents' grave in the Catholic cemetery. Then she went to the Jewish cemetery, where she placed flowers on the grave of Herr and Frau Qualla. When she came home she was angry. The Qualla grave was neglected. The iron fence around their plot had rusted, and the ground was overgrown with weeds. The Qualla children, she told me, had forgotten their wonderful parents. Darling Resi! Humble house servant, Gentile Austrian countrywoman of Adolph Hitler, who, on her own holy day of Christian remembrance, laid flowers on the neglected grave of two forgotten Jews and proved that not all people of any country are bad.

The November sky was wintry gray when I saw a strange kind of cloud, intensely black, moving across it. As the cloud came nearer and lower, I saw that it was made up of enormous black birds. "Resi! Come quick!" I pointed out the window. *"Raben,"* she said matter-of-factly. *"Schnee Kommt."* Ravens! The words of Poe's famous poem repeated themselves in my head. If those were ravens, then no raven ever "perched upon a bust of Pallas, just above my chamber door." The birds I watched were bigger then turkeys. British critics accused Poe of plagiarizing Dickens, charging he stole the poem's idea from *Barnaby Rudge.* The accusation was ridiculous. Poor half-witted Barnaby's pet raven and

Poe's ominous bird have nothing in common. Poe was no ornithologist and, like most Americans, he confused ravens with crows.

Resi was right about *Schnee.* A big snowstorm followed the ravens, as they settled down for the winter in the Vienna woods. To Fritzl's horror, a raven occasionally foraged in our garden and sent him scampering indoors, where he crouched, staring out the window at that awful paradox—a bird that could scare a cat.

Bunches of twigs, sprinkled with artificial frost, appeared in shop windows along with Christmas toy displays. They were a warning to the Austrian children to be very, very, *very* good. If they were not good, Grampus would leave those sticks on Christmas Eve to beat them with and Saint Nicholas would leave them no presents. Grampus, that legendary anti-Santa Claus, never did put in an appearance during the Christmas season as far as I could see. A Viennese Christmas custom I could vouch for, thanks to Resi, was the washing on December 24 of every window in a home until each was sparkling clean. If the windows of a house were dirty, the Christ child would not visit there. After Paris, where the French had treated Christmas as a quiet religious holiday, the Viennese celebration was exhilarating. In spite of the city's impoverishment, its gaiety caught up everyone, including ourselves, in a week-long round of exuberant parties, culminating in a big bash on New Year's Eve.

The Fodors, the Gunthers, and we combined forces and funds to give a New Year's Eve party for the correspondents' group. We held it on the spacious second floor of the Gunthers' rented mansion, where there was plenty of room for dancing. Newspaper people have a gift for the convivial, and I have never known them to give a party that was not a success. Ours was no exception. There was an abundance of good food, good drink, and good talk.

A roast suckling pig was the *pièce de résistance* on the buffet table. In the Viennese tradition, each guest was served a tiny piece of its ear, with the admonition to carry it at all times, like a rabbit's foot in America. It would bring us something we were all going to need desperately—luck. Never again for many years would there be such carefree New Year's festivities as on that eve of 1931—not in Vienna, not anywhere in the civilized world.

SIX

ᔐ

MARRIAGE

STORY
THE ONLY MAGAZINE DEVOTED SOLELY
TO THE SHORT STORY

The only purpose of Story is to present, regularly from one place, a number of Short Stories of exceptional merit. It has no theories and is part of no movement. It presents short narratives of significance by no matter whom and coming from no matter where.

It is not an anthology, but a sort of proof-book of hitherto unpublished manuscripts. Some of the stories will doubtless appear later in other, perhaps more permanent pages, and the rights remain vested in the authors, to whom communications may be addressed, or to the Editors of Story, 16 Poetzleinsdorferstrasse (xviii) Vienna. Thus the magazine is withheld by the editors from public sale in England and the United States, but may be obtained in Vienna, Paris, Nice, Budapest and Berlin.

Only short stories are considered, and if and when any articles are used, they will be as rare as Short Stories of creative importance are today in the article-ridden magazines of America.

This announcement appeared on the first page of the first issue of *STORY,* vol. I, no. 1. It was dated April–May 1931. 1931! The year the Great Depression began.* If ever there were babes in the business woods, they were Whit and myself. Whit had been allowed to graduate from the Salt Lake City High School on his promise that he would never take a job as bookkeeper, and I had got a passing grade in mathematics at Latin School because my algebra teacher caught me in study period reading a copy of Tennyson's poems concealed behind a textbook, and she loved Tennyson. The only times Whit and I discussed money in connection with the magazine was as to how we could finance its publication. *STORY* was not conceived as a money-making enterprise but as a crusade.

Our ignorance of commerce was proved by our starting a magazine in a depression. It was more immediately demonstrated to us when we decided to splurge on a printed cover to camouflage my crude mimeographed pages. Olivia Dehn, like her brother, the well-known Adolph Dehn, an artist, designed the cover for us. It was a simple, modern design, stark in comparison with the magazine covers then in fashion. The word *STORY* in bold black type extended diagonally across a bright orange background. At the bottom of the page were printed in smaller type the city, Vienna, the date, April–May, and the price, Sch. 3.20, approximately forty-five cents in American currency. Knowing the price of printing in the United States, with trepidation we approached Herr Hollinek, a printer with a Buchdruckerei in

---

* The Depression did not begin with the Wall Street stock market crash in October 1929, as many people suppose. There was panic in America then, much selling of stocks and loss of jobs, but nothing like the devastation that lay ahead. That began in May 1931, when a New York bank, alarmed by the sudden apparent imminence of a union of the Austrian and German Republics, withdrew support from Vienna's Kredit Anstalt, the biggest bank in Central Europe, and one of the world's most powerful. Its collapse shattered the global, interwoven financial and political structure, which, like Humpty-Dumpty, could not be put together again. Not for many bitter years, at least.

Steingasse. The price to print several hundred covers the smiling Herr Hollinek quoted to us *was* a shock. Whit turned to me in amazement and exclaimed, "Why, that's less than for a few handbills in New York!" It was little more than a dollar. My poor mimeograph-blistered fingers! It had never occurred to me to investigate printing costs in Vienna, where everything was expensive but printing was cheap.

Right away we wanted to know how much it would cost to print an entire issue of the magazine. What *The American Mercury* paid me for a single article, $150, would pay for two issues of *STORY!* On the spot we told Herr Hollinek we would like him to print future issues. But before signing a printing contract, could we please see his presses and typesetting machines? Of course, he assured us. Unfortunately, at that moment his manager was out. Another time would be fine. Several futile trips to Steingasse followed. The office was always open, but the plant itself was closed to us. Either the manager was absent again, or it was a holiday unknown to us, or there was some other mysterious, inexplicable reason. Finally we said we were sorry, but we would have to seek another printer.

At that, Herr Hollinek broke down and confessed. He had been ashamed to show us his equipment. He was ashamed because we were Americans who came from an efficient country full of wonderful machines. And he—he—well, the type in his shop was set only *by hand!* I wanted to hug him. *STORY* was going to be printed in beautiful handset type on rag paper! And all for seventy-five dollars an issue. And no more my struggling with mimeograph stencils! Screamer! Screamer! Screamer! As printers call exclamations.

No critic could have determined the future trend of the magazine from that initial issue. We ourselves never thought of doing so. The contents were literary short stories, and that is all we cared about. They made for eclectic reading. Whit led off the issue with "Herr Qualla," a story about Resi's old employer, which could not be called a *roman à clef* because the door was wide open to identification. A second story by Whit, "A Day in the Country," was based upon an excursion on which I went with him (instead of taking part, as I was scheduled to do, in the ceremony that opened transatlantic telephone service between Paris and New York). The best-known contributor to our issue was Romer Wilson, Edward O'Brien's wife, whose "A Poor Relation" was about how the heir to a rich man felt on his father's death. Edward had sent the story when we wrote him that we were starting a magazine. Romer was a member of the family that owned the Sheffield Steel Works, so she knew about life among the very rich. The contributor best known today was a beginning writer then, Kay Boyle. Her story, "Rest Cure," depicted an author dying on the Riviera. Many readers have thought the writer was D.H. Lawrence; I myself guessed that it was Kay's close friend, the brilliant Ernest Walsh, founder of the Paris magazine, *This Quarter.* It was his death and suspension of *This Quarter* that led the Jolases to start *transition.*

Oliver Gossman, our Scottish friend, wrote one of his delightful whimsies "Penny Whistle," about "a widow woman" and "a beggar man." Franz Kafka would not have been ashamed to have written "The Crime of Pessimism," by George Balint, the Hungarian author. The hero was sentenced to be hanged for neglecting his "laugh duty"; he refused to be amused by life in a dictatorship. A simpler and moving tale, translated from the German of Ernst Decsey, was "The Great Wheel," which told of the devotion of an old servant in a country inn to a pet pig. A story of my own was the much-reprinted "One with Shakespeare," describing an ecstatic moment in the life of an adolescent girl. The last item in our table of contents was "Portrait of a Contemporary at 70-odd," Whit's account of an evening he spent with Frank Harris, during Harris's last years in Nice.

There were only 167 copies of the first number of *STORY,* and they had to be doled out sparingly. Copies went to the *Sunday London Times Literary Supplement, The New York Times* and *New*

York Herald-Tribune's book review sections, to Edward J. O'Brien as editor of *The Best American Short Stories,* and to Blanche Colton Williams, editor of O'Brien's imitator, *The O. Henry Memorial Award Collection.* Miss Williams wrote me that she was not interested in little magazines published outside the United States and please not to send her any more. Isabel Paterson, on the other hand, as the editor of a page of literary gossip in the *Herald-Tribune* Sunday section, sent me a friendly letter and wished us luck. Isabel also used the publicity item I sent her. In it I had said that not only lemmings but also short story writers were on the march that year. If she or any reader considered it rather ambiguous, I was never told. Too late I realized that I was not being as clever as I thought: I had compared short story writers to rodents rushing to commit suicide!

Of all publications, the first to applaud *STORY* was the august *Sunday London Times Literary Supplement.* It declared that *STORY* was an important development that should be watched. Lewis Gannett wrote in his *New York Herald-Tribune* book review column that Whit and I had built a "better mousetrap." It was the *only* mousetrap.

Sylvia Beach's "Shakespeare and Company" was the first bookshop to receive copies. A handful were also distributed, as we announced in our opening statement, to stores in Vienna, Nice, Budapest, and Berlin. Our first problem with distribution was in Vienna. Dealers at first were scared to display it; because the cover was orange and black, the Hapsburg colors, it looked to them like monarchist propaganda. A friend who was an editor of the socialist *Arbeiter-Zeitung* intervened, and they stopped hiding it.

Splendid manuscripts from well-known and unknown writers multiplied geometrically; bookstores in America and Britain, disregarding our statement that *STORY* was not for distribution in their countries, sent us orders, and one day toplofty Herr Polizeibeamter arrived at our door, saluted the Divinity with the standard Viennese greeting, "Grüss Gott," and handed us an imposing document. It was a subpoena ordering us to appear in court. We were being prosecuted under the Austrian law forbidding publication of any magazine, newspaper, or book by foreigners. We could be both fined and imprisoned.

Viennese friends advised us to see Dr. Max Kulka, leading Austrian liberal lawyer, well read in English and European literature. He was a man so amiable, reassuring, and free of legalistic jargon that, after a few minutes in his office, we were calling him Max. He became a precious friend. All the law required, he told us, was "a whipping boy"—a citizen who willing to assume all responsibility for *STORY*, financial and legal, in case we printed libelous or treasonous matter, and willing to go to jail if necessary.

"Kaputt!" said Whit. "That finishes us. We're only a couple of newspaper bums living on our salaries. How in hell can we find some damn fool willing to go to jail for us?"

Max laughed. "You've found him," the wonderful Max Kulka told us. He would lay his life and fortune on the line for us by becoming our responsible editor, our *Verantwortlicher Schriftleiter,* and keep us out of prison.

Our Yugoslavian string man, whose dispatches from Belgrade were monotonously matter-of-fact, startled me one day by submitting a short story addressed to me as editor. The story was so histrionic, so wildly foolish, that I became disgusted with it and with him and rejected it immediately. He was, later on, furious, and rightly so. To evade censors, and thinking that I was smarter than I was, he had disguised a dispatch about a sensational palace coup, involving a king who was assassinated, as fiction. If not for my shortsighted editorial hubris, Whit and I would have been the first to get the news out to the world.

The increasing mail coming to *STORY* included letters from various publishing houses addressed to authors, care of us. "My heart leapt up" whenever I beheld the return addresses of illustrious book publishers on impressive envelopes. "We're making our point," I told Whit. "They see now how important short stories can be." My elation ended when I saw the uniformity of the letters. "I have read with admiration your story," or "Your story shows great talent, . . ." and all summed up their praise the same way: "If you are writing a novel, I would be honored by an opportunity to consider it." "Damn!" I said. "Damn! Damn! Damn!"

We went ahead with a second number of *STORY*. Spared the time and labor of mimeographing, it was easier. And if ever brand-new publishers received encouragement, we got it, sooner than expected, from Edward O'Brien. He wrote asking permission to reprint four stories from the first issue of *STORY*—the most ever chosen from a magazine in a whole year, let alone a single issue. One, Oliver Gossman's Scottish tale, he asked to reprint in *The Best British Short Stories*. The other three selections, for *The Best American Short Stories of 1931*, were Kay Boyle's "Rest Cure," Whit's "A Day in the Country," and my own "One with Shakespeare." Such unusual recognition by O'Brien drew excited attention to *STORY*. In an introduction to the anthology he declared that *STORY* was "the most important development in English literature since Wordsworth and Coleridge published 'Lyrical Ballads.' "

I was in bed with a cold when Resi brought O'Brien's letter to me, asking permission to reprint my story. Whit was up and at work in our office in the next room when he got O'Brien's request for his story. He came into my room to show me his letter. I was out of my mind with joy, and I held out my letter to him, "Look! Look! O'Brien wants to reprint my story!"

"Congratulations!" His voice was subdued. "I got a letter, too. Asking for my piece."

He quickly went back to the office before I could read his letter. Later he returned with a sheaf of papers, financial statements issued by the Hungarian government. "Better do the report on these right away. They're important." But I slept with O'Brien's letter under my pillow that night.

Robert Musil sent us a story, and we printed it in our second number. Called "Catastrophe," it was more like a poem than a prose piece. In language as graceful in English as I was told it was in Musil's native German, it told of a hare pursued and captured by a dog, who in turn is pursued by a man who takes the hare to cook for his own dinner. It seemed a fable, yet no moral was drawn.

The Viennese were impressed that "the great Musil" had sent us a story. "The great Musil"? Neither Whit nor I had ever heard of him. We printed the story because we liked it. The Viennese were horrified at our ignorance. Musil, they informed us, was one of the century's great writers, ranking with Proust, with whom he is often compared, Kafka, Rilke, and Heinrich Mann. They declared that Musil had shown our new little magazine a tremendous honor.

Literary reputations undergo bizarre sea changes. The great Shakespeare himself was long forgotten and ignored in his native England, and resurrected only when German audiences in Berlin went wild over his plays. When I arrived in France in the Twenties, Jack London and Upton Sinclair were considered by the general French public as the most important modern American authors. When I arrived in Austria in 1930 indignation was boiling over the award to Thomas Mann of the Nobel Prize for Literature the previous year. It was felt that Heinrich Mann, his older brother, deserved it more. Marlene Dietrich was playing in a film "Blue Angel" adapted from Heinrich Mann's *Professor Rat,* and I went to see it. Dietrich's acting was magnificent. It made her lasting reputation, but it was Heinrich's story I loved. (I also love Thomas's short stories, or novellas, particularly *Death in Venice* and *Mario the Magician.*)

The second issue of *STORY* was as eclectic as the first. It was the last number in which most of the contributors were known to us personally. A stranger was G.M. Noxon. He wrote a collage of conversations ("Bordeaux") in a French railway carriage, some in French, some in English, giving a composite impression of

French art, law, and family life, all accented by the total silence of two colonial African soldiers, who knew neither language.

I felt a great personal satisfaction that a circle had been completed, an ambition fulfilled, in the publication of "Fog" by Carter Brooke Jones. He was one of the unhappy old *Smart Set* ex-contributors I'd met in California who had first made me want to start a short story magazine. A love story of a boy and girl on a fog-bound Golden Gate ferryboat, "Fog" recalled the days in San Francisco when the city's life was less sophisticated. Other authors included Jay Dratler, with "Dark Victory" (about a white girl and a black boy); Ira V. Morris with "The Kimono" (the tragedy of a man whose wife sleeps with his brother), and Laurence Vail, Kay Boyle's husband, who wrote his "Thunderstorm" in a stream-of-consciousness style, more experimental in 1931 than now, of a man suffering great emotional stress. Among the remaining stories was "Neighbors," by Oliver Gossman, my own "Samarkand,"* and Whit's finest, "Sherril."

"I want to be respectable," Whit announced to me one afternoon during *Jause,* when we were drinking tea in the Viennese fashion, with milk, sugar, and rum—a change from the omnipresent coffee with whipped cream.

"Sounds awfully dull," I commented. *"Epater la bourgeoisie* is much more interesting."

"Well, I'm tired of being unconventional, of living like a Bohemian."

"Bohemian!" I repeated, and I thought of the most dismal

---

* As soon as I received readers' reactions to my story, I knew I'd botched it. I'd intended to portray two romance-starved housewives who arrive in Moscow on their way to fulfill a life-long dream of visiting "golden Samarkand," but who have been domestic slaves so long that they are trapped by feeling it their duty to stay and tidy up the revolution-shattered communist capital. Because I described the shabby condition of the Russian streets and buildings, no worse than slums anywhere, readers thought I was writing anti-Russian propaganda. The women were—like my readers?—like Pavlov's dogs.

Sunday I'd ever spent in Europe, a rainy Sunday in Prague, the capital of Bohemia. "I'm going to write an article for Mencken, exposing the Bohemians. They're frauds. Getting credit they don't deserve for carefree living, when they have the world's worst Blue Laws!"

I laughed and recalled how, with every bookstore and news-stand closed up because of Prague's Blue Laws, and me unable to go to bed without something to read, I'd found some old Czech newspapers in the hotel lobby, had taken them up to my room, and had held them in front of me and tried to figure out Czech, which I didn't know at all, just to have something to read.

"It's a deep, biological urge," Whit went on, to explain why it was he wanted to be married and have a child.

"So!" I thought. "So that is what he was driving at when he said he wanted to be 'respectable.'" From what I had seen of married unhappiness, I was not enthusiastic about that institution. But babies? I loved babies. When I was a little girl, before baby-sitting became a profession, I begged mothers to let me take care of their offspring. As I grew older and became aware of the suffering in the world, I decided it was cruel to bring more children into the world when there already were so many un-loved, neglected ones already here. I would adopt some, I'd decided, and now I told Whit so.

"Nothing doing," he said. "I want my own kid. It's a deep biological urge," he repeated.

I had won the argument about starting *STORY.* Whit won the argument about starting a baby. But he still wasn't satisfied. Early one morning before I even had my usual *Frühstück* of coffee with *Schlagobers* to brace me for the day, he demanded, "Will you marry me?" This was too much, and I broke down and cried.

Realization that I was in a socialist city and could have a socialist ceremony reconciled me. There would be no nonsense about veils and wedding marches. It would be a simple, rational affair. Max Kulka agreed to take care of the legal arrangements. John Scott, the American vice-consul, agreed to be best man.

Only they knew our plans. We hadn't told even the Gunthers. I bought a simple, short dark dress. The ceremony would take place in the Rathaus, the Vienna city hall, before a justice of the peace. Or so I thought.

When we arrived at Max Kulka's office to pick him up on our way to the Rathaus, Whit in an everyday business suit and I in my informal short dress, Max presented me with an enormous, baroque wedding bouquet, dripping with white satin ribbons and tiny silver, tinkling bells. At the Rathaus, the chamber into which we were ushered was not the plain, justice-of-the-peace office I had visualized. It was a chapel, all done up in red plush, with a lectern in front. Preceded by a page boy bearing a satin cushion, a dignified official entered in a magisterial robe. The page boy approached us where we were seated in the front row and held the red satin cushion in front of Whit. Whit looked at it. Max tapped him on the shoulder and whispered, "Your ring—the wedding ring!" It was a double-ring ceremony! Whit took off his big garnet ring, with its heavy silver mounting, and placed it on the cushion, into which it sank almost out of sight like a lead weight. I put down a ring Whit had given me in Paris, a small, exquisite thing of linked turquoise circlets. The magistrate gave a long talk, as solemn sounding as a sermon, of which I understood little. It was in erudite, guttural *Hochdeutsch,* and my German was Resi's lowbrow *Wienerisch.* Finally he stopped, Whit and I exchanged rings, and were no longer lovers but a respectable, bourgeois married couple.

I wanted to avoid appearing with my beautiful, tinkling bouquet on the wide steps of the impressive, stagelike entrance of the Rathaus. Max showed us to a small exit on a side street. As we opened the door, a friendly, familiar voice shouted, "What's all this? A wedding? Who's being married?" It was the poet and playwright Alfred Kreymborg* and Dorothy, his wife, whom we

---

* Alfred's experimental poetry made him famous in the Twenties and Thirties, and his radicalism got him blacklisted in the hysterical Fifties.

had been seeing a lot of during their stay in Vienna. We invited the Kreymborgs to join Max Kulka, John Scott, and ourselves for lunch on Cobensl, a high hill in the Wienerwald, with lovely views of the city.

"Sehr schön," a smiling Resi told me when we got home, "your bridal bouquet." She seemed not at all shocked, as I was worried she would be. The wise woman had guessed all along that Whit and I were not married. I sighed with relief when the day was ended. But Whit was not going to let me forget I was now a wife. "It's time," he declared, "for your marital duty."

SEVEN

〜

DAVID

The first sign of the direction American writing would take in the Thirties came to us out of Chicago. It was a story called "A Casual Incident," of a hungry, homeless boy warding off the advances of a "cruising" homosexual. We accepted it for *STORY*'s third issue. It was by James T. Farrell, the first and one of the most important of the new "proletarian writers." The following year would see publication of his novel, *Young Lonigan,* the first volume of the now classic "Studs Lonigan" trilogy.

He was twenty-seven years old, Farrell wrote us. After telling us that he had been educated in Chicago public and parochial schools and had studied law and social sciences (in which he won a scholarship at the University of Chicago), he said, "I have done considerable bumming, and have worked as a clerk, filling station attendant, reporter and once had a nondescript job in an undertaking establishment in which a friend and myself were considered as one man and received between us three dollars a week and a bed for hanging around there in the evenings." He was living in Paris but emphasized in his letter to us that he was not an expatriate, declaring, "My sympathies are almost wholly left wing and I subscribe to no Parisian literary credoes or movements."*

Farrell was a self-proclaimed Marxist, both as a writer and as a political activist. American proletarian writing came of age in the Thirties. A better term for the writing it referred to might be socially conscious writing, for it was inspired by social injustice laid bare in America for all to see, as never before.†

Not all the "proletarian" writing *STORY* received during the Thirties was as good as Farrell's. Far from it. There was some awfully faked writing called "proletarian." I hated the kind that had what I call a "conversion ending." This was as contrived as stories in the worst of the slicks. The main character was a hard-hearted rich person or a bigoted racist, but through some *deus ex machina* of a revelation he was shocked into a realization that poor people were not shiftless, but exploited, or that blacks and Jews were really fine fellows. There was another kind where working-class life was painted an unalleviated black, the author not realiz-

---

* "I was living in Sceaux-Robinson," Farrell has written, "just outside of Paris from Porte D'Orleans, and late in the summer, or early September, 1931, I sent the manuscripts of two stories, 'A Casual Incident' and 'Spring Evening' to STORY Magazine in Vienna. I had heard of it, and that it published stories. I received a reply from Whit Burnett, accepting both stories, and, I believe, particularly praising 'A Casual Incident.' He seems all of his life to have considered it a classic of its kind." Farrell found Whit "a litte bit pompous," and notes that "his beard added pomposity to his appearance." Martha, he writes, "was more direct, but when they were together, she seemed more in the background. Not that Whit precisely hogged attention. He looked it; he looked like a man who was more important than he actually was. . . . My own feeling is that it was Martha's fate, as it is of many women in our society, to find a man who was inferior to her." —ED.

† *The Oxford Companion to American Literature* defines proletarian literature as "the name applied to the school of writing that contends that experience is primarily conditioned by the social, economic and political environment and that the author is able to understand this environment by Marxist theory, which explains the dialectical relation of class cultures to the prevailing economic and social structure. During the Depression, when they flourished, proletarian writers contended that it was life, itself, not the Communist party, that forced them to be interested in such phenomena as strikes, agricultural and industrial conditions, and persecutions and oppressions of racial minorities and the working class."

ing that a little light would have accentuated the gloom of the shadows. One example I remember was a novel about factory girls in a town that was named, which angered the girls themselves. The author wrote that the girls, to help keep their families alive, turned over all their earnings to their mothers and had no money to spend on pleasure. "That's a damn lie!" one girl exploded. "Our mother gives my sister and me each fifteen cents out of our pay every week to buy an ice cream soda. We have pleasure!"

William Faulkner could hardly be categorized as a proletarian writer, and he was doing some of his best work in the Thirties, as were Katherine Anne Porter, Thomas Wolfe, Willa Cather, Ellen Glasgow, Caroline Gordon, Robert Penn Warren, Stephen Vincent Benét, and others whose fiction was not greatly motivated by social-consciousness. Still, it must be admitted that the list of Thirties writers who did write important socially conscious stories with permanent literary value is a much longer one. Some are Sinclair Lewis, Nelson Algren, F. Scott Fitzgerald, Vardis Fisher, Jack Conroy, Irwin Shaw, Howard Fast, Waldo Frank, Ernest Hemingway, John Steinbeck, Clifford Odets, William Saroyan, Richard Wright, Susan Glaspell, Erskine Caldwell, Michael Gold, Pietro di Donato, and more.

Well-known, even famous, names appeared more and more on the manuscripts *STORY* received.* Several came with notes saying, "You may have seen my work in the *Saturday Evening Post.*" Or the magazine mentioned might be *Collier's*, or the *Ladies Home Journal,* or *Cosmopolitan,* or any one of the other mass circulation magazines of the period. The author would add, "I hope

---

* *STORY* would, within its first dozen issues, publish, in addition to Farrell, Musil, Gossman, Decsey, Morris, Boyle, Vail, Whit and Martha, stories by, among others, José Garcia Villa, Ralph Manheim, Manuel Komroff, George Albee, Peter Neagoe, Conrad Aiken, Alvah Bessie, Charles Kendall, O'Neill, E. Gimenez Caballero, E.P. O'Donnell, Eugene Jolas, Tess Slesinger, H.E. Bates, John Cowles, Noah Fabricant, Mikahail Zoshchenko, John Fante, L.A. Pavey, Pietro Solari, L.A.G. Strong, and William Carlos Williams.—ED.

you will like this story I am sending you because serious fiction is what I want to write." It was sad how many of those manuscripts agreed with what one best-selling author told a friend of mine who asked him, "Whatever happened to the kind of writing you used to do? I like it better." The man looked unhappy, sighed, and explained, "I wrote one for the money and I've never been able to get back my virginity."*

Traveling writers, editors, and publishers interested in *STORY* came directly to the Pötzleinsdorf house instead of meeting us more casually at the Louvre Stammtisch. Many became friends. Among them was Thayer Hobson of William Morrow Company, and his wife, Laura Hobson, who had not yet written *Gentlemen's Agreement.* Another was Donald Friede, of Covici-Friede, the firm that published Steinbeck. Donald had financed George Antheil's sensational *Ballet Méchanique* while we were in Paris, although we had not met him or Antheil then. At the ballet's premiere, ladies' hats blew off and men raised their umbrellas against the gale that roared through the hall from one of the instruments—an airplane propellor. George, a short, fair young man, and Beshki, his dark-haired wife, became regular visitors to our house. George brought a group of composers and musicians weekly for—and I'm still startled by the fact—a poker game, when nary a note of music was sounded, although Whit, the music maniac, was host! George was in Vienna arranging for production of his *Transatlantique,* the first opera by an American to be produced in Europe.

---

* Yet there *was* a Herman Melville! Rich and famous though he had become, Melville was able to cast aside writing the superficial adventure yarns of the South Seas, which had brought him commercial success. Instead he wrote the magnificent classic *Moby Dick* and the equally magnificent group of short stories, "Piazza Tales." That collection includes "Bartleby the Scrivener," often called "America's greatest short story." Both books were failures, and Melville died broke and forgotten. Melville's fate is a shame on the Philistines responsible for the kind of society we have. His last beautiful short story was rejected by a magazine editor for fear of "offending the religious sensibilities of the public and the congregation of Grace Church."

David

STORY acquired a circulation manager to take care of local distribution, incoming subscriptions, and the mailing of copies. I am sure he was the most unusual circulation manager an American magazine ever had. He was a handsome young Parsee newly graduated from Oxford University and detained in Vienna by a tragic *contretemps.* Like many foreigners in Vienna, he became the victim of a misunderstanding with his landlady. Many once rich Austrian women, now old and widowed and temperamental, managed to hold on to their grandiose apartments at a prewar rental and supported themselves by renting parts of them. Whit and I had first lived in such a decaying, baroque apartment, and Whit too had become entangled in a dispute with poor, nervous old Frau Doktor Saxl, over her missing chamber pot.

Soon after we moved to Pötzleinsdorf, Whit had a letter from the Frau Doktor asking him please to return her chamber pot. Whit wrote saying he was sorry, we did not have it. Back came a furious letter accusing Whit of stealing the chamber pot. Whit, lacking a proper chamber pot vocabulary in German, got Frau Schwartzwald, our secretary, to write that we did not use chamber pots, that we had found her nice bathroom adequate. His was an incredible lie, another letter informed Whit. Everybody used chamber pots. And no, she didn't want the money Whit offered. That particular chamber pot was priceless. It was the one her late, beloved husband had used.

Far more serious was our worried Parsee's trouble with his landlady. She made him lose his ticket to Paradise. What the cause of her unhappiness with him was I could not imagine, because, although he was a courteous, intelligent person, she had him arrested. In the station house, according to universal police practice, he was searched. Everything he might use to hang himself was taken from him—his tie, belt, shoelaces, and his sacred Parsee girdle. In the court next morning he was acquitted and freed. The police returned to him his tie, belt, and shoelaces, but not the girdle.

143

The Parsees, I learned, after he came to work for *STORY,* are Zoroastrians, a Persian religious sect which migrated to India in the eighth century and settled in Bombay. They are nature worshippers, revering all aspects of nature—fire, earth, and water. To avoid contaminating nature, they expose their dead on "towers of silence" to be devoured by vultures. Their excellent schools make them one of the best-educated groups in India, and they are also one of the richest. The Parsees celebrate a boy's entering puberty with a special ceremony, during which he is presented with a girdle and the command never to be parted from it. It will ensure his entrance to heaven.

The Parsee told me he did not dare return to India without the girdle. His family would be too upset. Besides, he himself felt disgraced at having been deprived by the police of the badge of honor worn by a good Parsee. So, instead of including the "grand tour" of Europe he planned after leaving Oxford, he felt forced to stay in Vienna and recover his girdle. He engaged a lawyer and was taking court action to make the police return it. They denied all knowledge of it. I have no idea what a Parsee girdle looks like because when I asked him, *STORY*'s circulation manager was too shy to explain. I am convinced someone in the police station stole it as a curio. When we left for Spain the following spring, the poor young man was still trying to get it back.

In addition to our needing a circulation manager, another sign of *STORY*'s growth was our need, because of the increasing number of manuscripts we received, for a rejection slip. It was impossible to send the authors personal letters, as we had done in the beginning. So back to the mimeograph machine in the *Journalitzenzimmer* I went to run off copies of a rejection slip I had composed. Until that time magazine rejections were the chilliest, haughtiest documents imaginable. Their effect on the unfortunate authors receiving them was sadistic. I have been told that my rejection slip helped thaw out some of the ice in the rejection slips of other magazines. I hope so. As time went by and the excellent stories sent us were many more than we could use, we would add a personal postscript to a good one to let the author know we liked it. "Dear Contributor," *STORY*'s rejection slip read,

This, alas, is a rejection slip. And, heaven knows, the editors, who have had their own full share of them, have no affection for them.

It has been found, however, that it is physically impossible to enter into correspondence with everyone who has been kind enough to send in a manuscript. And the editors have had to resort to this.

It is, fortunately, thus far our only recourse to formality. And you may rest assured that this manuscript, like every other that comes to STORY, has been sympathetically read and carefully considered before it is now, finally, for one or perhaps more reasons, put back in circulation.

Thank you for letting us see the story.

Cordially,

THE EDITORS

The summer of 1932, the last we would spend in Vienna, although we did not know it, was happy, as was the early fall. We had many house guests, newspaper friends from New York and Paris, and many, many writers interested in the magazine who stopped by for brief calls, often to leave a manuscript. Hospitality as we experienced it in Europe was far more expansive than in America. Never was there a hint of the saying often heard in the States, "After three days fish and visitors stink." Weekends extended from Thursday to Tuesday, and for house guests to stay for weeks and months was not unusual. When I mentioned this custom in America, more than once someone has said, "I hope they paid their share." In Europe, the hosts I knew would have been insulted if a guest offered payment.

Resi had decided likes and dislikes among the guests. The

only time I was angry with her was when she told me how she treated I.V. Morris, the novelist. Ira, tall, slender, and handsome, with a languid manner, looked like the last of a long line of effete French marquis. In reality he was a hard-working, conscientious young writer worried about his first novel. He belonged to a rich Chicago meat-packing family, his father was American ambassador to Sweden, and he was used to retinues of servants. Maybe it was this that bothered Resi—that he treated her casually. None of the rest of us was rich enough to take a servant for granted.

"Herr Doktor Morris," she horrified me by telling me on the day of his departure, "I fixed him." She told me that what she had been doing was taking his breakfast tray up to him early in the morning, before she left for six o'clock Mass. He was so sound asleep she would have to shake him awake. Sitting him up in bed, she would plunk the tray before him and leave for her morning devotions. When she returned an hour later for the tray, she said, Ira would be sitting there looking at his untouched breakfast. Poor Ira! When in later years I saw him in his parents' sumptuous Manhattan apartment, with its gold piano, or in his French chateau with its private chapel, and I remembered him confronted with that breakfast tray at 5:30 in the morning, I would be torn between wanting to apologize and wanting to laugh.

A guest Resi adored was Edward J. O'Brien, who spent a month that summer with us. *"Herr Doktor Besucher."* Her eyes sparkled like those of a girl in love when she spoke of him. Edward could talk with her in fluent German, an advantage neither Whit nor I possessed. More important, he showed her the exquisite consideration that made him loved by many others who knew him.

He spent hours discussing Ira's writing problems with him and helped many other writers, reading fiction they sent him, and, if it was good, recommending it to magazine editors and book publishers. Hemingway was not the only writer he first made eminent. The world of letters is forever indebted to O'Brien, together with Raymond Weaver, for saving Herman Melville from oblivion: in 1923 he made a stirring appeal for recognition of America's great forgotten author. As for Whit Burnett and myself, there are no words strong enough for the gratitude we owed him, as do all the authors whom *STORY* was able to publish, because of the critical support he gave the magazine.

There were surprising facets to Edward's character. Of Irish ancestry, he was an ardent Anglophile. Born and raised in the world's most technological nation, the United States, he abhorred all mechanical objects. Extremely decorous, almost shy in both appearance and conduct, he was a dedicated nudist, not just sunbathing for health and pleasure but practicing nakedness as a rite, outdoors in summer, indoors in winter. Giving an impression of remoteness from petty matters, he loved gossip. He told me some scandalous behind-the-British-scenes tales that would make front-page headlines in America.

He was going to become a British citizen, Edward said, as soon as his small son, an heir to the Sheffield Steel Works, reached the age of eighteen. As the child of an English mother and American father, the son then could choose either American or British citizenship, and Edward did not wish to deprive him of a free choice. Like Edward, I too was of Irish ancestry (on my father's side some came in the 1790s, on my mother's, in the early 1800s), but, though I reveled in Irish literature, I never felt any fealty to Ireland.*

---

* In the many years during which I lived in Europe, I did not visit or wish to see Ireland, yet back in America I become a raging, infuriated Celtic chauvinist every Saint Patrick's Day. I cannot stand, cannot endure, I want to scream at the "begorra's" and "Paddy's" in phony brogue littering newspaper columns and TV programs. And never a mention of Yeats, A.E., Moore, Shaw, Joyce, O'Casey, or any of the other marvelous writers who illustrate Oliver St. John Gogarty's answer to an Englishman who demanded, "What's the matter with you Irish? You're always fighting us, you refuse to join the Commonwealth, you hate our guts, yet

Long before Edward wanted to change his citizenship, long before the "Lost Generation" of the Twenties, expatriation had been popular with American writers. It began with Irving and Hawthorne, continued through Henry James, Stephen Crane, down to T.S. Eliot, Ezra Pound, and Ernest Hemingway, to the present.†

Edward pinpointed his reason. "Americans have made gods of their machines and become their slaves," he wrote in his book, *Dance of the Machine,* which damned all mechanization. He quoted with approval Samuel Butler: "I do not think America is a good place to be a genius . . . America is about the last place in which life will be endurable at all for an inspired writer of any kind." To explain his theory as to why much American writing was slick, Edward declared, "In a mechanical civilization, to the writer *technique* is a generic term for labor-saving devices to alleviate his own fatigue and that of his readers."

Nudism, according to Edward, revived the classical Greek approach to life. The ancient Athenians reverenced all beautiful things and saw a healthy human form as clean and lovely and to be admired, not despised, as in Puritan prudery. He invited Whit and me to spend an evening at his Viennese nudist club and, overcome by curiosity, we went. It was a bore. Clothes can make people more interesting, I discovered. After I undressed in a cubicle, like that at a bathing resort, I had a terrible time mustering courage to go forth. Assuring myself that I was not completely naked (I was wearing eyeglasses), I bravely stepped out. Any

---

† To quote myself from an introduction to an earlier book, "There have been many reasons for this emigration, cheaper living and lower taxes, the perspective that distance can give a writer on his native material, the stimulation of foreign peoples and sights, but the prime one is the reason that makes the short story popular in the United States. The great speed and high pressure of life here drive writers to seek the more contemplative, less mechanized ways of living in the security of an older, more settled civilization."

sense of shame vanished in a few minutes. I concentrated on people's faces and tried to ignore their bodies. I watched the faces swimming around in a pool, gathered around tables to play cards or chat. Not a hint of an orgy. It was as dull as a church social. I never went again.

Edward's dead wife, Romer Wilson, had planned to write a definitive biography of the Brontës, and Edward was familiar with the vast amount of material she collected. The father of the three famous writing sisters, Charlotte, Emily, and Anne, was an Irishman named Patrick Prunty. As curate of Haworth church on the bleak Yorkshire moors, which his daughters made famous, he changed his name to Brontë.

Romer Wilson had to abandon her plan for the Brontës biography, Edward said, when she discovered the hushed-up scandal in the family. British libel laws, far stricter than American, made publication impossible. Every now and then in some literary review such as that of the *Sunday New York Times* there is a guarded hint of a Brontë scandal, but Edward spelled it out for us. A child was born of an incestuous relationship in the Brontë family, he said, and descendants of that child are living today in England.

More startling was the story Edward told me when I visited London in 1938, after the abdication of the duke of Windsor. It was fortunate that T.E. Lawrence had been killed in a motorcycle accident the previous year, Edward said. The duke and Lawrence had been conspiring with Adolph Hitler to turn the British government into a dictatorship. Their plan was to model it after the Italian Fascist pattern, where King Victor Emmanuel reigned as king and Mussolini was dictator. If their plan had succeeded, Edward explained, Lawrence, who was then play-acting as Private Shaw in the Royal Air Force in the same way he had done when posing as an Arab in the Middle East, would have become dictator. The duke would not have abdicated, but would have remained as monarch (King Edward VIII), and Britain and Germany would have become close allies. As Edward described the fantastic plot to me, I remembered that the first trip the duke of Windsor took after abdicating was to visit Hitler in Germany.

Edward's delight was almost childish when he was gossiping in Vienna; he told us how the formidable British intellect, Bertrand Russell, philosopher and mathematician, came to *him* for information about contraception. It was shortly after Dora Russell, with whom he started a school, became Russell's wife, and neither knew how birth control was practiced. Russell expressed great relief when, thanks to Edward, he finally learned.

Because Pötzleinsdorf was on the edge of the Wienerwald, friends who lived in other parts of Vienna gathered many pleasant Sunday mornings at our house for a day-long outing in the woods. Resi made dozens of *Aufschnitten,* open-faced sandwiches, which we packed along with her cake and fruit, and we set out on one of the most beautiful walks in the whole wide world. Edward teased us by calling our walks "pub crawling." Of course we stopped at a beer garden or a "Heurigen," an open-aired restaurant where they served new wine, but in between we covered many miles of tree-lined, flowery forest paths and, occasionally, climbed a small mountain. Sometimes we climbed up to Hollandischerdorf—the Javanese village the Empress Maria Theresa constructed in the eighteenth century in honor of visiting Dutch royalty—replete with thatched huts and open market and Far Eastern detail. There we drank sweet, cold water from the deepest well in Europe. Other times we climbed up Kahlenberg, had a beer there, and, if especially energetic, walked over the ridge to neighboring Klosterneuberg and ventured down its steep, spectacular trail to the Danube's shore. "Far away and long ago," but so wonderful to have been there.

Two more issues of *STORY* were published in 1931, each an important milestone for the magazine. Our September-October issue was significant because it published that first story by James T. Farrell. But for the third time the magazine disappointed me.

We were still offering fine short stories for sale, yet there wasn't a nibble—kind words aplenty but no butter for the parsnips. It was interesting that not a single author of any of the flood of manuscripts coming to us mentioned pay. But I had walked on picket lines where poor pay was the cause of strikes and knew from my reading how many great writers had died in poverty; and I knew, too, that the writer was an Atlas supporting a prosperous industry—in New York then the largest industry was publishing and printing—and it all seemed so damned unfair.

The November-December issue was the last *STORY* issue in 1931, marking completion of our first year as publishers, and it held a Christmas present for me. It was the most cosmopolitan issue we had published yet. Its authors included Peter Neagoe, the Rumanian writer, with one of his warmhearted stories about Transylvania peasants, and Fritz von Unruh, the German author of *Verdun, The Sacrifice,* the first pacifist war book, whose story in the magazine based on a visit to Trotsky in exile on a Turkish island is still a magnificent depiction of the Russian leader. There was also a lyrical love story by José Garcia Villa, a Filipino poet who lived in America. Until I reread his story recently I had forgotten that Villa had woven numerals into his story, long before a similar experiment by Delmore Schwartz (which I had thought was original with the latter). Villa showed more courage than Schwartz. After giving me permission to reprint his story in *The Best American Short Stories,* Delmore wrote asking me to delete the numerals because students at Harvard, where he taught, chanted the numbers after him when he passed them on the campus. I pleaded, in vain, to keep the effective numerals. I reprinted his story as he wished but never liked it as much again.

The most exciting story for me in the year's final issue of *STORY* was Mikhail Zoshchenko's "A Slight Mistake," but not because of its literary value, although his humorous tales are classics of the postrevolutionary period in Russian literature. "A Slight Mistake" was a gleeful satire about a three-month bureaucratic program designed to liquidate illiteracy among factory workers. When I opened a letter from *The New Republic* and read an offer to buy the Zoshchenko story, I shouted to Whit in jubilation, like a shipwrecked castaway, "A sale! A sale!"

"Meet the family!" was how Whit announced to people in the fall of 1931 that I was "expecting." As if anyone needed to be told! I had arrived in Vienna five feet tall and weighing ninety-eight pounds. Now, owing to Resi's cooking and Whit's parental ambition, I was almost as wide as I was high. Vienna was not the United States, where pregnant women are advised not to overeat: "Remember, now you must eat for two!" I was constantly urged. Not only was I admonished to eat for the next generation but also to drink beer for it. Before the First World War, when Vienna was a rich world capital, upper-class women hired peasant women as wet nurses and lavished vast quantities of beer on them to assure an abundance of breast milk.

I found my obstetrician only after making the rounds of the plush-parlor reception rooms of his colleagues, who bristled when an upstart young American woman dared ask what delivery methods they used. They retorted by quoting the chapter of Genesis: "In sorrow thou shalt bring forth children." This curse upon Eve was engraved over the entrance of the century-old Frauenklinik, Vienna's big public hospital for women, as divine authority for the founder's ruling against all experiments in pain-easing obstetrics. Dr. Burger, however, was tenderhearted and told me that he was a modern obstetrician who believed in making childbirth as painless as possible. "I use the best, the safest, the newest method, '*chloroform à la reine,*' " he said. "Only I don't use chloroform anymore; I use ether. Little whiffs of ether toward the end. It's called '*à la reine*' because it was invented to help out Queen Victoria."

Dr. Burger agreed with my choice of the Rudolfinerhaus, about which I had written a newspaper feature, as a birthplace for my baby. This little lying-in hospital, beside the Beethoven Brook, which sang its way out of the Wienerwald, was founded in 1882 by a group of aristocratic women inspired by Florence Nightingale. For the first time in history princesses and duchesses rolled up their sleeves and went to work as nurses. Construction was not completed until 1894. In 1889 Crown Prince Rudolph and his *Liebchen,* the pretty young Baroness Maria Vetsera, were found mysteriously dead in scandalous circumstances in the royal hunting lodge at Mayerling. To please old Emperor Franz Josef, who believed to the day of his own death that he had fooled the public into thinking his son's death natural, the new hospital was named after the dead prince, new theories about whose murder or suicide still made page-one copy for Viennese newspapers in the Thirties.

When I was there, nurses at the Rudolfinerhaus continued to be drawn from the upper classes. Many had titles from the old aristocracy that they did not use; they were called instead by the name given all nurses in Austria, *Schwester* ("sister"). There was one exception. The hospital midwife had the quaint title of "Stork Mama." The group of blue-clad nurses followed a rigid discipline, and its members pointed proudly to signs in every room saying that it was forbidden to accept gratuities. They were the only well-bred women in Vienna known to do manual work.

Stork Mama greeted me at the door like a gracious hostess and showed me to my room, which had two beds, only one of which was to be occupied. Then she summoned the smiling young, fair-haired, brown-eyed *Schwester* who was to be my private nurse and who would accompany me and the baby home, to take care of him there. This *Schwester* helped me unpack. When she arranged a set of the baby's clothes from bonnet to booties on a bed as though he was already lying there in them, I had an eerie feeling.

Whit, absent in Czechoslovakia on a news story, was alerted by telephone that I was in the hospital. He arrived with a basket of enormous hothouse grapes to find me wandering around the hospital. "Where is he?" he demanded.

"Who?" I asked.

"The baby, of course."

"He isn't here, yet."

"Damn! I was hoping it would be all over by the time I got here. I'm going to John's. I'll be in touch."

The Gunthers' villa was not far away, and a party was in progress there in honor of Bruce Bliven, the editor of *The New Republic,* who was visiting Vienna. Whit said that when he told John I was in the Rudolfinerhaus, he asked him not to mention it. "Here," John had said and poured him a stiff drink. Then John turned and announced to the party, "Whit's having a baby!" There was a cheer and, during the next couple of hours, delegations from the party came to the Rudolfinerhaus to give me moral encouragement, some still holding on to glasses of their own encouragement. I did not know whether Bruce was among them because I had never met him. (When I did meet him in New York, he told me that his most vivid recollection of that trip to Vienna was that someone was having a baby.)

My son was as considerate about arriving in the world as he was to be all his life. I had left the Pötzleinsdorf house at about four o'clock in the afternoon, and, at ten minutes before eight that evening, he was born. He came so quickly that Dr. Burger did not have a chance to pretend I was Queen Victoria. I had pain but not the long drawn-out agony most mothers endure. And I heard my baby's first tiny cry. Whit arrived in time and waited outside the delivery room. As I was being taken to my own room, the first thing he said was, "Here's your David for you."

David was not the wizened, little, red squawking monkey of a creature I had been led to expect all new babies were. He did have a shocking mat of black hair, unknown in our blond families, but it soon turned gray, fell out, and was replaced by bright yellow. Otherwise he was a picture-book baby, pink and white and dimpled and perfectly formed. His first picture, taken when he was two days old, with Frances Gunther holding him while he looks over her shoulder, shows him wide-eyed and alert with already well-defined features. We had chosen his names beforehand, David Benjamin. A worried nurse asked me if I knew those names were Jewish. When I told her yes, I knew they were from the Old Testament, she went away looking puzzled.

For two days after David's birth I experienced an hallucination. I do not know how common it is among new mothers, I never heard of it. Everyone suddenly seemed to be a baby. The doctor, the nurses, my visitors, everyone in the whole world was a baby who needed mothering. I tested my illusion by thinking of people far from the hospital. It still held. I thought of the derelicts on the Bowery. They, too, had been sweet little babies who needed to be burped and to have their little bottoms powdered.

About the third day I was brought back to a bizarre reality. Did I want to sell my milk? I was asked. I had more milk than one baby could use, and good prices were paid for mother's milk. I started to protest, "I'm not a dairy!" but restrained myself and said that if there were mothers in the public ward downstairs who had no milk for their babies, I would be glad to give them mine. Then began an awkward ritual. There was no wall plug in the old-fashioned hospital room, so a vacuum cleaner nozzle was attached to my breast with a long hose snaking through the partly opened door to an electric pump somewhere outside in the hall.

As feature editor of the *Los Angeles Daily News,* editing five-dollar-winning contributions from readers, I used to marvel at how silly the "My Most Embarrassing Moment" feature was. What happened one afternoon while I was sitting up in bed being pumped made me more understanding. Pembroke Stevens, for whom I substituted on the *London Daily Express,* came to call. Now "Pem" was one of the handsomest men who ever lived, and one of the most sartorially elegant. He usually wore a dark blue blazer with a brilliant gold crest embroidered on the pocket. When he arrived in all his glory at the Rudolfinerhaus he so dazzled the young nurse at the reception desk that she gave him the number of my room and told him to go right up. He pushed wide open the door. Blup. Blup. Blup. The vacuum nuzzling my breast was throbbing away. Pem took one look, dropped the pretty flowers he was carrying, and disappeared. "My Most Embarrassing Moment"? No, indeed! It was poor Pem's.*

---

* I did not tell this episode in the article "Blessed Event in Vienna," which I wrote for the *Mercury.* Both I and the *Mercury* would have been too prudish in those days to have published it.

EIGHT

∾

AUFWIEDERSEHN, VIENNA!

I was afraid that Dr. Darwin Lyon might send my baby to the moon. When he asked me why I had not had him as my doctor, I told him so—as gently as possible, of course, because he was a kind man, and, like the other American correspondents in Vienna, I was fond of him.

"You don't trust me," he said sadly.

Trust him? Trust *him!* When we all knew he was as crazy as a loon? Sending rockets into outer space and collaborating on wild experiments with another nut named Goddard way off in Massachusetts and talking about interplanetary travel as if it would begin on an hourly basis the next day. It was a shame, I thought, but he really was cracked.

A lanky, nervous man in early middle age, Dr. Lyon told me that he was named after an ancestor, Charles Darwin. He was one of the only two American physicians at that time who had ever been licensed to practice medicine in Austria. He arrived in Austria at the end of the First World War, with a Red Cross mission, and stayed. The Viennese loved him for the help he gave them and paid him a respect he never got from his fellow Americans. All one evening he tried to make me understand how interplanetary voyaging was inevitable. The human race was to him like bees grown too numerous for a hive. We were getting ready to swarm. So, like bees, we would send out scouts to test new environments. More and more exploratory ventures would be made, and, to support the explorers, there would be man-made satellites circling the earth. Those satellites would be flying laboratories equipped with the most modern instruments and manned with crews of technicians . . . but those whirling laboratories strained too far my wish to believe, and I remember no more of Dr. Lyons's long discourse.

Once he wrote from the Italian Alps saying he had successfully launched a rocket into outer space. Did any of us rush to the cable wires to let America know of his achievement? Not a one of us took the report seriously. Not William Shirer, not Robert Best, not John Gunther, not Whit Burnett, not I. We were too smart. Today we know that the "nut" named Goddard whom Dr. Lyon mentioned so often as his colleague was none other than the now celebrated American physicist Dr. Robert H. Goddard, renowned as the genius whose rockets propelled the world into the modern space age. It was not Dr. Lyon who was crazy but we correspondents.

Resi and the United States government did not agree on baby care. Again, as in the case of Dr. Lyon, I now know too late how blind I was. Resi, who never had a child, would have made a better mother than I. Her delight in David was a joy. When I arrived home with the baby I found on the door to his room a poster made by Resi. Colored with bright crayons and decorated with hand-drawn daisies and many curlicues, it announced in big letters, "WILLKOMMEN KLEINE DAVIDL!"

Before Dr. Spock's book on baby care was published, the bible of many American mothers was a book issued by the Child Welfare Bureau of the United States government in Washington. I know now that the book, with its cut-and-dried rules and admonitions, was a typical, unfeeling, unimaginative bureaucratic document. It could have been composed by a hard-boiled army drill sergeant. But it was followed faithfully by innumerable, conscientious mothers, especially American women like myself living in foreign countries who felt a need for guidance from home, lest we be led astray by alien customs.

"Der Bubi schrei!" Resi raced many times to tell me when his nurse was not there.

"It's all right, Resi," I'd say. "It's bad to pick him up when he cries." But oh! how I myself wanted to!

"Vielleicht der Kleine hungrig ist."

"It is not his feeding time yet. He must learn to wait."

"Aber—"

"Resi, I *have* to follow the American book!"

"Das verdammte Buch! Jesu, Maria und Josef!"

Today I echo Resi with my whole heart. "That damned book!" Next to picking up a tiny baby when he wept, it said that the greatest crime was to give him a pacifier, said to cause teeth to grow crooked and to distort the shape of the mouth. What fury Linus's security blanket would have aroused in the book's cold-blooded, priggish authors! I was supposed to be a fairly intelligent young woman; yet they had me so convinced of the rightness of their views that, the few times I did pick up David and cuddled him when he cried, I felt that I was a wicked mother. And he was such a beautiful, good-natured baby! But even if he had been the homeliest little creature on earth, no baby can have too much love.

Every American and English mother I knew in Vienna advised me to buy a kind of diaper made only in France. On his next trip to Paris I asked Whit to buy five dozen of them. "Five dozen!" He was appalled. *"Sixty* diapers for *one* little baby? Are you sure?"

"Well, some of them will be soaking, and some of them will be in the wash and some of them—"

"OK, OK, You're the boss."

That is what Whit said when he didn't agree with me but reluctantly let me have my way. It meant, "Watch it, sister! If you're wrong I'm not responsible." On his return from Paris, he told me, "Well, I got your damned diapers."

"You mean the baby's. I stopped wearing them a long time ago."

"You wouldn't think it funny if you knew the trouble they gave me at customs. I had a bitch of a time getting them into Austria because I didn't know their German name."

"*Windel.*"

"You bet it's *Windel* and I'm never going to forget it!" Whit described what had happened at the Swiss-Austrian border. The big pile of cloths he carried mystified the Austrian custom inspectors. The more he tried to explain, the more suspicious they became. Exasperated, he twisted a diaper about himself to demonstrate. When the inspectors saw a tall, dignified, and angry bearded American wearing a diaper, they were overcome. *"Yoh! Yoh! Windel!"* they guffawed. *"Ganz bestimmt!"* All was clear. American men wear diapers. They let him pass.

What they did not know, in their concentration on my baby's diapers, was that they also let pass a beautiful diamond ring that Whit had bought for me in Switzerland. Not that he had tried to smuggle it. He simply had forgotten all about it in the excitement of the ridiculous argument.

Considering the news Whit brought back from Paris and his talks with Bill Bird, our European manager, that ring was a horrendous extravagance. But it took us, like all Americans, some time to comprehend the economic catastrophe that had overtaken the world. This was especially true of Americans, like ourselves, living abroad and not seeing first hand the much-vaunted American prosperity crumble before our eyes. We could understand its happening in Austria. Austria had lost a war. But America? That never-defeated land of bountiful promise? Incredible. Yet now Fodor's melodramatic prediction a few months before that the

Kredit Anstalt's collapse meant disaster ahead seemed an understatement when compared with Whit's report of a cataclysm in the United States. "Everything's going to hell," Whit said. "Nobody knows what'll happen to the country. Suicides and bank crashes and unemployment all over the place. Some of the biggest subscribers to our service are quitting. Advertising and circulation are way off. New York says we must economize. More mailers and fewer cables. Our stringers have to go wherever possible. Last words Bill said to me when I was leaving were, 'Remember! Cut expenses to the bone! Because things are godawful!' "

"So you bought a diamond ring!" He put the ring on my finger. It fit perfectly. "It is beautiful!" I told him. "I love it but —but after what Bill Bird said, should you have spent so much money?"

"Well—well—we can always hock it." How could anyone foresee that the time was near when pawnbrokers would be confronted with such a glut of diamonds that many refused to take them? In a depression, diamonds are not necessarily a girl's best friend.

Whit had exquisite taste and had given me many lovely pieces of jewelry; most were set with semiprecious stones and none as costly as this ring, with its little diamond, rainbow-hued as a dewdrop in the sunshine, centered in a circle of small pearls. With one exception, it was the last piece of jewelry I remember Whit giving me. The exception was a startling contrast to this dainty ring from Switzerland. It was a silver replica of a prison cell door, with tiny realistic bars, padlock, and chain, made into a brooch. It was a replacement for a pin, presented to me before I knew Whit, by the Woman's party, to commemorate my four days in jail. I had lost the original pin, and Whit obtained another from the party as a Christmas surprise for me. (He hated it and said he wished he had seen what it looked like first.)

When I met Whit's mother for the first time I recalled that she had surprised me with what seemed unusual criticism of a son from a mother to a daughter-in-law. She said, "I never thought Whit would find a girl who could live with him." Moreover, she advised me, "If anyone is going to save money in your family, it will have to be you. Whit can't. He spent fifteen dollars on a necktie when he was making twenty-five dollars a week." Mrs. Burnett did not know that while I had read about economic determinism and agreed with Karl Marx about it, economics never determined my own spending. In spite of Bird's warning to "cut expenses to the bone" and Whit's Paris report that hundreds of thousands, including newspaper people, were losing their jobs in the States, we went ahead with another issue of *STORY.*

That issue, the first that would appear in 1932, is notable for the appearance of another "unknown," who was, like James Farrell, to be one of the Thirties' most important authors. He was Erskine Caldwell. As with Farrell, we had not met him. We became friends with both young men later. Caldwell's story, "Indian Summer," was set in the Georgia back country, whose sharecroppers Caldwell made famous in *God's Little Acre* and *Tobacco Road.* A lyric about two boys and a girl just reaching puberty and the sexual awakening of one of the boys and the girl, it did not have the startling realism and earthy humor of those novels.

I was not enthusiastic about a story, "The Maker of Signs," that Whit had chosen for the issue. The main character was an old philosophical eccentric employed by a religious sect to paint roadsides proclaiming "God Is Right!" and "God Is Love!" The story was not bad, but it was one Whit had written years before in California. Instead of going forward with his writing, as I'd hoped he would, Whit was pulling old manuscripts out of a trunk. Compared with his *transition* stories, written with the encouragement of Eugene Jolas, the old stories were weak and dated—and far inferior to "Sherril."

I wish that, like Henry Adams, who omitted all mention of his wife and their relationship from *The Education of Henry Adams*, I could avoid in this story of *STORY* my inevitably one-sided comments about Whit. But our working and emotional lives were so interwoven it is impossible to separate them. I was disappointed that Whit was not writing his fiction. Since O'Brien chose "One with Shakespeare" for reprinting, I myself, encouraged, had been writing stories in what little time I had free from the baby, the press, and the magazine.

Whit did not enjoy reading manuscripts. I am a compulsive reader and loved it. Whit was interested in makeup, layouts, typefaces, and the technical side of production, as well as wording of announcements, indexing of authors and stories we published, and maintaining a file of reviews and publicity items. Since all this bored me, I was more than content to have him take care of it. I think he would have been perfectly happy if I alone chose the stories. I do not remember his ever disagreeing with any of my choices, except on one occasion, after the fact, when I had turned down a story, "Saint Katie and the Virgin," by John Steinbeck, and the story went on to attract attention when published elsewhere.

I cannot emphasize too strongly that it was easy to make good choices from the material we received because we had no competition. It was to be a bone of contention with us for years as to which should come first, reading manuscripts or taking care of the production problems. I thought the manuscripts should be read first; Whit felt he needed my help on what he was doing.

Because we were amateurs, editing *STORY* was a simple business, not time-consuming. We accepted or rejected the stories and sent those we liked to the printer. Except to correct misspellings, we made no changes and asked for no revisions. I think now it was fine that we did not. We escaped the homogenizing that goes on in many magazines and gives them a boring uniformity. The soundness of our system is proved by the fact that any number of those unretouched stories are still being reprinted in anthologies and textbooks.

Whit bought a moving picture camera and projector and, instead of writing, took hundreds of shots of Viennese scenes. With various kinds of gadgets, he spent hours clipping them, editing them, and joining them in a sequence. I was invited into a darkened room to view the result. Those movies were full of pigeons! Until I saw them in Whit's films, I did not know how many pigeons strutted around Vienna. "Pigeons on the grass, alas," said Stein. Alas, said I.

I said to Whit, "I would die if I thought I could not write."

"You *would?*" It was not a question but an exclamation of incredulity. He was shocked. I do not believe it ever occurred to him that writing could be that important. Why did it not register on me that I had never heard him lamenting, as did John Gunther, that he needed time for his fiction writing? Declaring that he would like to throw over newspaper work so he could write only short stories and novels? Or mourning the loss of a fiction market as did the old *Smart Set* contributors I knew in California? I was blind, obtuse, and self-centered. And I had created a situation that years later would torture the three of us—our child, Whit, and myself.

(When I told Whit I would die if I thought I could not write, I spoke the literal truth. When I was eight I started a novel, never to be finished.

When I was eleven, I was the first in my class to have a short story published in the Latin School magazine. When I was fifteen, I was an unhappy, dowdy girl among beautifully dressed classmates from pleasant homes whose unworldly father told her, "Youth is its own adornment,"

I ran away but was returned to more misery. I thought of suicide. One morning before class I took an overdue theme to Miss Gerrish, my English teacher. What happened then is told, with names changed (one character is based on Louise Bogan), in my story "One with Shakespeare." Miss Gerrish read the theme, gazed out the window for a long moment, looked back at me, and I quote:

> "Let me give you a pointer, my dear."
> Elizabeth automatically looked toward the blackboard ledge at the chalky pointer until the words my dear bit into her mind. My dear! Miss Cox had called her my dear.
> "You have a spark of the divine fire," Miss Cox said. "You should make writing your vocation."
> Elizabeth flamed. Miss Cox, my dear, themes about immigrants, blackboards and desks whirled and fused in the divine fire.
> Miss Cox marked *A* in the red pencil at the top of the theme and Elizabeth said thank you and went away.

I was no longer a miserable girl in dowdy clothes, embarrassed among self-confident girls who mastered waltzes and fox trots while I earned pocket money memorizing poems by Milton and Shelley for my father. I was going to be that most important of beings, a writer! I forgot about suicide. My wonderful teacher had given me a future.)

Like most Americans traveling abroad, I was constantly surprised by what happened to prices when translated from foreign currencies into American dollars. Many things seemed either much too expensive or too cheap. I have stopped telling people that when I first went to Paris in the Twenties a clean and passably comfortable hotel room could be had for ten cents a night, so obvious is their skepticism. Or that I could have an excellent *table d'hôte* dinner at Michaud's on the Boul' Mich' for five cents (in American money) and, if I wanted to be extravagant, an elaborate one for seven cents. I read recently that Hemingway was bitterly envious of James Joyce because he took "his tribe" to dinner every night at Michaud's while Hemingway and his wife Hadley could afford to eat there only twice a week. When I mentioned in a Columbia class the deep impression little things often can make, and that it was seeing pork chops in a New York shop window for seven cents a pound that finally drove home to me the full impact of the Depression, a student exclaimed, "Those were the days!" I had to explain that pork chops were seven cents a pound because many people in the Thirties did not have eight cents.

Austrian currency acrobatics were the most antic Whit and I encountered. We finally got it through our heads that in Vienna things were expensive and people were cheap. Printers' labor was cheap, so we could put out an entire issue of the magazine for seventy-five dollars. A baby's nurse cost us fifteen dollars a month. I have forgotten how much Resi's wages were, except that I was so upset by their smallness that I raised them on her first payday. After the collapse of the Kredit Anstalt, all money transactions in Austria became exasperatingly complicated for foreigners.

Before the Kredit Anstalt collapse we had patronized the black market in currency only once, when Whit made a round of coffeehouse back rooms to obtain two American dollars in cash. They were required by United States law to pay for registration of our son as an American citizen at the embassy. Whit said it was easy to find bills of larger denominations, but singles and twos seemed nonexistent, and the law was exigent in stipulating two American dollars in cash. Those he found were torn and filthy, but these ragged scraps of paper made David an American, instead of Austrian, citizen.

Although we knew Americans—some of them even tourists staying only a few days—who patronized the black market, we felt it was a sleazy, dangerous business controlled by crooks. We deposited our American checks, as required by Austrian law, in

rented a furnished house, so we did not have John's worry. We did have a three-month-old infant and a new magazine. And our beloved Resi. And Fritzl, a cherished cat.

When the ax did fall, it fell on us. The Consolidated Press was dissolved and the *Chicago Daily News* stayed intact. True to their promise, the Gunthers urged us to live with them until we found other work in Vienna. It was a hopeless prospect. Sooner or later, we knew we would have to leave Vienna, taking with us the baby and the magazine. But Resi? To move a woman of her age from country to country with our limited financial resources was impossible. We were damned, however, if we were going to abandon her in a city so plagued by unemployment as Vienna. William Shirer, dear, kind Bill, who had returned from a lengthy assignment in India, came to the rescue. Bill said his wife, Tess, and he would love to have her as their cook. That left Fritzl's problem still unsolved. Leave him behind in a place where people hated cats as much as did the otherwise *gemütlich* Viennese? No. Yet how to manage during international travel all three—a nursing baby, a magazine's bulky paraphernalia, and a cat with his private toilet?

Because they had relatives in the city, Donald and Ann Friede stayed longer in Vienna than did most visitors, and we became good friends with them. Whit and I had been charmed by the loveliness of Yugoslavia's Adriatic Coast, its picturesque ancient towns, magnificent beaches, mild climate, and low prices. We decided to go there, to try to get by with free-lance foreign correspondence, article writing, and *STORY.* The Friedes planned to go to Majorca from Vienna. Donald was rapturous about the island's attractions. He urged us to go to the Spanish island instead of to Yugoslavia. I associated Majorca's location in the Balearics with Caesar and his enthusiasm for the Balearic slingers in his *Gallic Wars.* Having hated to translate his militaristic "All Gaul is divided into three parts," I kept to our Adriatic plan.

It was Fritzl and Ann Friede, though, who decided our destination. Ann was petting Fritzl, who was purring happily in her
lap, when I mentioned that I felt badly about asking a vet to
euthanize him, but I did not know how I could manage with both
a baby and a cat on a long trip. Ann looked at me with tears in
her beautiful brown eyes. "Don't kill Fritzl! Please don't! If you
come to Majorca, I'll take care of him on the trip." So it was
decided. Donald would go ahead to make house arrangements,
and Ann and Fritzl would accompany Whit, the baby, and me to
Majorca.

Ann was one of the loveliest, sweetest-natured children I have
ever known. Child she was, still in her mid-teens, although married to a much older man. It was Ann who gave me my first
glimpse of how hard life can be for a child of divorced parents.
Her marriage to Donald had been a bonanza for the sensational
press. They were gone only a day on their honeymoon to the
Caribbean when it was discovered that their marriage was illegal
because Ann was below the legal age. A startling mistake, since
her mother's new husband was Arthur Garfield Hays, one of the
most celebrated liberal lawyers in the country. Frantic messages
recalled Ann and Donald immediately to New York. This trip to
Vienna and to Majorca, after a second ceremony—a legal one—
was a belated honeymoon.

Of course there were any number of witticisms about Donald's "robbing the cradle." The sharpest barbs were aimed at
Hays for his alleged ignorance of marriage law. Any lawyer who
was the stepfather of an illegally married young daughter would
have been ridiculed, but Hays's critics took special relish in his
predicament. Reactionaries were delighted because he was famous as a lawyer who had served on the defense team in the
Scopes "monkey trial" and in the Sacco-Vanzetti case. The French
have a proverb about "fruit of a first marriage losing importance
when a second marriage follows divorce." If Mr. Hays had been
Ann's own father he would have realized her age.

From Ann's description of her misery at home and her brother's marrying at seventeen to get away, I believed that Donald, far from "robbing the cradle," may have felt sorry for the girl. He could be foolish and sometimes a bore, but he was a kind man. I never sensed either shrewdness or guile in Donald. He and Cornelius Vanderbilt were much alike. Donald, too, was from a mo ieyed family—Donald's much less so—and he had the same eagerness to be an important book publisher that Vanderbilt had to be a big newspaper publisher, the same eagerness to be friends with writers that Vanderbilt had in regard to journalists. Both were led up the garden path by men they trusted.

Donald told me that creditors of his firm, Covici-Friede, called a meeting to discuss its liabilities. "I went to the hotel meeting happy," he said, "because Steinbeck's book was selling so well I knew we had nothing to worry about. Then I learned for the first time that Pat Covici had made Steinbeck's contract out to himself, not to our firm."

!!!POVERTY PARTY!!! read the heading on the invitation to the last party we were to give in Vienna. Printed like a handbill on cheap butcher paper, it invited friends to join us for an evening of beer, bread, and cheese. We bought a barrel of Gösserbrau, which we set up in the kitchen, and many loaves of the delicious, crusty Vienna bread, and kilograms of German and Italian cheeses. Our personal belongings had been packed—pictures taken down from the walls, bookshelves emptied, and the stripped, bare look of the living room and dining room seemed just right for a hearty, informal gathering.

Beer, bread, cheese. After three years in Vienna hadn't we learned what the city's tenderhearted people were like? We had not. The poor, jobless Burnetts were starving if that's all they could afford to serve at a party. No wines, no *schnapps,* no tortes, no *patés* and cold meats, no chocolate cakes and apple strudels— it was heartbreaking! Before seven o'clock in the morning of the day of the party, the first of a procession of delivery wagons arrived at our door, and the driver left two roasted chickens and a ham. More chickens and hams followed, then roasts of beef and bottles of wines, even champagne, and boxes of pastries, along with flowers. By ten o'clock I was on the telephone begging for mercy. Please, please, we were only joking. We wanted to laugh at the depression. But people in Vienna, who had learned from devastation by war and real poverty what starvation is, could not see the joke. Thinking it over, I saw the meanness of joking about food when so many in the world were hungry, and I was ashamed of myself.

It was a good party, nevertheless. Many guests, with the same idea, came in laughing and holding up a string of frankfurters, saying, "Look what I brought!" We festooned the frankfurters from picture hook to picture hook along the bare walls. Bill Shirer was bartender, filling tall glasses with the Gösserbrau—people seemed to prefer it to the expensive wines, bottles of which stood unopened on the dining room sideboard. The party had been under way for less than an hour when Bill Shirer came rushing from the kitchen. "The beer's all gone!" he told me. Oh, no! Impossible! Had the dealer cheated us? Bill turned the spigot to show me. Not a trickle. But beer we had to have. Past nine o'clock and all the liquor stores were closed. Perhaps the Green Anchor, the little restaurant up Pötzleinsdorferstrasse at the top of a hill, would sell us a barrel. It was against the law, but the friendly owner knew us. A delegation of men guests went to see.

Soon there was a bumping sound of a barrel tumbling over cobblestones down the hill to male chanting of the Alpine song, "Hi-li, hi-lo!" The singing men lugged the barrel into the house and set it up in the kitchen. The spigot was pulled from the first barrel to use on the second. A foaming geyser showered us with Vienna's best brew. The first barrel was almost 100 percent full. Bill Shirer is the best foreign correspondent I know and the worst bartender.

Now we had two barrels of beer, and the party was on its way to record-breaking success. Whit did his party specialty, singing "Heaven Will Protect the Working Girl." The ribald stanzas about the country girl who comes to the big city with its wicked ways, when sung by Whit with his unsmiling face, always brought down the house. We joined with gusto in shouting the chorus line, "For heaven will protect the working girl!" The wonderful I.W.W. hymn, "Hallelujah, I'm a Bum!" was especially appropriate, and we sang it with tremendous enthusiasm. For the first time in the almost three years we had been living in the house, next-door neighbors sent a message that we were disturbing them.

Despite much consumption of salty cheeses and pickled herrings, there was an awful lot of beer left over the next day. It seemed a shame to abandon good Gösserbrau. I tacked up a cardboard sign on our front door, "FREE BEER INSIDE! BRING A PITCHER!" Nobody came. Proper Viennese do not accept free beer from eccentric Americans.

Donald Friede wired from Majorca that he had rented a charming house, that there were plenty more available for us, that the island's beauty was enchanting and prices unbelievably low. "Hurry and get here!" But poor Ann Friede. Poor Fritzl. Ann came down with measles the day before we were to leave. Our departure arrangements were so final we had to go ahead. A cousin would take care of Ann and accompany her to Majorca as soon as she was well enough to travel. Now Fritzl had no one to take care of him on the long trip across four countries, Austria, Italy, France, and Spain, plus the overnight boat trip across the Mediterranean to Majorca. So I held Fritzl in my arms and wept while a veterinarian injected the drug that sent a little gray cat on his own trip into eternity.

David was a three-month-old infant when we left Vienna. When we were in America and he was old enough to voice a protest, he was indignant about having been taken to so many countries before he was old enough to enjoy seeing them. Tiny though he was, he had a most important role on our trip. Because of the strict currency laws, Austrian officials staged a savage hunt for money being smuggled abroad. Passengers were searched like criminals, and their luggage opened and spilled out onto the train floor. To my delight, during all the commotion, David did not pee-pee once. When we got to Italy, the American money in his diaper was still dry.

As we had prepared to leave Vienna, Nazi swastikas were being seen more and more in public places throughout the city. A reason for the neglect by the Qualle children of their parents' graves in the Jewish cemetery, which had so angered Resi, finally dawned on me. They were scared and had fled. When the train crossed the Austrian border I was relieved that we were leaving behind Hitler and his obscene tirades. It would be wonderful, I felt, to relax in the sunshine of the Spanish island paradise so ecstatically described by Donald. I had never heard of a man named Franco

NINE

∽

MAJORCA

Four pages! Horrified, Whit and I stared at one another. The Majorcan printer was telling us he could print only four pages of *STORY* because that was all the type he had. As we stood talking with him in his small print shop, which opened to a court-yard where washing hung from lines, chickens pecked around our feet. On his arm, the printer held a little girl who hid her face from us against his shoulder, while another child, sucking a thumb, clung to his father's leg. The man gestured at an ancient foot press, his chief piece of equipment. "A museum piece," Whit muttered.

Smiling, the little man, short and dark like all Majorcans, waited patiently while Whit and I tried to decide what to do. We had discovered there were only two printers on the island. One was in the employ of the small weekly newspaper and did not do job printing. The other was this friendly paterfamilias. There were plenty of modern, well-equipped printers on the Spanish mainland, but they were a day-and-a-night's sail away on the weekly Barcelona boat.

Previous issues of *STORY*, published in Vienna, had averaged eighty pages. Four into eighty makes twenty. We asked him how long it would take him to print four pages. He could do it in a day, he said. Could he, we then asked, print four pages, redistribute the type, and print successive sets of four pages each until he had printed eighty pages? Yes, he said. It would be a long, tedious process, involving many visits to his shop to correct proofs, approve the final ones, and watch them come off the primitive press. But we had to settle for it.

"I knew we were moving a magazine and I asked about prices and climate and scenery, but never once thought about printing!" I lamented on the way home. "How stupid can one get?"

Whit was even more mournful. "I looked forward to some fishing. I've never tried deep-sea fishing. Fat chance of that now!"

One hundred twenty-six Calle del 14 Abril in Palma was the most beautiful place we would ever call home. A white-painted, two-storied villa, it stood on a high slope in El Terreno, Palma's lovely suburb. One entered from a roadway at the back, walked through spacious, high-ceilinged, white-plaster walled rooms with mosaic tiled floors and carved, heavy, dark Spanish furniture, to a wide veranda in front—and stopped, breath snatched away. There for miles before one was the great blue bay of Palma under the bluest of Mediterranean skies. Red sails of fishing boats dotted the bay's waters, and the golden sandstone walls of the Palma cathedral, the fourth largest in the world, glowed in the sunshine. The wharves and buildings of the little city of Palma were almost lost in this magnificent sweep of the earth's beauty.

From the veranda a flight of many steps led down past a series of terraces, each terrace wide enough, with its trees and shrubs and flowers, to be called a garden, to a sandy beach lapped by clean, gentle waves. A gardener, paid by the owners, lived in a cottage beside the house and took care of the upkeep. For all this we paid as rent a lot of pesetas that came to nineteen dollars a month in our American money.

But there was no Resi. As advised by the two sisters who

owned the house, we engaged a cook and a general maid. For our first dinner, to which we had Donald Friede as guest, I asked the cook to prepare a meal so dull I was ashamed of it—roast chicken, green peas, mashed potatoes, a salad to be mixed at the table, and a pastry bought from a shop in town. I found out what the cook did with the peas: she put them in the oven without water and baked them until they were shriveled pellets. The appearance of the chicken and potatoes made analysis of their preparation impossible. Donald Friede was hysterical when he saw the chicken. "You asked a Majorcan woman to cook a *whole* chicken? Oh, no! Would you ask an American woman to cook a whole cow?"

He explained. Only a single leg, or a wing, or half of a breast of a chicken was bought at a time. It was finely shredded and scattered over a *paella,* the most common native Majorca dish. This resembled an Italian pizza, except that its foundation was rice instead of dough. As with pizzas, there was a variety of *paellas,* the most popular being made with fish or vegetables.

The dinner marked the beginning of my language difficulties with the cook. I had been surprised on arriving in Majorca to find that the islanders did not speak Spanish, as I had thought everyone in Spain did, but their own native Majorcan, a blend of Barcelona's Catalan, France's Provençal, Moorish, and ancient Phoenician. I did not dare leave my baby until I found somebody trustworthy, whose language I understood, to take care of him. I knew no Spanish but could get by in French and German. It was not easy to find such a person on the island, so I felt fortunate when I heard of Paquita, who had lived in France, and knew French besides her native Majorcan. She could be my interpreter with the cook as well as help me with the baby. Like all Majorcan girls, she was closely guarded in traditional, Spanish fashion. Mama was her chaperone.

The two arrived together, Mama to interview me, Paquita to be interviewed by me. Both wore the Majorcan costume—ankle-length, full-skirted black dress, plain white apron tied around the waist, and little white cap atop a heavy braid of black hair hanging down in back. Paquita was a pretty girl of seventeen with a nice smile. She's too young to be a regular nursemaid, I thought, but she can baby-sit. Mama, who spoke a slow, careful French, was a most serious person. She asked about my husband's occupation, how many servants I kept, what kind of cooking we did, asked to see the baby and wanted to know if he was healthy, how many hours of the day Paquita would be expected to work and, of course, how much the pay would be. I watched Paquita's face when I showed the baby to her and her mother. I liked Paquita's tender expression as she looked down at David in his crib. Her mother and I reached a financial agreement and, after much earnest talk to Paquita in Majorcan, which I could not understand, Mama left, saying she would be back the next week to take Paquita to Palma for her day off.

After the mother's departure, I sent Paquita to her room, telling her that when she had unpacked and was ready, I would explain about taking care of the baby. Half an hour later, a stranger came out of her room. The stranger was wearing a bright red blouse, a short bright blue skirt, and bobbed hair.

I gasped. "Paquita!"

"*Plus moderne, n'est-ce-pas?*" she demanded, her cheeks dimpling mischievously. "*Très Américaine!*"

"*Mais votre mère—?*"

Paquita put a finger to her lips and winked. She was making me a co-conspirator. I was frustrated. She was only being a normal seventeen-year-old girl hungry for the fashions of 1932 and not the centuries-old style of the island, picturesque though they were. But I could visualize a stern mother whisking her away from my house of iniquity, leaving me without a nursemaid who could speak a language I understood. Besides, I liked the girl. I had once been seventeen and rebellious, too.

Whit was amused when I told him. "'*Très Américaine,*' huh? She's been inspecting the girls off the cruise boats." Every so often a big, white vessel steamed into the bay, and passengers came ashore for a few hours.

"The mother will take her away and I'll be left with no one to help with the baby."

"I'd leave that to Paquita to worry about. She's fooled the old lady thus far. She'll manage."

Whit was right. The next week, on the day her mother was to come, Paquita was demure again in her ankle-length black dress and white apron. Once again a pigtail, pinned to her head under the little white cap, hung down her back.

Before that day came around we went to the printer's to see our four pages of his proofs. His greeting was subdued. The proofs he gave us were speckled all over with many little black slug marks.

We looked at him with surprise. He looked back at us with sorrow.

"Oh, Señor! Señora! I am most sorry but I cannot print your nice magazine."

"You can't? Why?"

"Yes, why?" I echoed Whit.

"You use too many *w*'s."

"First time I've ever been accused of that," said Whit. "What's wrong with *w*'s?"

"There are no *w*'s in the Spanish language. I do not have enough in type for them."

Neither of us could speak for a moment. All the words in English with *w*'s started racing around in my head. Who, when, where, why, what, word, world, wife, wolf, work, now, how, show, cow, write, whether—oh, God! I thought, ours is a language of *w*'s!

"Could we buy some?" Whit asked.

"Si, Señor, it might be possible."

"Where do you get your type?"

With the address he gave us, we went home to write to the

type foundry in Madrid which might sell us some *w*'s.

"How many do you think we should order?" Whit asked me.

"Millions," I answered. "It's the only letter in the English language."

"Seriously."

"A couple of thousand, at least, I think. And don't forget capital letters, too."

After we mailed the letter to the Madrid type foundry, emphasizing the urgency of our need for *w*'s, Whit declared, "I'm not going to hang around, waiting for a bunch of *w*'s. I'm going fishing." Off he went to join a group of new friends for a fishing cruise of several days. I did not go. I could not leave the baby with a brand-new nursemaid, but even if I could, I would not have gone fishing. I hate killing for fun. One of the reasons I liked Whit when I first knew him was his telling me he had hunted only once. "I pointed my gun at a bird," he said, "the bird looked at me and I looked at the bird. I put my gun away and never went hunting again." His dedication to fishing was a surprise and a disappointment. (People keep repeating the superstition that fish have no nervous system and do not feel pain. That is obvious nonsense. Why do they writhe in agony, then, when hooked?)

With Whit gone, I spent every minute I could with the baby. Each day he was a new miracle. With his bright yellow hair, black-lashed, dark blue eyes, pink-and-white skin, regular features, and perfect little body, he seemed too wonderful to be real. His sweet nature was another marvel. He seldom cried but smiled often or gurgled a cheerful, baby laugh. I felt love so great for him I sometimes wept for the joy of it. David gave me more happiness than anyone I have known.

I have never forgotten the afternoon that I saw a man travel his first inch. I had taken David from his crib and placed him on my bed. I heard a little grunt and after a couple of minutes another. I looked at him. Slowly, and with great effort, he was pushing his body forward. It was not yet creeping. It was an inner urging of his body to go forth. I thought, dear baby, so many, many miles await you!

When David slept, I kept his crib beside me while I worked. We had left the material for our final Vienna issue with the printer, and he was very faithful about sending proofs—*not* four pages at a time! The Vienna post office was also efficient about forwarding our mail. The amount of our correspondence was increasing by leaps and bounds. A surprising number of stories came to us from continental countries, Sweden, Russia, Germany, France, Italy, Hungary, Austria, and Spain, by their native writers. Among those we received from England were stories by such outstanding authors as L.A.G. Strong and H.E. Bates. Farrell and Caldwell continued to send us stories, along with many other Americans. Newcomers among them included William Carlos Williams and Manuel Komroff. The latter, whose warm personality was recognizable in his letters, was later to play an important part in *STORY*'s history.

Whit came back from his fishing trip deeply tanned and enthusiastic over the prospect of more such trips. A few days after his return a small but very heavy package arrived in the mail. It was our *w*'s, and we hurried with them to the printer. *STORY*'s publication deadline for its first Majorcan issue was getting dangerously close, and the stories for its contents were all chosen; so we implored him to do the job immediately. He protested at first, explaining that picking out the slugs and replacing them with the new letters and running off more proofs would take some time and that he had other customers' work to do. Finally, he said he could have the new proofs ready for us the next day.

"*Mañana! Mañana!* I'm goddamned sick and tired of this shuttling back and forth!" Whit protested. I was exasperated, too, but I did not remind him at that moment that each issue would require many more shuttlings to correct twenty sets of four-page proofs. If I had, there might never have been another issue of *STORY*.

"At least our *w* problem is solved," I commented. How optimistic I was!

The printer's weary *"Buenos dias, Señor, Señora"* the next morning puzzled me. He sounded like a very, very tired man. When he gave us our page proofs I understood why. His ancient, worn type could not compete with our brand-new letters. Now all we could see were *w*'s!

"Shit!" yelled Whit. "Shit, shit, SHIT! Those goddamned bastard *w*'s! What do they think they are? One single, solitary letter in the alphabet and look at them! The bastards!"

I laughed. I couldn't help it.

"And you! *You!*" Whit turned on me. "Who had the bright idea to start a magazine? When there are no *w*'s in the Spanish language!"

"Señor, please!" The printer pointed through the doorway and across the courtyard full of children, chickens, and a donkey, at his small house, where his wife was scowling at us from a window. "My youngest, the infant, sleeps!"

"Huh? Oh! I'm sorry. But what do you suggest we do with this mess?"

"Make those new letters old."

So we did. We sandpapered those *w*'s, we stamped on them, we hammered them and hurled them around to give them in an hour all the wear and tear the printer's other type had endured for many years. We finally subdued them so that they lost most of their prominence. But I have been *w*-conscious ever since.

Instead of being an arduous bore, as we had feared, the installment reading of the proofs, four pages at a time, became a pleasant routine. Sometimes Whit went to the printer's, sometimes I, but more often we both went. We marked the proofs the printer had ready, and, while he made the corrections, we played with his bevy of children. We took them sweets, but they seemed to enjoy much more laughing at the funny mistakes we made, mispronouncing the Majorcan words they tried to teach us. The proofs corrected and OK'd, we repaired to a café terrace on the Rambla, the hilly main street that ran up and down through the heart of Palma until it ended at the waterfront. We had a glass of the good local wine, accompanied by the wonderful native olives, stuffed with anchovies, and watched the happy throng go by.

And it was happy! We could have traveled "the wide world over" and not found a greater contrast to the despair of the unhappy, war-devastated, poverty-stricken Vienna we had left than this prosperous, contented island in 1932. The very air, with its bracing sea breeze, was unlike the *Föhn,* the enervating Alpine wind that plagued Vienna. The chattering, laughing people who passed us as we drank our wine included Spaniards of all kinds. The Majorcan women, in their white-aproned, white-capped black costume, looked alike. The men varied. There were Basques in their berets, down from the north, laborers in red woolen belly bands, from the island's copper mines and marble quarries, Barcelona business-suited men, over from the mainland, Africans from Spanish Morocco, and a great medley of sheep herders, vintners, peasants, and fishermen. If a cruise boat was in, there was also a flock of tourists, mostly American, inspecting us all, including Whit and me, as if we were specimens in a museum.

The Rambla scene was exhilarating because the people showed such a feeling of emancipation. Two years before they had rid themselves of a dictator: Primo de Rivera had been forced to resign and go into exile. Only a year before our arrival, they had toppled King Alfonso XIII from his throne. He, too, became a fugitive in a foreign land. Now there was a republic in Spain. For the first time in their long history, Spaniards were tasting freedom and loving it.

The long-discontinued magazine *Vanity Fair,* published for many years by Condé Nast as "a sophisticated review of contemporary art and society," has said Whit and I "led the migration" that made Majorca a popular resort. I am glad it is not true. I would hate to be responsible for what recent photographs show Majorca has become—Miami-like, with high-rise buildings, huge neon signs, crowded waterfront, and all. In 1932 Majorca was so unspoiled it was almost primitive. I remember only a couple of small, three-story hotels. Flowering gardens and sandy beaches rimmed the waterfront, except for those docks at the foot of the capital, Palma, which called itself a city but was really a town. Unlike Miami, however, the climate was not very warm, save in midsummer. The many writers from the cold, damp, foggy countries of northern Europe who have written rapturously of balmy weather on the Riviera and other Mediterranean places are contrasting it with the rigor of their native climes.

Two famous lovers, George Sand and Frédéric Chopin, who in the early nineteenth century went to the island seeking a romantic retreat, were the first to put Majorca on the literary map. They did not find the bliss there they expected. In her book, *A Winter at Majorca,* the French novelist tells of their unhappy experience. Like many of the unconventional migrants in my time and, probably, at the present time, they were not popular with Majorcans. George Sand shocked them and Chopin terrified them. Devout Catholics, the Majorcans were scandalized that the novelist and the composer were living in sin in their beautiful old monastery at Valldemosa. Even worse, in some ways, George Sand wore *trousers!* When word spread that the frail Chopin had tuberculosis, the Majorcans panicked. They forced the two to flee the island.

A sensation weirder than George Sand's trousers was titillating both Majorcans and the Anglo-American colony when we arrived. Jean Hoyt, Tallulah Bankhead's sister, and even more wayward than the notoriously unconventional Tallulah, had appeared on a beach in a topless bathing suit. A police officer had thrown his coat over her shoulders and rushed her off the beach. She was warned never to appear again in public with uncovered breasts. The next day Jean returned to the beach with her breasts covered. Bright rings of red, green and blue paint encircled them. She was arrested and ordered deported.

Jean Hoyt belonged to a group of what today's gossip columnists call "the beautiful people," men and women with too much money and too much leisure, who had settled on the island. Many of the women were divorced, and handsome young men, the first gigolos I had seen, were in solicitous attendance on them. Not once but several times I heard that rooms in a hotel across from the villa belonging to one rich woman were in constant demand because she and her entourage of a gigolo, a lesbian lover, and a monkey could be viewed, all taking a bath together.

Mary Dahlberg lived in the monastery at Valldemosa where George Sand and Chopin had stayed. She was a pleasant woman, the handsome, dark-haired former wife of Schulte, a cigar-store magnate, and, at the time I knew her, living apart from another husband, Bror Dahlberg, "the celotex king." She invited Whit and me to a party in her monastery "cell." The monastery, except that it was in beautiful countryside, reminded me of the Palais-Royal in Paris, where Colette had an apartment. Like the Palais, it was built around a tremendous courtyard, with gardens more extensive than those of the French structure. A chapel stood in the center.

Until that evening I had thought of a monk's cell as a tiny, spartan cubicle with walls bare save for a crucifix and furnishings as bleak as those in a penitentiary. Instead, the cell Mary rented, like others in the monastery, was as big as a town house, with two stories, spacious reception, living and dining rooms, and kitchen on the first floor, and bedrooms, a library, and study on the second. I was assured the layout was identical with the original, built for monks from the nobility ages before. Only the furnishings were modern. The party guests, in expensive evening clothes, were more circumspect than those at some newspaper parties I had attended, but there was no praying, fasting, or celibacy.

American and English writers were scattered all over the island. Robert Graves and Laura Riding lived at Deya, on the other side of Majorca from Palma. There the scenery was grander, with mountains and caves famous for their stalactites. Miss Riding was pointed out to me in Palma one day, and I almost spoke to her. I wish I had because she and Graves, as I learned after we left the island, operated a small literary press, the Seizin Press, in Deya. Genevieve Taggard, the poet, was living on a Guggenheim Fellowship near us with her small daughter, and we became friends. Theodore Pratt, a frequent *New Yorker* contributor, and Charles O'Neill, fresh from editorship of the Dartmouth *Jack o' Lantern,* were on the island, and contributed stories to *STORY*.

There was an abundance of empty houses for rent on the island. Their low rent attracted writers and painters. The reason for their vacancy, I was told, was that the more prosperous families customarily built a house every time a baby was born, in order to guarantee it a future home. (With the perspective I now have on Spanish history, I am convinced those houses, many of them large villas, belonged to aristocrats who had fled when, in 1931, the year before we arrived, King Alfonso and the dictatorship had been overthrown and the Spanish republic established.)

A real mystery to me was, and still is, Spaniards' absolute unawareness of the fact that animals feel pain. I know they are not deliberately sadistic. In every other respect they are among the kindest people I have met. They are wonderfully courteous to strangers. They adore children—a sign of their love for them was the candy necklaces I never saw anywhere else. These were necklaces strung with brightly colored hard candies, instead of beads, on which children could suck while they wore them—and create lovely, sticky messes down their fronts. More than once, a friendly Majorcan draped one on David. He was too young to want candy, so I was able to deprive him of it as soon as the beaming donor was out of sight.

No consideration was shown animals, however. Packs of dogs,

neglected and hungry, roamed, scavenging streets and fields. I loved to lie and listen to the tinkling music of sheep bells as it came down to me from the hills in the quiet night. One night I was startled by the weak mewing of tiny kittens. I still heard it in the morning and traced it to the garden of neighbors. They were sitting on their veranda, laughing and chatting, when I interrupted to tell them I heard kittens crying in their garden. "Oh, yes," and the laughter seemed to increase, "we killed their mother yesterday." "But the kittens! What will happen to them?" I asked. "They'll die off," they replied.

When I heard of a movement among the English and American residents to start a Society for the Prevention of Cruelty to Animals, I gladly joined. Many Majorcans, instead of scoffing as I expected, were interested. We invited them to the first and last meeting, quite a fair-sized gathering. We discussed first the misery of the many homeless dogs. When the problem that confronts every new organization arose—the question of financing—a middle-aged man in the audience asked for the floor. *"Señores* and *Señoras,* gentlemen and ladies, it is always easy to raise money for a good cause in Majorca. All we have to do is give a bullfight." So much for the Society for the Prevention of Cruelty to Animals.

When Whit announced he was going to a bullfight, I raised no objection, and he did not ask me to go along. He knew only too well how I felt. Since it was Sunday, Paquita and the two maids were off. David and I were alone in the house.

I heard the harsh scream of a peacock at our front door. I ignored it. It's one of the neighbor's birds, I thought, taking a walk for itself. Countless beautiful peacocks were kept on the island. Peacock Island would have been a good name for Majorca. Besides being beautiful garden ornaments, the birds acted like watchdogs, raising a raucous clamor when an owner's premises were entered. The peacock cry at my door became louder, insistent.

"What *is* the matter with that bird?" I wondered. "Can it be hurt?" I went to see.

When I opened the door, a slight, dark-haired man in his thirties was standing there laughing.

"I'm Bob McAlmon," he said.

Robert McAlmon! In Paris I had heard his name innumerable times. I knew he was a writer, publisher, and close friend of Joyce, but I had never met him or read his work. "A spokesman of the post-war nihilistic pessimists of the 'lost generation' " is how *The Oxford Companion to American Literature* describes McAlmon. In his biography of Joyce, Richard Ellman says, that Joyce "treated McAlmon as a colleague and was pleased to find some resemblance between their short stories." In Paris I'd heard an account of how, when the husband of Joyce's typist had destroyed her copy of the Penelope section of *Ulysses* because he considered it obscene, McAlmon had dropped his own work to do the recopying himself. In turn, Joyce suggested the title *A Hasty Bunch* for a collection of McAlmon's short stories (a new edition of which was published in 1977).

McAlmon, the youngest of a Presbyterian minister's ten children, was married to Winifred Ellerman, the daughter of Sir John Ellerman, one of the richest men in England. They were separated, and she was living in Switzerland with H.D. (Hilda Doolittle), the American Imagist poet, and writing poems of her own under the name of Bryher. No one, including writers, to whom I have mentioned Robert McAlmon's name recently has recognized it. Yet McAlmon was more important than many of the period whose names are famous today. He used his father-in-law's riches to help many writers. Before Harriet Weaver endowed Joyce, McAlmon provided him with $150 a month. In New York, before he came to Europe, and, to his surprise, married a rich woman whose status as Sir John's daughter he did not realize until he met her family in London, he and William Carlos Williams, together with Nathanael West, published *Contact,* an avant-garde magazine. When he arrived in Paris and had money, *Contact* became Contact Editions, a book press. McAlmon's book publishing partner was William Bird, who, as European manager of the Consolidated Press, was our boss when we worked in Vienna.*

After that first visit, McAlmon came several times to our Palma house. There was a tautness about him, a frigidity in his brilliantly blue eyes, that made me guess he was under terrific tension. I felt there was something in him that might snap at any minute. At the same time, he seemed lost and lonely. I never saw him with any friends.

McAlmon, and not any of the players, was the star of a Palma little theater group's premiere. His performance upstaged them all. For weeks after, he was more avidly discussed than the cast, the scenery, or the direction. Because the playwright's sister directed the group, they had chosen that dull old standby, *"Outward Bound"* for their first production. I was being thoroughly bored by its cargo of souls heading for an afterlife and wishing I could escape when, from high up in the theater's empty gallery, came a peacock's cacophonous cry, repeated again and again. It was, of course, Bob giving "the bird" to *Outward Bound.* There were shouts from the audience of "Quiet!" "Hush!" The peacock salute continued. The players could not be heard. The curtain was

---

* A *New Republic* reviewer, Dan Pinck, paid this posthumous tribute to McAlmon in 1958: "By 1925, in the pre-dawn of our literary renaissance, McAlmon had already—and *first,* in some instances—published Ford Madox Ford, Mina Loy, Ezra Pound, Norman Douglas, Djuna Barnes, Havelock Ellis, Edith Sitwell, William Carlos Williams, H.D., James Joyce, Gertrude Stein, Marianne Moore, Marsden Hartley, Wallace Stevens, Kenneth Burke, Glenway Westcott and Kay Boyle." Edward J. O'Brien had been the first to publish Hemingway when he printed his short story, "My Old Man." McAlmon and William Bird were the first to publish a book by him, *Three Stories and Ten Poems.* True to form, Hemingway later rewarded McAlmon by punching him in the face, splitting his lip. Using the title of McAlmon's 1938 memoirs, *Being Geniuses Together,* Kay Boyle in 1968 contrived a fascinating literary duet by interweaving her own memoirs of the twenties with alternate chapters of McAlmon's.

lowered and people yelled, "Get the police!" When the police arrived, McAlmon had slipped out and was gone.

McAlmon and I agreed about both Gertrude Stein and bullfights. Although he had published at his own expense Stein's *Making of Americans,* which he considered her only worthwhile book, McAlmon called her "a spoiled rich child." Most of her writing, he told me, was baby talk. I said I thought she had fooled the critics into thinking she was garbed in glorious raiment when really the Empress had no clothes on. Bob roared. "Gertie nude! What a sight that would be!"

He kept away from the Palma bullfights.*

The cook did not appear one morning. Instead I received an angry letter from her in excellent English probably written by one of the scribes who sit in little booths in public places to serve those who cannot write. She was quitting, she said, because "I have never been so insulted in my life. I, a grown woman and an

---

* In his memoirs he tells what happened when he and Hemingway saw their first bullfight together. "At first it seemed totally unreal, like something happening on the screen. The first bull charged into the ring with tremendous violence. When the horses were brought in, it charged head on and lifted the first horse over its head. But the horns did not penetrate.

"Instead of a shock of disgust, I rose in my seat and let out a yell. Things were happening too quickly for my mind to consider the horse's suffering. Later, however, when one of the horses was galloping in hysteria around the ring, treading on its own entrails, I decidedly didn't like it. I have since discovered that many hardened Spanish *aficionados,* and in one case I knew of, the brother of a bullfighter, had to look the other way on such occasions. Hemingway became at once an *aficionado,* that is, a passionate bullfight fan or enthusiast, intent upon learning all about the art. If I suspect that his need to love the art of bullfighting came from Gertrude Stein's praise of it, as well as from his belief in the value of 'self-hardening,' it is only because his bullfight book [*Death in the Afternoon*] adopts such a belligerent attitude in the defense of bullfighting."

Again, "nothing is more horrible than a bad bullfight, and the clumsy killings of the bulls are more horrible than the horse part of the fight. The lost, baby-calf look of wondering stupidity on a bull's face is heartbreaking, particularly when it is a brave bull but does not want to fight or charge horses. It is complete nonsense that all bulls are naturally attacking and fighting animals. Even goaded by torture, some of them remain brave, and fight only to be let alone."

experienced, high-quality cook, have been given orders by a seventeen-year-old girl!" She had the sensitive pride of all Spaniards, and I was sorry I had offended her. Perhaps Paquita had been saucily self-important in passing on my requests. I decided that trying to cope with Majorcan marketing and cooking in a language I did not know was too difficult. A reasonably priced *pension* was down the road, and Whit and I arranged to have lunch and dinner there. Paquita and the general maid could fix their own meals and I would prepare the baby's food.

I was lunching at the *pension* when an unfamiliar Majorcan hurried to my table. "Excuse, Señora," he said, "do you know the Señor McAlmon is in prison?"

"What? Oh, no!"

"Yes. For some days. I have been taking to him his food."

"But why?"

"For going on the Barcelona boat when not a passenger. He has a trial this afternoon. He should have a friend there."

I jumped up. "Of course, he should. I'll go." Damn, I thought, and Whit's off fishing!

I was frightened when I learned it was the Guardia Civil that had arrested McAlmon. The Guardia, a paramilitary national police force, was a hated legacy from the old régime. Majorcans lowered their voices when they spoke of it. Jay Allen, the *Chicago Tribune* correspondent who had been a friend in Paris, had been transferred to the Madrid Bureau, and I telephoned him. As always, Jay was wonderful and promised to help.

McAlmon's crime was committed by Majorcans and foreigners alike, all the time. I myself had done it often—going on board the Barcelona boat to bid good-bye to friends who were sailing —and had never heard of any law against it. But McAlmon had objected when stopped by the Guardia, and had been knocked down, handcuffed, his ankles shackled, and dragged through the streets of Palma to the jail. It had been vicious treatment to inflict on so slight a man, but then the Guardia was notorious for its brutality. No Majorcan would have dared question an order from it.

At the door to the courtroom I was asked for my identity papers, which a foreigner in Spain was required by law to carry always. In my excitement I had forgotten them. Now I, too, was arrested, but not taken to jail. I was told to stay in the courtroom. I begged to go home for my papers. I told them I had a small baby there who needed me. "Please sit down, keep quiet and wait," I was told.

Paquita was at the house and could be trusted to take care of David through the afternoon and evening. Whit had said he would be home for dinner, which, in keeping with Spanish custom, would be at nine o'clock or later. It was late afternoon before Bob's case was called and, looking weary and unkempt, his face bruised, he was brought into the court. Half-heartedly he waved to me.

The bored-appearing magistrate motioned me to the front of the room and assigned a Majorcan to stand beside me as interpreter. By then I was so upset about the baby that I made little sense. I did say I knew many important persons in New York and Paris who admired McAlmon as a writer. I do not remember whether I mentioned Joyce. It wouldn't have mattered, as his name would have meant nothing to them. Later I was furious with myself for not thinking to remind the magistrate that Spain's greatest writer, Cervantes, had also been arrested and imprisoned, not once but several times.

Bob was found guilty, of what I did not know. He was also ordered to stop disturbing the peace by imitating peacocks and to leave Majorca by the next boat. I was found guilty of breaking the law by not having my identity papers with me. I was fined something like fifty cents in pesetas and freed.

All was serene when I arrived home. The baby was fine and smiling. Paquita had not missed me. I telephoned Jay Allen in Madrid to tell him what had happened. He already knew. He said that as soon as he got my call, he contacted a friend in the Republican government who was promised by the Majorcan authorities that they would not be hard on Bob. I suppose Jay also cabled an account to the *Chicago Tribune,* but I forgot to ask him. Whit came in soon after I got back. When I told him how different my day had been from his out on the water, he said, "McAlmon should not have tangled with the Guardia Civil. They're tough babies." Which, of course, was true. Bob's behavior belied the popular notion of effete poets.

There was a great booming of cannon fire one morning. We rushed to the front veranda. A long line of battleships had entered the bay and was approaching the Palma docks. Mussolini's Italian navy had dropped in to pay an alleged friendly call and to show how mighty he was. It was a tactical maneuver for what lay ahead. All that was to happen in Spain for the next seven years, including one of history's bloodiest civil wars, was a dress rehearsal by the great powers for the Second World War. Every afternoon, while the fleet was in the bay, right at the siesta hour, Fascist planes buzzed our rooftops. Dogs barked, peacocks screamed, but the most terrible cries were those of frightened children. I held David close in my arms at such times and thought of the millions of mothers who had clutched their children thus.

The Italian fleet left after a few days. It had succeeded in its mission, to cow the people of Majorca and to assess the island as a base for shelling the Spanish mainland. Uneasiness was in the balmy air. I felt it when I heard people wonder why there were young German men camping in remote spots on the island, or what mysterious things were happening on the neighboring island of Minorca that travel to it should be forbidden. Juan March, one of the richest men in Europe, had his home on Majorca. When his name was mentioned, Majorcans looked wise and secretive. His fortune was rumored to have been founded on smuggling, an activity so common on Majorca that peddlers of smuggled goods came openly to my house, offering Swiss watches, French perfumes, Italian silks and, most common of all, cigarettes almost prohibitively taxed in Spain.

I do not remember meeting Juan March, but I do recall meeting a friend of his, who, I was told, paid frequent visits to March, coming all the way from Corunna in Spain's most northwestern tip to see him. I met the friend at the home of a Majorcan where Whit and I, with half a dozen other guests, were having late afternoon coffee and drinks. A small, dapper, black-mustached army officer, he was introduced to me as General Francisco Franco, former commander of Spain's Foreign Moroccan Legion. He bowed to me. There was no shaking of hands. His name meant nothing to me that afternoon, but I am now glad our hands did not touch. A year later, in 1933, General Franco would become the military commander of Majorca. Three years after that, the same year Hitler came to power in Germany, he would lead an army mutiny against the Spanish Republic.

The only time I ever had to sleep on a roof it rained. Ann and Donald Friede, a pretty girl cousin of Anne's, Max Kulka, our "whipping boy" from Vienna who was visiting us, and I arrived in Ibiza after a day-long boat trip from Majorca. Whit had stayed home to supervise Paquita's care of David. I have mentioned that Majorca, when we arrived there in the spring of 1932, was so unspoiled as to be almost primitive. Ibiza *was* primitive. And quite wonderful. To savor the quality of life in Ibiza before it was destroyed by Franco, read Elliott Paul's lovely classic, *The Life and Death of a Spanish Town.* The story of Santa Eulalia, the village where he had lived and had loved its simple, warmhearted people, is one of the happiest books I have ever read, despite its sad end.

The whole town of Ibiza, the island's capital with the same name, was at the dock to see the Majorca boat arrive. It reminded me of what I had read of small western nineteenth-century towns turning out for the daily arrival of their one train. Girls and women of all ages, whose dress seemed to have more touches of bright color than those of the Majorcan women, fishermen, laborers, and farmers were there, and two old people in wheelchairs were given front-row places. The children were countless and included lewd, upward-peering small boys who scampered in and out from under the widely spaced boards of the gangplank, forcing female passengers to draw close their skirts.

There were only two tiny inns in the town of Ibiza and neither had any rooms vacant. Nor could anyone tell us of a private house that might have rooms for rent. "Don't worry," we were told. "It never rains at this time of year in Ibiza. There are benches in the square or a sandy beach where you can sleep." We returned to the first inn for supper. The owner took pity on us. He would give us pillows and blankets and we could sleep on his roof.

The second-story rooftop was certainly no mattress, but we had pillows for our heads and blankets against the chill. It was a fine, starry night, we could look out over the Mediterranean, with its long reflections of bobbing lights on the fishing boats, and I could think about Astarte, the site of whose shrine I would visit the next day. Astarte, Astarte! Such a beautiful name, I thought, when I first saw it in my ancient history textbook at school; it belongs in a poem. The emphasis of the ancient history class was on the Greeks and Romans; of Astarte I learned only that she had been the Phoenician goddess of love, corresponding to the Greeks' Aphrodite. The beauty of her name stayed with me. Now I was on the island where Astarte's shrine had drawn women from all over the ancient world, women who came with votive offerings to gain for themselves the love of a man or the birth of a child.

My sleepy mind wandered from the goddess to her people. The Phoenicians had invented the alphabet. Before them there had been only cuneiform wedges and hieroglyphics. Like the Jews and the Arabs, the Phoenicians belonged to the Semitic race. All were extraordinary. The Phoenicians gave us letters for our books, the Arabs numerals for our mathematics, and the Jews monotheism for our religion. My gropings in ancient history stopped It never rains in Ibiza at this time of year? Then what was this liquid splashing on my face?

Grabbing our pillows, blankets, and travelling bags, we made for the opening to the inside stairs and huddled on them. They were horribly uncomfortable. Max left to explore and did not come back. I went to look for him. From a room with an open door I heard a woman's angry voice. I looked inside. Comfortably ensconced in an easy chair, Dr. Max Kulka, well-known Vienna attorney, was sound asleep. Lying in bed, the bedclothes drawn tightly up under her chin, an excited woman was scolding him in an unintelligible dialect. Shades of Charles Dickens and Mr. Pickwick in the wrong hotel room! But this was 1932 and the scene was pure Thurber.

For the first time in the more than two years I had known Max, I learned that he was deaf in one ear. The ear happened to be the one turned toward the woman in bed. That roof was awfully hard. Those narrow stairs were terribly cramped. That overstuffed easy chair was delightfully soft. I wonder.

With his great black beard and plump figure, Elliott Paul, dressed in a spectacular suit of bright red sailcloth, greeted us the next day in Santa Eulalia, nine miles from the town of Ibiza. I had not seen him since the days we both had worked on the *Paris Herald*, but he looked exactly the same.

"Just in time to pick the corn for lunch!" he declared with gusto, knowing what a treat it promised the Friedes and myself as expatriate Americans. Until I reached Hungary I never saw corn served to human beings in Europe. It was considered fodder fit only for animals. And in Hungary, where it was called something that sounded like Kukurutz, it was overcooked in very salty water and served without butter. The only American restaurant in Paris made a fortune during the corn-on-the-cob season each year.

Elliott has written about how amused the Santa Eulalians were when they saw him gnawing at corn on the cob. Children grunted, "Oink! Oink!" as he passed. It was important hog-raising country, and Ibizinos grew acres of corn for the pigs but themselves never touched it. Today they eat it. During the civil war when their village was laid waste and they were starving, they remembered how a crazy American had eaten corn, and in desperation they tried pig's food. It saved their lives.

When I mentioned Astarte to Elliott, he knew immediately where her shrine had been. The place was a gold mine of archeological treasures, he said, and a strict law forbade digging there. Many lay so close to the surface that a heavy rainstorm would reveal them. A small museum had been built to house them, but before that the villagers had collected them and given a number to him. He gave me one, a small clay head of Astarte with a Byzantine headdress. But all I saw when he took me there was ordinary farmland.

When I left Ibiza to sail back to Majorca it was to face economic reality. Thus far our stay in the Balearics had been a long holiday. After coping with the daily grind of newspaper jobs and editing the magazine at the same time, work on the magazine only was play. I no longer remember how much money we had when we arrived in Majorca, but I doubt if it was more than a thousand dollars. Neither of us had earned any money while there. Material for any number of *Mercury* articles abounded, yet I never once queried Mencken about them. We became lotus eaters, which happens when people who have been used to high prices find themselves in a place where everything seems incredibly cheap.

David had his first birthday in Majorca. On November 5, 1932, he became one year old. He was a healthy, happy child, strikingly blond in contrast with the dark-complexioned Majorcan children. We had to call a doctor for him only once in Majorca. The doctor paused in the doorway before entering and called down divine blessings upon all in the house, examined David,

who was crying in pain, diagnosed the trouble as colic, and pre-
scribed a dose of castor oil, which David recovered without. I had
heard my doctor father say too many times that castor oil was such
a violent cathartic that it should be given only in extremely rare
cases. The island's infant mortality rate was 40 percent. David was
at least twice the size of a Majorcan baby of the same age. His diet
was utterly different from theirs. Fresh milk was scarce on the
island, so I bought imported dried whole milk for him. He also
got lots of protein from eggs, another food not given babies in
Majorca. Paquita reported to me that the woman from whom we
bought vegetables was upset when she learned I was feeding
David spinach. She declared I should be reported to the police.
But the high infant mortality rate occurred among the Majorcan
babies fed on a diet that she approved, which consisted, after they
had been weaned, mostly of starches and sweets. David was not
only healthy, he was quite intellectual. He could be kept quiet for
all of fifteen minutes by giving him a magazine whose pages he
could turn.

In spite of what must have impressed some people as publishing flightiness in moving an American magazine from one European country to another, our subscriptions and bookstore sales
continued to grow, as did the number of flattering reviews. Edward O'Brien's choice of eight of our 1932 stories for reprinting
in *The Best American Short Stories* attracted widespread attention.
For the second time, his selections from *STORY* were the most
ever chosen from any magazine in one year.

Whit's last good pair of shoes had given out, and he had been
reduced to a pair of cheap espadrilles for all occasions. Since Whit
was fussy about his appearance, the espadrilles were an ominous
sign of worse economies to come. If we, and the magazine, were
to survive, we had to get some money. We wrote letters to New
York to sound out the possibility of a publisher's financing
STORY. Although Lewis Gannett, a well-known critic who did

book reviews for the *New York Herald-Tribune,* had given *STORY* enthusiastic reviews, he wrote us that it was hopeless to think of continuing *STORY.* No literary short story magazine would ever succeed in the United States. He was sure, however, that we could get good jobs with a publishing house and he would be glad to recommend us.

A warm, friendly correspondence had grown up between Manuel Komroff, one of our best-known contributors, and ourselves. In one letter he wrote us that everywhere he went in New York he heard comments about *STORY.* "Not since *The American Mercury,"* he reported, "has a new magazine made such a stir." He was the author of several successful books. We wrote to him. Would he know of someone who might finance us? Komroff sent us a letter, both exhilarating and depressing. Harry Scherman, president of the Book-of-the-Month Club, and Bennett Cerf and Donald Klopfer, owners of Random House, wanted to talk to us. Come to New York at once, he wrote. Go to New York? How? We were down to our last fifty dollars. Not even enough for boat fare. I laughed and cried at the same time. Laughed because I was proud such important publishers liked the magazine, cried because we would lose this wonderful opportunity. When Whit faced a crisis, he went fishing. Now Whit went fishing.

While he was out on the briny deep, a letter came for me from Boston. Here I hesitate. If what I am about to write were in a story submitted to the magazine I would marvel that any would-be author could devise such a crude *deus ex machina.* And I would send the manuscript back pronto. The Boston letter informed me that the Foley estate litigation finally had been settled and asked where I would like my share sent.

As I wrote earlier, I had forced myself to blot out all thought of any money ever coming from my trust fund. "The Estate!" How many times while growing up had I heard those words! And the family fights and the lawyer who sold much of the property to a Peter Larkin (who turned out to be a straw man) and how long the public had been allowed to use a path across a corner lot because somebody had fallen on it and was suing and could collect only if he proved the public had been using it for a certain number of years and a newspaper story calling me a "little heiress" and . . . and . . . when one got right down to it the whole hullabaloo was over really little. In 1816, my great-grandfather bought a tract of land in what was known as "the fair green village of Roxbury." Today it is one of the worst slums in the nation. Over the years, streets were laid out and houses built, many of them the typical Boston three-deckers. My father remembered catching trout as a boy in a stream on the property. In my own childhood, it was a pleasant middle-class neighborhood of mostly professional people who sent their children to the famous Roxbury Latin school, a private school not to be confused with equally famous Boston Latin, a public school.

I came off better than the characters in *Bleak House.* Court costs left them nothing at all of the Jarndyce fortune. I was getting only a few thousands or so, picayune compared with the family's expectations, but oh, what it meant, coming in a depression and at this particular moment! On to Harry Scherman and Bennett Cerf and Donald Klopfer! We could sail for New York now!

TEN

∽

STORY
IN AMERICA

W e sailed for America in ex-King Alfonso's old suite on a Spanish Royal Mail Liner. The bathroom had His and Her Majesties' tubs. We bathed in His Majesty's and washed diapers in Hers. We arrived in America after a long, slow, but fascinating voyage along the Spanish coast, during which we stopped in every large port before we entered the Atlantic.

When we came into New York harbor in the dark of night, the beauty of the city's many towers, soaring skyward and jeweled with lights, was thrilling. It was the last time I was to think of New York as beautiful. Noise, confusion, and dirt overwhelmed us after we landed. And rudeness.

At our third meeting with Bennett Cerf, he said, "I might as well give you the money for your magazine." It's going to be taken from me tomorrow anyway."

"Why?" I asked.

"There's going to be a revolution."

Revolution! As a young woman I had heard the word in the Boston Socialist party headquarters, under the Washington Street elevated tracks, where textile mill and shoe factory workers from

Lawrence and Lowell sang "The Red Flag." I had heard it in the I.W.W. hall on New York's Lower East Side, where miners and ranch hands who rode freight trains from the West sang the Wobblies' hymn "Hallelujah! I'm a Bum!" I had heard it on a Norfolk, Virginia, dock, where Italian crew members in mutiny against Mussolini, refusing to return to their ship, roared "The Internationale." I had heard it on the "Boul' Mich" in Paris, where night after night before the execution, faculty and students of the Sorbonne marched, chanting, "Justice pour Sacco et Van-zetti! Liberté pour Sacco et Vanzetti!" And I had sympathized! But to hear it spoken of as an imminent event in an elegant suite of offices on East Fifty-seventh Street (just around the corner from Fifth Avenue and a cluster of Manhattan's hotels), was for me more of the dizzying world-turned-upside-down I found in Amer-ica after my seven years abroad.

Bennett Cerf's prediction of an imminent revolution seemed strange. (I had yet to see the enormous Diego de Rivera mural, glorifying Marx and Lenin, in the main lobby of the newly built Rockefeller Center, and to learn that it was now popular to be a communist, and the reasons why.) Until Bennett's abrupt declara-tion, and since our arrival a few days before, Whit and I had been on tenterhooks. We had had two previous conferences with Ben-nett, Donald Klopfer, and Harry Scherman.

Each man had a distinct personality. Bennett, intense and talkative, was the most vivid. He should have been an actor, I felt. He would have upstaged an entire cast. Donald was steadier, more reflective, and I liked him. Harry, who apologized for chewing gum, because, he explained, he had an ulcer and was having a terrible time breaking the cigarette habit, was the most genial. It was with Harry that we were to have the closest associa-tion.

When we parted late that afternoon, *STORY*'s future had been decided. The magazine would be brought to America, and,

instead of a bimonthly, it would become a monthly. Its office
would be at Random House* All five of us would have an equal
share in a corporation to be formed, and Whit and I, as editors,
would draw weekly salaries of thirty-five dollars each. Contributors would be paid, to start, twenty-five dollars a story. The first
American issue was to be ready for distribution in early March
and would, in accordance with magazine practice, be dated ahead
—April 1933.

We were amazed by the enthusiastic reception given the magazine in New York. H.L. Mencken gave us a flattering full-page
advertisement saying *The American Mercury* welcomed *STORY* to
America, and he invited us to lunch at the Hotel Algonquin. The
lunch was not in the hotel restaurant, where the famous Algonquin Round Table (with Harold Ross, Dorothy Parker, Alexander Woollcott, James Thurber, E.B. White, and other *New
Yorker* celebrities) was then attracting a crowd, but upstairs in the
quiet of Mencken's room.

Unlike many photographic subjects, Mencken looked exactly
like his pictures. He was then fifty-three years old, of stocky build,
round-faced, round-headed, with brown hair parted in the middle, and wide eyes of a light Delft blue. What his photographs did
not show was the sweetness of his smile. When he smiled his face
had a softness one would never have associated with the savage
iconoclasm of his critical writings.

Over the Algonquin's bootleg cocktails he told us that he was
resigning as editor of *The American Mercury.* As soon as I said that
I was sorry to hear it, I realized the irony of the situation. Once,
I knew, I had sat in the *Los Angeles Daily News* city room sympa-

---

* One reason Random House was interested, which I didn't realize at the time
because I was very inexperienced in the whole business of publishing, was because
they saw us as a good scouting arrangement to bring authors to them. They got
Saroyan that way. Until that point, they'd been a reprint house. Now they were
planning to bring out trade books.

thizing with the writers there who complained that Mencken had forsaken a fiction magazine, the old *Smart Set,* to become editor of the more factual *American Mercury,* and now I was the editor of a fiction magazine, sitting in Mencken's hotel room and telling him I was sorry he was quitting *The American Mercury.* (I did not mention to him that it was his leaving the *Smart Set* that made me think of starting a short story magazine. I now wish I had. I would love to know what he would have said.)

"After five years, an American editor ought to be sent to a nice quiet place like Mexico," he explained, talking of his leaving the *Mercury.* "If he keeps on for ten years he'll wind up in a madhouse." He sighed, laughed a little, and said, "Let's have another drink." And he went on to complain of the lack of good beer under Prohibition—which he reviled. He also said he would send us some short stories his wife, Sara Haardt, had written before her death. She was a good writer, and we were glad to publish them when he sent them from Baltimore.

Because of his ridicule of our national mores— his delight in lampooning what he called "the booboisie"—Mencken aroused much popular American antagonism. His attackers failed to realize how much he resented Europe's patronage of American culture. His answer to foreign patronizing was his masterly work of linguistic scholarship, *The American Language,* which emphasized the ways American usage had enriched the English language. Contrary to what his critics believed, Mencken was no radical. His social consciousness was limited. When, supported by many well-known writers, office workers at his publisher's went on strike, Mencken plowed his way through the long picket line, chaffing those pickets he knew. Mencken's great value to American literature was as a catalyst. Dreiser, Lewis, and Anderson are among the important American authors indebted to him for their success. And he was kind to a great many lesser figures such as Whit and myself.

The New Republic also gave us a luncheon, and the Meeting Place, a literary club of the period, gave a cocktail party in our honor (at which a coat I had bought the day before was stolen). The Pen and Brush Club invited me to speak. During the question-and-answer period I was asked if, since I called myself Miss, my baby was legitimate. We were receiving close to a hundred manuscripts a day.

Harry Scherman sent out an elaborate test mailing to a list of writers, informing them that they would be happy to know of a new magazine devoted to short stories and based only on literary merit (regardless of names), and would they please subscribe. The response was the greatest he had ever received. Practically all said they would be delighted to subscribe, and would we please deduct the price of a subscription from what we paid for their manuscripts, which they were sending us.

We knew personally more authors, both well known and unpublished, than most magazine editors now do because so many writers brought their manuscripts by hand to our office.* Often they did not have the money for postage. Tennessee Williams, Malcolm Lowry, Cornell Woolrich, Nelson Algren—they all brought their manuscripts personally. One of the first of the American contributors who had sent us stories while we were in Europe, and with whom we became friends after arriving in the States, was Erskine Caldwell, whose first novel, *Tobacco Road,* had been published in 1932. He was an earnest, broad-shouldered, tall young man, and I remember how he kept taking some silver

---

* "The impression of the office was one of utter happy confusion," Irwin Shaw has written. "The two staffs seemed cosily intermingled. Since they made no suggestions about changing anything in my stories, there was no occasion for conferences." Later, when Martha was editing the *Best Stories* series, she dedicated one year's volume to him. "When I gained some fame and a modicum of fortune with my first novel, *The Young Lions,*" Shaw went on, "she wrote an introduction to that year's volume gently chiding me by saying that *The Young Lions* was a long, disguised collection of short stories."—ED.

coins out of his pocket and counting them. He explained that he
had just enough paper money for train fare back to his home in
Mount Vernon, Maine, where he had left his family, and that he
had to guard every penny.

"We would have starved last winter," he told us, "if we hadn't
found a big sack of dried beans in a dark corner of the cellar. They
had lain there forgotten since the Spanish-American War, but
they were still good. Those old beans kept us alive."

Erskine was in New York because he was to be tried on
charges, brought by the Society for the Prevention of Vice, of
aleged obscenity in his new novel, *God's Little Acre.* Unlike John
S. Sumner, the society's director, Magistrate Greenspan, who
tried the case, was an intelligent man. He found that *God's Little
Acre* had "not been written by its author primarily to provide
lascivious thoughts for morons." Many of the classics were still
banned then, and Joyce's *Ulysses* was still forbidden entry into the
United States, but public opinion on literary censorship was
changing. A short time later, Magistrate Nathan Perlman, who
tried another friend of ours, Frances Steloff, owner of the Gotham
Book Mart (arrested for selling a copy of André Gide's *Autobiography*), wrote a vivid twenty-page opinion when he acquitted her.
"The heroine of the American novel is no longer the pink-
aproned girl making cookies in the kitchen," he wrote. *"Hamlet*
shocked all the Cromwellian Puritans and shocks nobody today.
. . . Some years ago," he went on to note, "a superintendent of
schools in Brooklyn was upset by the recitation in our public
schools of Longfellow's poem, 'Building of the Ship,' because the
ship was described as leaping 'into the ocean's arms.' "

Whit went with Caldwell to the court, where I was to meet
them for lunch. When I arrived, the trial was over, and Erskine
had been acquitted. A very excited Maxim Lieber, his literary
agent, was trying to convince Erskine that he should leave by the
next plane for Hollywood. Somebody named Jack Kirkland had
telephoned from Hollywood, wanting to dramatize *Tobacco Road.*

A dazed Caldwell yielded and was whirled off by Lieber to the airport. Whit and I had lunch alone. Erskine never ate any more Spanish-American War beans. As a play, *Tobacco Road* had a continuous run of 3,182 performances.

Erskine invited me to the opening night, and I shall always be sorry that I could not be there. But David had the croup and I could not leave him. Whit didn't go either. Erskine told me he had kept a seat for me, which stayed empty. He had desperately needed moral support, for he thought, when the audience roared with laughter at the lusty bawdiness with which he depicted sharecropping Jeeter Lester and his family, that the audience was laughing at him because of the poor writing job he'd done. Not until hours after the curtain fell did he grasp that the audience was laughing with him and not at him. By week's end the lines at the box office showed what was to come—that Erskine was to have one of the great all-time theatrical successes.

Truman Capote annoyed me, as he had a habit of doing, when he once told a *New York Times* interviewer that "a boy has to hustle his book." Erskine Caldwell was no hustler. His writing possessed a sincerity lacking in most of Capote's work. Erskine is a quiet man and a prolific writer of many novels and books of stories. They have been very popular in paperback reprint editions but receive little attention from today's critics. Nevertheless, Caldwell must be considered one of the major writers of the Thirties. Especially fine are his collections of stories, such as *Kneel to the Rising Sun,* which was a sensation when published in 1935. No other writer, with the possible exception of James Agee (whose *Let Us Now Praise Famous Men* so parallels Caldwell's *You Have Seen Their Faces*), has written as powerfully of southern sharecroppers.

The most heartbreaking writer to visit my office was Malcolm Lowry, separated from his wife and dismally lonely in the United States. Except at *STORY,* his work, including a novel, was being peipetually rejected. For weeks he visited my office everyday, sat around for a while, looked at books and magazines I had lying about, and disconsolately departed. Once he disappeared. When he returned he told me he had been placed for observation in Bellevue.

There were "closet" authors too, who came with stories in hand. One was Morris Ernst, the well-known liberal lawyer. "The two M's—masturbation and menopause—are the best defense for a woman arrested for shop-lifting," he told me one day when he handed me a story he'd just written which centered on such a case. He had been introduced to us a few days before as the lawyer who would be the attorney for *STORY*. Morris was as unlike Max Kulka as his native New York was different from Vienna. Morris was bright, sharp, shrewd, and ever alert. Max was gentler, slower to speak, smiled more, and gave an impression of great strength.

The stories Morris showed me read like case histories, as do most stories by lawyers, doctors, social workers, and other "closet" authors. Accustomed to an objective scientific approach when recording their professional experiences, it is difficult for them to think of their characters as sentient human beings and to write with feeling about them.

Nelson Algren's short story, "So Help Me," which I accepted during our first months in America, was one of many sad stories we were receiving that made me suggest to Whit that we should include in each issue a column, "End Pages," of light, informal, and amusing comment for the sake of our readers, who were already enduring much grimness in their own Depression-burdened lives. I would like to have followed the pattern of the ancient Greeks, who had clowns and satyrs scampering about in the theater during the most somber tragedies, and to have had humorous stories interspersed throughout the magazine, but good humorous stories are hard to come by, even in prosperous times.

At the time he sent us his story, Algren wrote, he was stranded in an abandoned filling station outside Rio Hondo, Texas. "So Help Me" was his first published story, a heart-piercing tale of a Jewish high school boy in love with a Gentile girl he has made pregnant. The boy's orthodox Jewish father forbids a marriage. ("Cut in two! Thy blood is not my blood!—We're cut apart!" the boy cries in his sleep.) A newspaper article says that men are needed to work on Boulder Dam, and the boy tells the girl he will go there, get a job, and send for her, but when he gets to Las Vegas, there are only eight jobs left and 4,500 men in the line ahead of him. He hitchhikes to New Orleans, hoping to get work on a ship, but falls in with a couple of crooks who exploit his innocence and involve him in a drugstore holdup that leads to his death.

When Nelson came to New York, we went to the Algonquin for lunch. The restaurant was almost empty that day, the Round Table without its usual coterie of celebrities. Nonetheless, the table in the corner fascinated Nelson. "So Thurber eats there," he said, in awe, looking across the room at it. Some time after he returned to Chicago, I had a letter from him inviting me to visit him at a new home he'd bought on the Indiana dunes. Meaning to tease him in his new role of landed proprietor, and in a flip mood one morning, I began my answer, "To hell with your Indiana dunes!" expecting that the rest of my letter would show that I was smiling as I'd said that. Nelson wired his New York agent, asking why I was mad at him. I told her to tell him that I wasn't. But Nelson has never forgiven me.

"Ernest Hemingway didn't go to Martha Foley to learn how to write." Thus Nelson began the Hemingway obituary he wrote for *The Nation*. That declaration must have mystified a lot of readers. It is the only obituary that ever made me laugh. Nelson has no sense of humor. (There are times when I have too much.) Nelson Algren is one of the country's finest writers (although I would not call him the best, as Hemingway did). It was my fault that our friendship ended, but every time I think of trying to explain it to him—even now—I find it impossible. Any explanation only seems to make it worse.

Since that time, more than forty years ago, I have become even more vexed with Nelson because of the mean things he published about Simone de Beauvoir. I met Simone once when she was in New York on a lecture tour and Richard Wright introduced us. She was a brilliant, beautiful woman, and the three of us stayed up until far into the morning, comparing French and American writing. She and Nelson had an affair later on during that same tour. They both wrote about it. I long ago learned, contrary to my early illusion about their chivalry, that men do kiss and tell. Perhaps what Simone wrote hurt Nelson, or perhaps it was no more intended that way than my own too-blithe greeting in my letter to him. (I do believe that no man should humiliate a woman by the kind of cruel ridicule Nelson heaped on Simone. So perhaps it is just as well my teasing letter ended our friendship when it did.)

Usually writers bringing manuscripts to the office asked for me, either because they thought Whit, being a man, was too important, or because people with a problem often find it easier to talk to a woman than to a man. Cornell Woolrich was one. I had never heard of him. A thin, shabby, shaking, hungry-looking man, he asked me, almost imploringly, "If I send you a story, will you please read it?"

"Of course," I told him. "That's why I'm an editor. To read manuscripts."

Reassured, he told me about himself. In 1927, when he was twenty-four years old, he had won first prize—$10,000—in a short story contest held by *College Humor,* then a large-circulation magazine. (Writing as I am now about Cornell makes me wish, as I have countless times, that I had kept a journal!) As far as I can remember, he said that there was a long hiatus in his writing after winning the prize, and that when he resumed writing his work was rejected. I remember his telling me of how his father had left his mother, and of how, as a boy, he had spent years with her roaming around the country in search of his father. I have never forgotten his leaning forward to me and saying earnestly, "A search for a father is a search for God."

The story I promised to read, which Cornell sent me, was the wonderful "Good-By New York," a skin-prickling tale of two people who have committed a crime; desperate to leave the big city, their stratagems to avoid detection, their near-captures and their terror, are told in writing far superior to that of the usual thriller. The praise given the story when it appeared provided Cornell with the renewed impetus he craved. He went on to achieve lifelong publishing success and is best remembered (popularly) for the movie "Rear Window." He wrote many mystery novels and short stories, using both the name Woolrich and William Irish. He won the Poe Award in 1949.

John Cheever was another writer who personally gave me a story, called "Homage to Shakespeare." It was one of his earliest. He was twenty-two years old and living then, he wrote later, "in a furnished room on Hudson Street . . . on the fourth or fifth floor in a company of unemployed seacooks and longshoremen and there was usually someone in the downstairs hallway yelling about the whores using the toilet." "Homage to Shakespeare" was not about the middle-class suburban characters who people most of Cheever's stories and novels, but about a middle-aged curmudgeon of a sailor, who in his youth, while working on sailing ships to the Orient, became infatuated with the works of Shakespeare. The infatuation becomes a lifelong obsession that leads to estrangement from family and failure in business, yet always provides intoxicating rapture.

Cheever's first name, on his manuscript, was spelled "Jon," for Jonathan. "You are going to spend the rest of your life cor-

wearing a beautiful corsage to identify her as the guest of honor, Zora was escorted by a group of white editors and authors to a table where she would be seen from all parts of the restuarant.

Another writing Dorothy whom I knew then was Dorothy Thompson. She was poles apart in every way from quiet-spoken Dorothy McCleary. Dorothy Thompson's voice was not loud; it was, simply, very, very emphatic, and she had strong convictions. Like her minister father, she preached you a sermon about politics and economics and you were supposed to be converted. If you weren't, the fine blue eyes in her otherwise plain face (a face, I thought, strangely like that of a simple farm woman) flashed scorn at you, and you were excommunicated. She was a large woman, and her scorn could, at times, be overwhelming. As long as you agreed with her, or at least did not openly disagree, Dorothy was pleasant company. For a while we were friends, not close, but friends. Hatred of Nazism united us.

Because she wrote articles for such liberal magazines as *The Nation,* she was considered liberal, whereas in truth she was so conservative as to be almost reactionary. As a newspaperwoman Dorothy was a vital, challenging American foreign correspondent in Berlin during the Nazi's rise to power. She had gone to Europe at the end of the First World War, with the Hoover Relief Commission. In Budapest, she met Josef Bard, whom she married. When the commission's work ended, she was out of a job. She asked Fodor to find her newspaper work. With the kindness he showed to all of us, Fodor arranged with the *Philadelphia Public Ledger* to give her part-time work at space rates. With Fodor as mentor, she progressed rapidly to a full-time correspondent's post.

She achieved international fame when she went to Vienna and, with Fodor there to advise her, wrote a series of widely discussed articles for the *Saturday Evening Post.* But when she wrote the book *I Saw Hitler,* prophesying that he would never come to national power, she almost lost her reputation for political astuteness. Hitler himself saved her. He obliterated criticism by giving her twenty-four hours to get out of Germany.

Dorothy wanted to write fiction. She was going to send me a short story, she said, and she had in mind a novel to be called *The Tulip Box*. She was so emotional in her speech that I was sure she would make a good fiction writer. The intense feeling with which she read me passages from her journal one evening at her Bronxville home also convinced me. That Dorothy was a snob I recognized early on in our acquaintance, but snobs have written interesting fiction—Proust, for one. And even Celine's utter loathing for the human race is often spellbinding. Dorothy never sent me the short story she was so enthusiastic about. Probably, like the novel she talked about at great length (even outlining to me its scenes in detail), the short story was never written.

Not until I read a letter to her second husband, Sinclair Lewis (reprinted in Vincent Sheean's reminiscences, *Dorothy and Red*), did I understand why Dorothy could not write fiction. Like John Gunther, Dorothy failed at fiction because she saw *things,* not people. Writing from Terre Haute while on a lecture tour in the Twenties, she describes with disdain "the cheapness of all standards, the shoddiness of all values." These she illustrates by citing the women's coats trimmed with cheap fur, priced at $25 to $39, the dresses for $2.99, the shoes for $5.50. Almost all the stores, she said, including the clothing shops, offered their goods on credit and installment plans. (And not a word of sympathy for the women who had to wear them!) "The houses are painted a dingy gray almost black with smoke. They usually have small front lawns, ragged and smoke-blackened. . . . The streets are a hodge-podge. And yet everyone seems contented. After my lecture yesterday a lot of women came up to speak to me and almost all of them said, 'Well, aren't we lucky to be living in America.' "

Her want of empathy is highlighted by the last lines of her letter to Lewis. "It is significant that Debs came from Terre Haute. He could not be otherwise than sentimental and ineffective." Where were Dorothy's vaunted brains? Ineffective when he amassed nearly a million votes while in a prison cell? Whether she agreed with his socialism or not, couldn't she see that Debs was revolting against the very conditions in Terre Haute that she criticized? Unlike Dorothy, though, he wanted to change them.

Another time she came to our apartment one afternoon, elated. She was hardly inside the door before she announced, *"McCall's* has just offered me a dollar a word for a 500-word article!" It was the most money she had ever received, and, in terms of present-day prices, was probably about $20,000. I too would have been excited. Over the cocktails (legal since Prohibition's end in 1933), she tried to decide how she would spend her new fortune. She kept changing her mind about a long list of things she had always wanted to buy and now could. As she left, she said, "My mind's made up! I'm going to buy a house in New Jersey!" She never did buy the house.

Dorothy was not the only famous conservative woman writer of those times. There was also Clare Booth Luce. The difference between them was that Dorothy used a blunderbuss and Clare a stiletto. I once saw an encounter between them at an evening party at the Gunthers. Dorothy was sitting near me, discussing with Walter Duranty, the *New York Times*'s Moscow correspondent, whether Hitler was sane or insane. Clare, not as beautiful as in her photographs, but still fragile and lovely and exquisitely dressed, arrived late. She sat down on the sofa beside me, took out an embroidery hoop, and added dainty stitches to a silken outline (of a cherub). We women, who had been sitting around relaxed, with highball glasses and cigarettes in our hands, immediately felt as big and clumsy as brewery horses.

An unwary Dorothy, meaning to be friendly, tried to draw Clare into her conversation with Duranty. "What do you think, Clare?" she asked. "Is Hitler sane or insane?" Clare looked pensive, pursed her lips, delicately inserted her needle in her embroidery again, and inquired, "Dorothy, if you were called to the witness stand, could you swear that you are sane?" We all waited for the answer. Dorothy reddened, looked flustered, choked on some words she started to say, and then turned back to resume her conversation with Duranty. For once, Dorothy's unwonted silence won her a victory.

Dorothy Thompson was married three times. The first two marriages, to Josef Bard, the Hungarian writer, and to Sinclair Lewis, the first American author to win the Nobel Prize, were disastrous. Bard, a handsome philanderer, squandered the money Dorothy earned on other women. After their divorce, Dorothy was grief-stricken for a long time. The acrimony with which the marriage ended is revealed by the heartbroken letters Dorothy wrote to Bard at the time, letters that are included in Sheean's *Dorothy and Red.*

"You think because a man is a good writer, he is a good man," Maxwell Perkins, the renowned editor, once told a young woman. "Well, they're all sons of bitches!" I disagree. I have known too many saints among them. The red-headed Sinclair Lewis, however, was not one of them. He was too often ugly-tempered and mean-spoken. But one look at his face and you knew he was to be pitied. His gaunt face with the prominent eyes (which Dorothy described as "pleading") was blistered all over with disgusting, inflamed pustules. The pustules could be removed agonizingly one by one with an electric needle, only to return later. Sheean says that Lewis had it done once, when he went to Stockholm to receive the Nobel award.

Dorothy told friends that she had vowed, during the agony of her divorce from Bard, that she would never marry another man unless she first lived with him for a year. "I lived only eleven months with Sinclair Lewis," she lamented. "Another month might have saved me." I got to know Dorothy best during the later years of her marriage to Lewis, when he had taken to calling her "the Talking Woman." Lewis I knew only casually, except for a memorable occasion when we both served on a literary prize committee, an account of which belongs in another part of this book.* A child she bore Lewis was a victim of their unhappiness. On my first visit to Twin Farms, their Barnard, Vermont, home, Dorothy showed me over the big, beautifully furnished house where she and Lewis lived. I saw no child's room. At the end of our tour, I asked, "Where's Michael's room? You didn't show it to me."

"He lives with the servants in our other house down the road," Dorothy explained. "Hal can't stand having him around, poor baby."

Dorothy's third marriage, which turned out to be happy, was to a Czechoslovakian painter, Maxim Kopf. He was a refugee from Hitler and they met when he was engaged to paint her portrait. He was *not* a writer. It is noteworthy that her first two unhappy marriages were to writers, which tends to confirm what Dr. Louis Bisch, Pearl Buck's analyst, was to tell me: "Two people in the same profession should never marry one another. Sooner or later they reach a point of competition." How silly, I said. If they love one another what difference does it make which one is successful? No one told me, "Look homeward, Martha!"†

Every friend of Lewis, and of Dorothy herself, Sheean relates, tried to convince him of the difference between the permanent historical reputation he had and Dorothy's ephemeral, journalistic one. It was no use, though, and many funny stories were told about them. Asked about a rumor that his wife might be a Republican presidential candidate, Lewis commented, "Fine, fine. I hope she's elected. Then I can settle down and write a column

---

* A Fiction contest jointly sponsored by the W.P.A. and *STORY* magazine. I found no written account of this occasion among her papers.—ED.

† I found the following handwritten passage among her papers: "I was always happy with Whit's success. That was why I had started *STORY*—to help him. He never complained when I sold a story. Once when it came up that I was selling my stories and he wasn't selling his, I explained it was because I had a commercial touch acquired from my tabloid newspaper experiences, while his were more literary and therefore really more important."—ED.

called 'My Day.' " Another time when asked about Dorothy, he replied, "I had a wife once but she vanished into the NBC building and has never been heard of since." And one does have to commiserate with Lewis in his rueful account of how one night he was lying in bed with Dorothy when the telephone on the bed table beside him rang. Answering it, he was told, "The president wishes to speak with Miss Dorothy Thompson." Lewis passed the phone to her. "There was the voice of the president of the United States," he said later, "traveling across my stomach to my wife."

My friendship with Dorothy came to an abrupt end through no wish of mine. She had dropped into our apartment late one afternoon at cocktail time. The Stalin-Hitler pact was then shocking everybody. Dorothy was vehement in her denunciation. "I have a feeling there's something phony about that pact," I said. "I bet each of those men has a dagger up his sleeve, ready to stab the other. I can never understand our relations with Russia anyway. Perhaps it's geography that controls them. It doesn't seem to be ideology. In our civil war, Czarist Russia sided with the North and in our last war Russia and we were allies. I have a hunch that if there's a Second World War we'll be on the same side again."

Dorothy, her face red, sprang from the living room armchair, strode across the room, towered over me, and yelled, "Martha Foley, you are crazy!"

I'm sure that if Whit had been there he would have agreed with Dorothy. And if Dorothy had given me a chance I might have agreed with her too, because I had no rational explanation for my hunch, even though it turned out to be right. But Dorothy gathered up her things and left. When we met at various gatherings later, we were friendly, but no longer close.

Russia could be incendiary for Dorothy. When Theodore Dreiser published his book, *Dreiser Looks at Russia,* Dorothy accused him of plagiarizing from her book, *The New Russia.* Lewis repeated the accusation in a belligerent encounter with Dreiser at the Metropolitan Club, whereupon Dreiser slapped Lewis's face. The whole affair was a farce, with which the press had a wonderful time. (Dorothy and Dreiser had both been in Russia at the same time. Both had been given the same Russian government handouts, and both had copied them.)

"End of the Depression," a lovely story by Mary Bolte, written after the Depression and reprinted in the *Best Stories,* throws poignant light on the lives of children during those years of the most painful economic strain the United States has ever endured. In this story, the only work a father (who has been an important executive) can find is door-to-door peddling. The thought of it is so humiliating that he refuses to do it. His children, wanting to help the family's finances, arrange, in typical lemonade-stand manner, a public sale of their toys and other prized possessions. Their shamed father takes the peddling job.

I don't think my own child knew about the Depression, because it was during the Depression years that he acquired a lifelong passion for, of all things, caviar. We were having a cocktail party, and among the canapés served with the drinks were a few made with caviar. When David took one, I expected him to make an awful face. Instead there was delight on his cherub's face and his little hand reached immediately for another. "No, no, young man," I admonished. "One is plenty. They're too expensive."

"Can I have some for my birthday?"

"Yes," I answered, and promptly forgot all about it. Came his birthday and a raft of presents, including his own private egg-beater, because he was always clamoring for the maid's when she needed to use it.

"Where's my caviar?" The sapphire eyes were troubled. "You promised!"

"Oh, David! But please wait until Christmas. I promise on my solemn word of honor that Santa Claus will not forget."

So, on Christmas morning, David found a small jar of caviar

in the toe of his stocking, as he did every Christmas morning
thereafter, until he was too old for a stocking and had to look
under the tree for it. David was a firm believer in Santa Claus.
Little Linda Margolies, a classmate, was crying because she was
told there was no Santa Claus. "Don't cry, Linda," David con-
soled her. "I'll prove there's a Santa Claus. I'll show you the
presents he brings me."

David began his education in Croton-on-Hudson, at Hessian
Hills School, when he was only twenty months old. He entered
the nursery class but, after investigating all the other classrooms,
decided he belonged with the thirteen-year-olds. The teacher,
Elizabeth Moos, who was also the school's principal, was amused
and did not shoo him out. On the second day he returned to his
own age group, where he learned to hang up his clothes, wash
the dishes he used, help clean the rest of the nursery as well, use
finger paints, draw pictures, weave mats, and other typical kinder-
garten activities. One of the teachers at the school, Alice Roth-
schild, was a gentle Quaker, always simply dressed, who used
thee's and thou's in her conversation. One day I met her on the
playing field, dazzling from head to foot in costume jewelry.
Ornaments glittered in her hair, large and small brooches flashed
from her dress, unmatched earrings dangled from her ears, chains
and beads were festooned around her throat, and bracelets and
rings adorned her wrists and fingers. I was almost afraid to speak
to such a crazy spectacle. "You are all dressed up today, Alice,"
I said. Smiling quite normally, she answered, "Thee are right.
More than I have ever been before." And she told me that the
previous day one of her first graders had given her a brooch. The
next day every child in the class showered her with their mothers'
jewelry, which she wore all day. Alice was that kind of teacher,
and Hessian Hills was that kind of school. I wish every child could
have the advantage of such schooling.

The children of many well-known parents, mostly writers and
artists, attended the school. One was the small son of Heywood

Broun, who, in the way of writer-fathers, often used his offspring as copy for his newspaper column. A friendly woman, visiting the school, asked the (literarily) exploited child (who today in his outrageously flashy clothes is a famous sports broadcaster), "And whose nice little boy are you?" Heywood Broun, Jr., replied: "You know goddamned well whose little boy I am!"

My own son's conversation was swiped from me by Bennett Cerf and reprinted in *Try and Stop Me*. It occurred while Whit and I were judges in the Doubleday Novel Contest. Most of our friends were writers, so that yearnings for the prize money were freely expressed in our house. (We would have liked it ourselves.) David loved to stand inside the kitchen screen door and talk to all the interesting people who came to the back door of a country house on a Saturday morning in the days before supermarkets and freezers became ubiquitous. The milkman came, then the vegetable cart man, then the grocery delivery boy. Finally the garbage man in his truck rattled to a stop.

"Hello," said David.

" 'Lo," said the garbage man, who was not loquacious.

"How do you feel?"

"Okay."

There was a pause in this fascinating conversation. Then David demanded, "How are you getting on with your novel?"

Sometimes I am sorry I gave away the title *The Literary Life and the Hell with It* to Whit. He and I had a fight, about what I now have no idea. He went into the sulks, and when Whit sulked it was no transitory matter but a sullen silence that could last for a week or more. I found the best way to end it was to interest him in something to do. It occurred to me that STORY had published enough "End Pages," all signed by Whit, although collaborated on by both of us, to make a book. I clipped them, put them together, and took them to him; he was sitting, enveloped by gloom, an untouched viola in his lap. "Do you know," I said cheerily to a sullen face, "do you know you have a book here? It's all ready to be published too!"

Slowly the dark clouds disappeared and the sun came out. "What can we call it?" he asked.

Feeling as I did at that moment—wanting to slap his withdrawn face—I gritted my teeth and said, *"The Literary Life and the Hell with It."*

EDITOR'S NOTE: Here the manuscript breaks off. In the Afterword I have tried to sketch in the rich and extraordinary story of Martha's remaining years at *STORY,* and of *STORY*'s years in America. But preceding the Afterword, I have included one additional chapter by Martha, discontinuous with the narrative she was writing of the early years of *STORY,* which I found among her papers: about Hollywood and the war years.

ELEVEN

∾

HOLLYWOOD AND
THE WAR YEARS

When Hitler invaded Austria I felt a terrible horror at what faced Vienna, that "rose-red city old as time," and its friendly people. I had once cabled a news dispatch about a demographic survey which estimated that 60 percent of the population was either Jewish or part-Jewish. Among those I thought of immediately was Max Kulka, the liberal lawyer who, as a citizen, had been willing to lay his life and fortune on the line for *STORY*. During Max's visit to us later, in Majorca, I had urged him to visit us in America. Now, on news of Hitler's invasion, I sent a cablegram, "Invitation still stands. Come immediately." Too late I realized what I had done; I had pointed a finger straight at Max.

My passport was in order, and, with a speed that amazed me, I was given a German visa immediately and was off to Europe in a couple of days. By being on the scene I hoped I could help Max and other of my friends. My first stop was London, where I stayed at the home in Canfield Gardens of Edward O'Brien and his wife, Ruth. It was toward the end of the week and I planned to leave for Vienna on Monday. Sunday evening the doorbell rang, and a maid told me there was a man—she didn't say "gentleman"— asking for me, and she didn't think she should let him in the

house. When I went to the door I saw why. It was Max. Unshaven, haggard, in wrinkled suit, he was a far cry from the
handsome, impeccably groomed Max I had known in Vienna. I
threw my arms around him and cried with relief that he was alive.

Over drinks in the O'Brien's comfortable drawing room, he
told us what had happened. He had not received my cable, but
he knew anyway that he was a marked man, and so went into
hiding. For two days and two nights he had not spent more than
four hours in any one place. Then the ambassador of another
country (not the United States) gave him falsified papers certify-
ing that he was a national of that country. Max warned me not to
go to Vienna. I said the German consulate in New York had not
hesitated to grant me a visa. "Of course. They know what you
wrote and said about the Nazis when you were in Vienna. They'd
love to get their hands on you." But how had he known I was in
London? "The underground." It seemed there was a well-organ-
ized grapevine of anti-Nazi Germans, both Christians and Jews,
working against Hitler, inside Germany and out. I was later to
receive copies of a minute newspaper they smuggled out of Germany.

Among the others of my friends who had escaped were the
Fodors. They had crossed the Danube into Czechoslovakia at the
very moment the German invaders were marching down the
Ringstrasse. The Fodors escaped so narrowly that their only
possessions were the clothes they were wearing. Fodor managed
to reach Robert Best by telephone. He asked him to go to their
apartment, where Best had been a guest so many times, and get
some of Martha's clothes to send to her.

When Martha Deane (a pseudonym) left radio station WOR,
for which she broadcast what was supposed to be feminine chat-
ter, liberally burdened with commercials, Peter Witt, who'd been
a theatrical entrepreneur in Europe, suggested me for the post.
I hadn't the slightest ability to speak in public (an ability I was to

acquire only much later, after having to lecture to university classes), but *STORY* needed money, so I agreed. Peter engaged a fellow refugee, Ludwig Donath, a well-known German actor, to coach me. Ludwig was a perfectionist and aimed to make me into an accomplished actress. Ha! For agonizing weeks I spent my lunch hours away from *STORY*'s office being drilled by Ludwig. It seems to me I spent hours on the proper delivery of single lines. One was in my telling of Princess Ileana's wedding in Bucharest. A butterfly, considered very bad luck in Rumania, had flown through a cathedral window during the ceremony. "And then— and then a pr-r-etty-y leetle bou-ou-terfly came in the ween-dow!" "Now again! Say loud the pr-pr-etty! Make it terrible it was a bou-ou-terfly!" Poor Ludwig was trying hard. I didn't get the job.

I did become good friends with Ludwig and his wife, Maria Champska. When he wasn't trying to make me into a world-shaking actress, Ludwig was selling poppyseeds to delicatessens for a living. Maria, a tiny, fair-haired little person, was selling Fuller brushes from door to door in Yonkers. It was safer for Maria, as a non-Jew, to stay in Germany, so it had been arranged for Ludwig to escape ahead of her, and he went to Switzerland. Maria was to star in a new play, and Goebbels had arranged a champagne supper in her honor after the premiere. It was a tribute to her very great acting ability that she could carry on successfully, with Goebbels in a box applauding her, when all the while she knew that, around the corner from the theater on a dark street, a car was waiting to speed her at the play's end across the border and into Denmark.

Ludwig obtained a part in a forthcoming moving picture production, and the Donaths went to California, where I was to see them again. One afternoon Maria got in touch with me to say that the Baroness Ruth von Berlau, a friend of hers, had written some short stories and wanted to know if I would read them and give her an opinion. I did and discussed them over coffee with the Baroness in the Los Angeles hotel where David and I were marooned because of the wartime housing shortage. When I mentioned my housing plight, she suggested I call up Salka Viertel, who might rent me the guest cottage in her garden. I did, and a throaty voice answered, "Ya, you come and see. Maybe you will not like it." We made an appointment for the following Sunday afternoon at 165 Mabery Road, Santa Monica, an address I shall always remember.

Entering a gate in a high iron fence surrounding a large house (slightly Central European in appearance), and a large garden, I went into the house and found myself in an enormous, book-lined living room filled with men, women, children, and dogs, all vocal. Before a fireplace on a coffeetable was a big *Kugelhupf,* a Viennese coffeecake, the like of which I had not seen since I'd left the banks of the Danube. A magnificent, tall, red-haired woman greeted me. She offered me coffee and a piece of the cake, which was even better than that I had eaten in Vienna. Some of her guests I recognized as old acquaintances I had not seen for a long time; others Salka introduced. It was a wonderful party, and I regretted not having brought my son on what I thought was to be a routine house-hunting trip. It got to be seven o'clock and I was embarrassed. I told Salka, "The Baroness von Berlau said you might rent me your guest house."

"*Ya, yawohl,* but maybe you won't like it."

She led me through a rose garden to a small house with splendid views of the ocean and the mountains. I was enraptured and said I wanted to rent it. Salka asked, "Sixty-five dollars too much?"

We moved in, and even before we were unpacked Salka took David into her big kitchen and opened the doors of a restaurant-sized refrigerator that was filled to overflowing. "Anytime you are hungry you take what you want," she told him. "I have three sons of my own who are big young men now. From them I learned something. You know what?" "What?" David asked, grinning. "Always the biggest part of a boy is his stomach!"

Bit by bit, I learned who this fabulous creature was, whose name I had not even known. She was a former European actress and writer and the author of most of Greta Garbo's scripts. Her house was Greta Garbo's address. Greta did not live there, but it was where tons of mail were delivered for her (to be tossed out unread) and countless telephone calls came for her (never to be returned). The Baroness von Berlau? She was the intimate friend of Berthold Brecht, an ugly dark man who was among those I met that first afternoon.

The cottage had a well-equipped small kitchen, and on my first day at Salka's I asked her to recommend some good shops for marketing.

"Don't you trouble," she told me. "You must be tired. You and David have dinner with us tonight." The first course may have been rich red borscht bounteous with sour cream, or it may have been long-simmered lentil soup dotted with juicy sausage morsels, or golden chicken broth in which floated *knödeln,* tiny fluffy dumplings. Whatever it was, it was a delightful harbinger of the flavorsome food to follow that evening and every evening at Salka's. Around the large table were Salka, of course, and on the floor beside her, Prince, the enormous German shepherd dog, a most important member of her household. Hans and Tommy, two of her sons in their early twenties, were there. (Peter, her third son, a writer, who was to marry the actress Deborah Kerr, was away in the European war.) There was a small black-haired woman named Olga, whose full name I never did learn, a Russian refugee who had been Lenin's secretary. She hardly spoke during the meal. And there was sweet delightful little Mrs. Steuerman—whom everyone called Grossmutter—a dainty lady in her eighties who was Salka's mother. Despite her age, she had traveled alone, or rather fled, from the Nazis, all the way across Europe and the Pacific to reach the haven of California. David and I had already been alerted to watch and intercept the postman before he could deliver mail to her; her youngest son had been seized by the Nazis and we were all sure of what had happened to him. But she sat by the window everyday waiting for his letter.

The next day I sneaked out of the garden, determined not to impose on Salka's hospitality. I was partway down the incline to the bottom of Santa Monica Canyon, when a bright, red, open convertible slammed to a stop beside me. "Get in." Salka commanded. "I'll give you a lift. Where are you going?"

"Down in the canyon." Down in the canyon we went, but when I asked Salka to let me off in front of a grocery store, she asked what I was going to buy in there. I told her some things for dinner.

She answered, "I'm going to see Thomas Mann. Do you want to come?" Did I want to come! I went with Salka up the other side of the canyon to the Pacific Palisades and the Mann residence. The Manns were not home, so I was not to meet them until another day. Instead, Salka drove me to see Ad Schulberg, the mother of Budd, to whom I had once given a college literary prize, and to show me Malibu, which I had never seen. I was surprised that Malibu was such a narrow unpretentious strip of beach bordered by bungalows, almost primitive by contrast with the kind of residence favored by most moving picture people. We had cocktails with Ad (or rather I did, because Salka was a teetotaller). By the time we got back to Mabery Road it was dinnertime. The inevitable happened. Salka insisted David and I have dinner with her. After that second wonderful repast, we agreed on financial arrangements for meals for David and myself.

Clerical workers in the moving picture studios were on strike, including Pauline, who had been Salka's secretary at Metro-Goldwyn-Mayer before Greta Garbo stopped acting, so we were well-informed of disputes in which actors and writers were taking sides. One afternoon the doorbell rang and I answered it for Salka. On the doorstep was Charlie Chaplin. On his chest was an enormous badge, *OBSERVER*. "I was there!" he said, grinning, to Salka, and pointing proudly to his badge. "I was there!" Along with other renowned Hollywood personalities, after the police had acted brutally he had joined a picket line that day and other days to help prevent further violence.

Chaplin was a man of intense enthusiasms. On perhaps the most vociferous evening I was to spend at Salka's, he came bursting in after dinner to announce that he had just read the world's greatest book. "What?" he was asked. *"The Decline of the West*. By Oswald Spengler. You should read it." As usual at Salka's, there were a number of writers. For a moment there was silence. It was a book all of us had read years before. Then the shouting began. "Charlie! You can't be serious!" "Charlie, he's a Fascist, a Nazi! He's right up Hitler's alley." "No, Charlie, no!" Chaplin was defensive and not easily convinced. After an hour's argument, he did what I saw him do at other times when ill at ease or bored. He went to the piano and tapped out a lilting London music hall tune.

I never told him, of course, but apart from admiration for his genius as an actor I had always felt sorry for him, ever since I had read *The Wind and the Rain*, by Thomas Burke. The closest I ever came to expressing my feeling was when I asked him if he ever heard from Thomas Burke. He gave me a casual answer of yes, something about Burke being all right, and I did not pursue the subject. Thomas Burke, of course, was the author of the collection of stories in *Limehouse Nights*, to be dramatized by D.W. Griffith as "Broken Blossoms." He and Chaplin had both grown up in Limehouse, and as boys had been friends. Like Burke, Chaplin had been very poor and knew many years of hardship before he went to America and achieved his first success. In *The Wind and the Rain*, his beautiful autobiography, Burke describes those years, and tells of the worshipful love Chaplin had for a neighboring girl who not only was indifferent to him but snubbed him cruelly. On his first return to England after his overwhelming triumph in the United States, London went wild over Chaplin. A parade was organized in his honor, and, with bands playing and crowds cheering, he was escorted through the city and through his old neighborhood of Limehouse, past the house where the girl he adored still lived. She was at the window. Radiant and proud, Charlie smiled and waved to her. She drew her head in and closed the window.

Oona, the daughter of Eugene O'Neill, Chaplin's teen-age wife, nearly always was with Chaplin when he came to Salka's. She already had one or two babies. A pretty, dark-haired girl, she sat silently knitting afghans. Chaplin had been known in Hollywood for his interest in young girls. Watching Oona, I wondered if she reminded him of another girl he had loved so desperately years before in Limehouse, and if the memory of that young childhood love explained the appeal young girls had for him.

Chaplin never really knew security, either emotionally or financial. We were once talking about a man who had millions, lost them, and was bankrupt and penniless. "How could a man have a *million* dollars and lose it?" he demanded. "A whole million! Is it really possible to lose a million dollars?!" I may be wrong, but I thought Chaplin was wondering if it could happen to him.

Like everyone else I knew, I took it for granted that Chaplin was Jewish. Salka came from across the room where she had been chatting with him, a look of surprise on her face, to say to a group of us, "Charlie isn't Jewish!" Salka herself was Jewish. "I told him that everybody thinks he is and why doesn't he deny it? He says because he doesn't care one way or the other. He doesn't mind."

(Another day I was sitting at breakfast on a glorious California morning, trying to decide whether I was enjoying more the heavenly weather or the heavenly *Gansschmaltz,* drippings from the pan in which a goose, lightly flavored with onion, has been roasted the night before. I was spreading it on good, mealy black bread when Gigi, Peter Viertel's first wife, came into the dining room. She was torn between anger and tears. A mare she owned was about to foal many miles away in the country. She wanted to be near it when it gave birth and had heard that a country club close by boarded horses. She went to inquire. Yes, she was assured, they had excellent stables and were pleased to board horses. All the arrangements had been made and they asked her to sign her name. "We are sorry," she was then told, "but we don't board Jewish horses."

I laughed and couldn't stop laughing. "Jewish horses! Oh, my God! Jewish horses!" Gigi was furious. "I don't see anything funny!" She was beginning to think I was anti-Semitic, when Irwin Shaw arrived and heard me laughing. Irwin is Jewish. He wanted to know what was so laughable. When I got my breath, I told him. It was his turn to roar. He said it would make a wonderful story and that he was going to write it. Jewish horses!)

Chaplin and Garbo. Two of the greatest actors of our time, and both had hideous childhoods; and both were misunderstood by a public that alternately idolized and reviled them. Chaplin was refused a return visa to come back to America when he had left on a European trip. Greta Garbo was mocked for saying, "I want to be alone." She was not posing. She was a frightened woman —not simple ordinary stage fright but absolute terror. It was why she stopped acting, why she refused to make public appearances during the war, for which she was excoriated by Hollywood gossip columnists.

She was so beautiful! So unutterably, poignantly beautiful! Hair dragged back, unpowdered, unlipsticked and unmanicured, in plain dark slacks and old sweater, her loveliness still took one's breath away. The first time David saw Greta he was twelve years old, an age when small boys are indifferent to feminine beauty. David, wide-eyed, watched her. Her every movement—sitting, standing, walking—was grace. When she turned her head, her profile was an exquisite cameo. When she looked straight at you and you could study the flawless face it seemed ethereal. David tiptoed to me and whispered, "Isn't she beautiful?"

She was the daughter of a poor butcher. He became ill, and her family, in those days before Sweden's ultramodern health plan, could not afford to call a doctor. Little Greta, a child not yet in her teens, half-carried, half-pulled her father onto a streetcar and took him to the big Stockholm public hospital. In the waiting room a nurse came up to them and asked the father what was the matter with him. He tried to tell her, but the nurse interrupted him. "Don't you know better than to remain seated when you are talking to a lady?" He struggled to his feet, collapsed, and died.

Greta went to work in a dressmaking establishment where she was a slavey doing manual labor. I remember hearing that one of her jobs was lugging great piles of heavy cloth on her shoulders. The rest of her story is well known. She got a job in a barbershop, was seen there and admired, and arrangements were made for her to enter a drama academy. But the fright she had known as a child never left her. She came to Salka's only when she was assured there was no one there she did not know well. I was told that the great love of her life was John Gilbert, and that she never recovered from his suicide.

Once in a while she, Salka, and I would have lunch, a very simple one in contrast to Salka's sumptuous dinners. Something like cottage cheese and a salad. If Garbo wanted a second helping, she would ask herself, "Shall we like more salad?" She was worried about her two geraniums which she had moved to a house she had recently bought. They would not bloom. Somehow this failure was significant. (In California geraniums grow tall as trees and almost as wild as weeds.)

As seen from Hollywood in the mid-Forties, literary life in the United States was strange. One part, on the West Coast, was the group of entrenched, professional, highly skilled, fabulously paid scenario writers. The second part, scattered through the country, was the serious, hard-working, dedicated-to-literature authors with moderate or minute incomes. Both these groups were jealously aware of each other. The third part consisted of European exiles bemused by the whole business. And last but not least there was a detached territory, William Faulkner.

When Vicki Baum, author of *Grand Hotel,* earnestly asked me if I thought if she sent a short story to a magazine in New York, it would be considered, I was startled. "Would they really bother to read it with *my* name on it?" She seemed doubtful when I told her they would. From that conversation and listening to the talk of others, I learned that the richly paid screenwriters had terrific inferiority complexes. A few may have had guilty consciences, but I have always felt that the successful writer of junk, to be convincing, must actually believe what he is writing. Whether my supposition is true or not, the Hollywood writers felt they were beyond the pale and were scorned by writers in the rest of the country.

And those latter writers? They were torn between bitterness and envy of the Hollywood contingent. Bitterness because inferior writing should reap such golden reward, and envy because, damn it, they would like some of that money too. The first night after our arrival in Los Angeles, David and I had dinner at the Westwood home of the young writer, Jay Dratler, a friend from my Vienna days, and his wife. We had just sat down to dinner when the telephone rang. Excusing himself, Jay answered it and told his wife it was his agent calling; "Sam" was at his agent's place and wanted to see him immediately. Saying he would be back as soon as he could, Jay departed, and we went on with dinner. Dessert was being served when Jay returned. "Sam bought it, Binks," he told his wife. "For fifty thousand."

Between soup and dessert Jay had sold and been paid fifty thousand dollars for an idea for a screen story not yet written. This was the story: A man and his wife are asleep in bed. The wife is having a dream that she is having an affair with another man. The husband is dreaming he is watching his wife have the affair and is jealous. Fifty thousand! I had always been fond of Jay, who is dead now, ever since I met him when he was a boy of nineteen, and I am not impugning his literary ability. He wrote a good first novel, *Ducks in Thunder,* but I am trying to illustrate Hollywood mores. Two weeks later Jay called me to say that the studio executives had decided it was illogical for two people to be having the same dream and could I suggest how to make it logical. I tried but I couldn't. Still later, a young writer, Polly James, receiving $150 a week as a studio "apprentice," was visiting Salka. "What are you working on now, Polly?" Salka asked her. Polly sighed. "The studio bought two story ideas. One is about a man and wife having dreams. His wife is having an affair and her husband is watching her. They paid fifty thousand for it. Then they bought a story about a bishop and his wife, who is in love with an angel. They paid seventy-five thousand for it. They don't want to lose the money so I am supposed to combine the two stories into one scenario." Polly sighed again. I did not see it, and my memory may be incorrect, but I am told the result was something called "The Bishop's Wife."

Another bizarre Hollywood custom was to brand a writer for life with the pay he received for his first script. Nanette Kutner, another writer unfortunately dead, told me she had been assigned to write a screenplay for Margaret O'Brien for an astronomical sum. When it was discovered how little she had been paid for another assignment years before, the promised amount was reduced to that low figure. A "witness" was an essential figure in all discussions concerning a picture. I found this out when Salka would ask me to be present when a producer, director, or actor came to the house to discuss any plans they might have for a picture. There was to be no trusting anybody.

As for Faulkner, most of his books were out of print, the Nobel Prize was in the distant future, and he was in Hollywood for what was called "peanuts"—a thousand dollars a week. I saw him ahead of me one day on Hollywood Boulevard, pausing to look in store windows. I had met him once years before with a group of friends in New York. It was a casual meeting that did not entitle me to interrupt his window shopping.

A story about Faulkner and Hollywood is well known but worth retelling. When he arrived at the studio that had commissioned him to come to Hollywood, he was ushered into a huge, palatial office and told it was his. "Of course, if you don't find it comfortable you can work at home," a producer told him. Then, as things went in Hollywood, he was forgotten for some months. At a story conference someone remembered him and suggested he would be the right man to do the screen treatment. "Get Mr. Faulkner on the telephone," a producer ordered a secretary. "We have just the story for you, Bill," said the producer chummily. "Get over here right away, sweetheart." "Sweetheart" was a Hollywood term of address for male and female.

"I can't," said Faulkner. "I'm home."

"Jump in a cab then."

"That'll take longer."

"Where the hell are you?"

"In my home in Oxford, Mississippi."

I did meet the Manns finally but remember no memorable talk among the group in Salka's living room that day or on other days when they were present. Mrs. Mann seemed to me much the livelier of the two, smiling and chatting sociably with everyone. Mann was not taciturn or aloof exactly, but he was not, as I remember, talkative. He did not look like the literary artist who had written *Mario the Magician* or *Death in Venice.* Instead, with his trim toothbrush mustache, neatly brushed hair, and expensive, conservative dark suit, he looked the typical businessman or insurance agent he had once been. Though I do not remember what he said, I liked him.

Brecht I simply did not like, in spite of his supposed irresistible attraction for women. He was, to me, an unprepossessing man with a "soup bowl" haircut, the sort mothers once gave small boys by placing bowls over their heads to make their hair even all around. I did not trust his eyes. My refugee friends were not only surprised but shocked to find how little Brecht was then known in the United States. I had seen *Mother Courage* and *Private Life of the Master Race* in German and found them interesting, but not, for me at least, as emotion rousing as they were meant to be. *The Three Penny Opera* was a different matter. There, of course, Brecht had as matrix Gay's *Beggar's Opera* and, as accompaniment, Kurt Weill's music.

Brecht brought Helli, his wife, when he came to Salka's, and I was to see his *"petite amie"* Ruth von Berlau only occasionally when I met her elsewhere. I am still grateful to Ruth for having found my small son and myself a home when we were stranded in the wartime housing shortage in Los Angeles. And I am especially grateful that she should have introduced me to Salka. But it was Brecht's wife with whom I was to become much better acquainted. Like Maria Donath, she had been an outstanding actress in prewar Berlin under her own name of Helene Weigl, and was to become also director of the big Berlin theater where Brecht's plays were produced. She was a wonderful cook and I often sat in her kitchen watching her work. Like her two children, for which she made them, I greedily devoured her spicy cookies delicious when freshly warm from the oven.

Helli was not happy, and she was much too thin. She was only too aware of Brecht's affair with the Baroness von Berlau, which, I was told, was the latest in a long string of affairs. I was also told that the baroness was the most determined of his lovers. It was not gossip but open knowledge in Hollywood, and openly conducted by both participants. I heard how Ruth went into the children's room one night when they were in bed and their parents were not home. She took them to a beach amusement resort, telling them they must be sure to let their father know what a good time she had given them. Another time Helli answered the telephone to be told it was the Los Angeles Hospital calling and asking for Mr. Brecht. Helli said he was out and offered to take a message. "Please tell Mr. Brecht his wife has been delivered of a dead child." It was poor, lovesick Ruth, who, knowing Brecht's devotion to his children, had gone to the extreme of trying to woo him away with another child.

"How long must a wife be patient with a husband who wanders?" Helli demanded. She said that when Brecht first started becoming interested in others she had left him and gone to her father in Austria. Her father was furious with her. "Are you crazy? You go right back to your husband!" When she returned, Brecht told her he was glad and that he would never divorce her.

So Helli, for the sake of her children, tried to play the Griselda role. (Griselda was the girl in the legend, you remember, who at her lover's request meekly dressed in wedding finery, another woman he said he would marry. The lover was so overwhelmed by such devotion that he married Griselda. My own theory is that Griselda felt supreme indifference to him.) I am probably wrong about Helli and Brecht, because I heard from friends who saw them after their return to Berlin at the end of the war that they were wrapped up in one another. Edita Morris, the Swedish-American writer, told me Ruth had been complaining to her about it. Edita said she tried to console Ruth: "You had your turn in Hollywood. Now it's Helli's turn."

A feud between Aldous Huxley and my son, David, prevented my ever getting to really know the Englishman. Huxley was connected with the Ojai school where David went. He had come across David and another boy having a snowball fight with oranges and scolded them. Whatever the words Huxley used, they cut David deeply. David seemed to feel I was disloyal when I told him I agreed with Huxley. I explained that oranges were a valuable food, as well as delicious to taste. When I was a child oranges were so expensive they were put in Christmas stockings as a special treat, and even now when they were cheaper, thou-

sands of American children seldom had them. But David glow-
ered at every mention of Huxley. Stoop-shouldered and slow-
moving, Huxley had the almost vacuous face of a near-blind
person.

Krishnamurti's and David's relationship was quite different.
Ojai, where David's school was located, is one of the loveliest
parts of California. Its beauty is often compared to that of India's
Valley of Kashmir. Like India, it was a mecca for Theosophists
because of Krishnamurti's presence there. Neither David nor I
were Theosophists, which is perhaps why the Hindu and David
became such friends. Even though Krishnamurti denied over and
over again that he was the "new Christ," the thousands of pil-
grims who flocked to Ojai all wanted to see and talk with him. His
hiding place, his refuge from them, was David's room at the
school. A Theosophist woman who heard my son knew Krishnamurti asked me if she could meet David. On David's next
vacation I arranged a meeting. She gazed at David with reverence. "You actually know Krishnamurti?" She asked in an awe-
stricken voice. "You saw him and talked with him? The new
Christ?"

"Sure," said David. "Krish is a nice guy!"

How do you tactfully ask someone if he or she is an American
citizen? One of my problems in editing *The Best American Short
Stories* has been the fact that some of the finest stories published
in American magazines are by foreigners. Authors reprinted in
the book must be Americans. That includes Canadians, who,
logically, are certainly Americans since they live on the American
continent, and for publishing purposes are so recognized. I've
had to make amends to good foreign writers by listing them on
a foreign honor roll. I have made mistakes. I do not know who
gets angrier, American writers who are listed as foreign or foreigners who are listed as American.

Christopher Isherwood had come to dinner at Salka's and was sitting across the table from me when I asked him that question. He was not annoyed but simply smiled and said he had taken out naturalization papers. Like Somerset Maugham, who had used him as the main character in *The Razor's Edge,* Isherwood was an avowed homosexual. He had brought with him that evening a boy in his late teens or early twenties who interested me more as a character than did Isherwood. He was a hard-faced kid with a too-wise look. I thought if Isherwood had brought a girl of the same type instead, she would have been immediately recognized as a gold digger. Isherwood himself seemed a pleasant, easygoing person.

Berthold Viertel, Salka's husband, was the director in Isherwood's *Prater Violet,* a story about the making of a film. Berthold was living and working in New York, where I saw him later. There was no divorce but an amicable separation between him and his wife. They wrote to one another constantly, and Salka occasionally read me parts of his letters. The separation of Max Reinhardt and his wife, Elsa, who was at Salka's nearly every day, was far from amicable, however. Reinhardt had taken another woman to Reno to divorce Elsa. Elsa was so distraught that she attempted suicide. To save both her pride and morale, Salka put Elsa in a car and drove her to Reno so that she might not be denied the woman's role of divorcing the man.

Madame Nijinski, the sad-faced wife of the great dancer, was also having a problem with her husband, but it was of a different kind. She was considering bringing him to Hollywood, and she wanted Salka's help and advice. As for Franz Werfel's wife, who called herself "Frau Mahler," after her first husband, the composer Gustav Mahler, she was blithely indifferent to Werfel. Although she had had two husbands, including Werfel, since Mahler, it was always Mahler this and Mahler that with her. And she let Werfel know plainly how inferior she considered him. Werfel died and Salka went to his funeral. She had liked Werfel and was saddened by his death. Yet she came home laughing. Frau Mahler wasn't there, she said. Instead, she had taken her pet turtle out for a walk.

Since so many writers gathered in the big living room, there were many literary arguments. I no longer remember everyone there the night they fell to discussing writers and immortality. I do remember that Clifford Odets, the author of the spellbinding play *Waiting for Lefty,* was there. Odets was a kind man who secretly did many acts of charity for other writers, so what he said that night about his own lasting reputation was incongruous. "You'll all be forgotten before I am," he declared. "One hundred and fifty years from now I can be on a ship in mid-ocean and people will say 'That is Clifford Odets.' I am the one who will be longest remembered!" Why he chose a ship's deck in mid-ocean 150 years later still puzzles me. I was not able to ask him then because there was such an outbreak of yelling directed at him.

But the most important inhabitant of the Mabery Road house was Prince, Salka's handsome German shepherd, who was not merely a dog. He was a character who made a lasting impression, sometimes with his teeth, on everyone who met him. At least two writers, Samuel Hoffenstein, the poet, and Edwin Justus Mayer, the playwright, were so fearful of him they carried heavy sticks when they came. Hoffenstein never let go of his stick a whole evening as he eyed Prince but clutched it so tightly his knuckles went white. Years later, Eddie Mayer and I got to discussing Prince. "A stupid dog!" said Eddie, "He couldn't tell friend from foe."

"Did you know he bit Greta Garbo in the behind?" I asked.

"He did?" Eddie laughed. "He wasn't so stupid after all. I always wanted to do that myself!"

Yet Prince could be affectionate and gentle. He and my son would roll over and over on the floor in the friendliest of wrestling matches. And he loved me to take him on walks during which he was always obedient. The trouble with Prince was that he was the victim of unrequited love. Iris Tree, the English actress, had a magnificently beautiful pure white Russian wolfhound, Luka. Prince was enraptured by her. He alternately pranced and got a silly look on his face when she was there. Luka ignored him. After she left, he moped for hours.

Word came that Peter Viertel, who had not yet written his first book to make him a reputation *(Black Heart, White Hunter)*, was returning from Europe, where he had been serving with the American army. When she learned the exact date of his arrival, Salka arranged that all the windows in the house would be dark and everyone would be waiting in complete silence in the living room. A good old conventional surprise party for the returning hero. He opened the door, and before we could speak, Prince took a flying leap and grabbed Peter by the thigh. It was a surprise all right.

I went with Salka when she took Prince to a distant estate where the owner wanted a watchdog. Prince knew something was wrong, because in the car he kept trying to lick first Salka's face, then mine. When his new owner led him away, Prince kept turning his head to look back at Salka long and sorrowfully. I felt he felt that we were betraying him. Salka wept all the way home. But, there was nothing else to do except to kill him. Poor Prince.

A telegram came from Columbia University asking me to give a course there. I was not interested. A second wire came, and Salka was impressed. I told Salka I could not accept the offer because no plane or train accommodations were to be had. She did not understand that I was only making an excuse. I really did not want to go. "I'll fix that!" she said, picking up the phone. "Peter can always get a plane." Before I could stop her she had arranged with Peter Lorre to get a reservation for me in his name. As P. Lorre I boarded a plane for New York and almost hoped the plane would crash. It would have been such a nice sensation for newspaper headlines. "Peter Lorre Killed in Crash!" And it would only have been me.

Far away and long ago. I never saw 165 Mabery Road again. Like Prince, I look back longingly at the kind people who gave my son and me shelter and affection at a time we needed them. The house has been sold, and they are all scattered. Some are dead, like darling Grossmutter and the son for whose letter she waited so long. Many are in Europe, from whence they had been driven by the Holocaust. In Switzerland, where she is often joined by Greta Garbo for long visits, is Salka herself.* Wonderful, wonderful Salka!

---

* Salka Viertel died, in Klosters, Switzerland, in 1978.—ED.

AFTERWORD

∾

Martha Foley did not live to complete her memoir. Her intention
had been to tell the "story of *STORY*"—to take her memoir to
the final months of 1941, when she left *STORY* (and Whit) to
become the editor for the annual *Best American Short Stories*. The
chapter she was working on at the time of her death—on *STORY*'s
first year in America—was fragmentary and unfinished, and lay,
its yellow pages neatly stacked, beside her typewriter in a manilla
folder marked "Work in Progress—Ch XII." Under it was another folder—"Research notes made for Ch. XII and passages for
later use," and under that—almost as if she knew she would never
finish the book herself—a folder with a pink three-by-five index
card taped to the front, stating, in bold capital letters, underlined,
and surrounded by exclamation points: *"IMPORTANT! DAVID/
ENDING!* Last paragraph to balance the first."

Martha had, clearly, never gotten over the loss of the two
important men in her life, her son, David, and her husband, Whit.
She could never admit much about David—she always spoke of
him glowingly—including the fact that he had been addicted to
drugs; according to her, he had been killed by incompetent doc-

tors during operations for ulcers.* Her life, during her last years, was so tied to him—to her loss of him—that she had originally entitled this memoir *Good Night, David.* In her notes she stated that she intended, in the last chapter, to "address David directly as in the opening part," and to set her remarks to him against a background of his telling her and Whit "the radio news of the Pearl Harbor bombing." "The world was never to be the same again nor anyone in it," she wrote, "nor anything, including *STORY* magazine." Among handwritten and typed yellow sheets, in which she talked to David of her divorce ("Divorce is a terrible thing to do to a child"), of the broken home he grew up in, of money troubles, of the "ulcers" that killed him and that he "endured so bravely," there was also a white index card, addressed to her publisher:

Norton! ! !
Ending! 'Good-night, my darling. Turn off the light, shut the door. David sleeps.

David remained, to the end, her little boy; and if she was unable to face the truth either of his life or his death, she could admit at times, to herself and others, how deeply the loss of Whit had affected her. Whenever, during the writing of her memoir, she came to a section where she had to write about him, she would be unable, for days and weeks, to write anything at all. She would become, by turns, angry and depressed—almost paralyzed—and

---

* But I found the following handwritten passage among her papers: "There are times when the emotions need an anaesthetic as much as nerves laid bare by a surgeon's knife. . . . For three months after my son died I stayed drunk. Really falling down drunk floor drunk onto a floor from which I had to be picked up. Happy people do not get drunk. Nor do happy people take drugs. They do not need relief from inexorable pain. The pity is that our society, always demanding visible tangibles, physical causes, mistakes symptoms for causes and damns the sufferer."

she spoke to me about this several times. She understood—this, more than thirty-five years after he had left her—that she had not, in her own words, ever gotten over him. ("Oh, Whit," she said to me. "He was such a handsome devil—I suppose I'm still carrying the torch for him.") She understood how hard it was for her to write about their years together, and—about this she seemed less self-aware—how hard it was for her to write about him with any objectivity or affection. "What do you think, Jay," she asked me one day, after she had been having special difficulty in describing what she'd felt toward him when they'd first met and had fallen in love. "What do you think? Am I too old for psychoanalysis?" She was then seventy-eight years old. We laughed together, and talked some more, and a few days later she telephoned to thank me—to tell me that our conversation had somehow unblocked her. She was writing again. She had, she said, decided not to enter psychoanalysis.

"With this issue *STORY* comes to America." The first American issue of *STORY* was published in April 1933, and in the announcement, Martha and Whit sketched in *STORY*'s extraordinary two-year history, and noted that, although Edward J. O'-Brien had stated in the *Best Stories* of 1932 that *"STORY* is now the most distinguished short story magazine in the world," and although *STORY* had a "really remarkable international reputation," at no time "did its circulation ever exceed 600 copies."

Things were to change, of course. During the next few years, its circulation would rise to almost 25,000; it would become a monthly instead of a bimonthly; it would found a readers' literary service, a radio program, a book publishing program, and would continue to publish stories by a remarkable range of writers, from the most famous to those who had never before published. The title page of this first American issue—the table of contents—tells us, more graphically than any description can, of the richness of the years to come. Under the masthead (*"STORY:* Devoted Solely to the Short Story") and the date (April 1933), are the following eleven stories:

"Nothing Can Stop It"by Elizabeth Wagner
"My Mother's Goofy Song"by John Fante
"Convalescence"by Kay Boyle
"Hamlet's Dagger"by Manuel Komroff
"Impulse"by Conrad Aiken
"She Walks In Beauty"by Martha Foley
"Masses of Men"by Erskine Caldwell
"Family Vitriol"by Mikhail Zoshchenko
"Time"by H.E. Bates
"Fisherman's Bride"by Charles Kendall O'Neill
"Black Jesus"by John Cowles

Then, in capital letters, is the information that the magazine is "PUBLISHED EVERY TWO MONTHS AT 20 EAST 57TH STREET, NEW YORK" (the offices of Random House), and that the editors are Whit Burnett and Martha Foley. The publishers are listed, in small type, as Donald S. Klopfer, president, Bennett A. Cerf, secretary-treasurer (both of Random House), and Harry Scherman, vice-president.* The issue appeared on the day before the banks closed, and issues would continue to appear monthly, for the most part, and always containing eight or more stories—and, later on, reviews, essays, letters, poems, photo-essays, novellas—until Martha's departure eight years later.

The next few issues included the first published short stories of Nelson Algren ("His full name is Nelson Algren Abraham,

---

* Of Harry Scherman, founder and president of the Book-of-the-Month Club, Martha wrote, in notes: "He was the most powerful man in American book publishing but few writers and practically no readers knew his name. Every book publisher did."

and he is Jewish and Swedish"), Frederic Scribner, John S. McNa-marra, Bernadine Kielty, Linda Henly, Alan Marshall ("Death and Transfiguration," a remarkable story about rural New Hamp-shire—Seabrook—that would elicit as much comment and praise as any story the magazine would ever publish), and the first story published in America by Malcolm Lowry, "a young English writer who has just completed his first novel, *Ultramarine,* sched-uled this year for London publication, Jonathan Cape."* They also included stories by Zora Neale Hurston, Ted Pratt, Faulkner, Coppard, and Zoshchenko ("Of William Faulkner, A.E. Coppard and Mikhail Zoshchenko, little need be said other than that these three are pretty generally recognized as the respec-tive representatives of the highest development of the contempo-rary short story in America, England and Russia").

In its third American issue (August 1933), *STORY* was doing so well that it declared to its readers that it was "in a position to announce its expansion from a magazine costing fifty cents an issue and appearing every two months to a magazine which here-after will cost half that amount and appear every month." Martha and Whit were at some pains to reassure their readers that "this change, which is largely a mechanical one and one which is in line with the policy of *STORY* to become more easily available to its readers and potential readers, involves no change in the editorial point of view.

"*STORY* will continue to be the medium, and, at present, the sole medium, for the presentation to intelligent readers of the new, significant writing in the short story form as it is being practised (if not printed) by the significant writers in America and

---

* Among Martha's handwritten notes about Lowry, I found the following, where she quotes herself saying to him, "I promise you that your book will be published. If Harper's won't do it, somebody else will. Please don't be dis-couraged. You are too good a writer. My promise came true—a lost man—Roseland. . . ." "I saw Malcolm unhappy but I never saw him drunk," she also wrote. "He was desperate for re-assurance. . . . He was so discouraged then. To be put in Bellevue was a terrible thing to do to him."

abroad," the announcement went on. "Reducing the price will entail no attempt to lessen the quality or vulgarize the appeal. *STORY* was brought to America as an experiment in the presentation of writing which generally was being ignored by the commercial magazines of this country although hailed critically when this same writing appeared in books. . . . With this issue's radical change in both price and frequency of appearance, the editors hope to bring *STORY* to an even larger reading public. . . ."

For the next issue, Bernadine Kielty, the wife of Harry Scherman, joined the magazine as an associate editor (she would remain for eight years), and George Cronyn, previously with *The Atlantic Monthly* and a short story writer and author himself ("his latest book has just been bought by Covici-Friede; it is a biography of Peire Vidal, a troubador of Provence in the time of the Third and Fourth Crusades, and entitled *The Fool of Venus"*), became business manager. The issue included stories by Marquis W. Childs, Martha Dodd (daughter of the American ambassador to Germany), R.C. Woods, Whit, A. Averchenko, Alvah Bessie, John Peale Bishop, and Gertrude Stein. ("A native of Pennsylvania, she prefers Paris, where for many years her salons in the rue de Fleurus have been famous and often deadly.")

In this issue Martha and Whit also introduced the first of many columns of "Notes"—informal and sometimes cloyingly cute remarks about writers and their work, especially about writers whose work was appearing in *STORY*. In this first column they noted the receipt of books published by *STORY* authors Komroff, Caldwell, H.E. Bates, José Garcia Villa, and George Milburn (about Milburn's stories, they wrote that "with William Faulkner's That Evening Sun Go Down they can take their place on any short story collector's shelf and stand up just as well several years from now as they do today"); they introduced Bernadine Kielty and George Cronyn to their readers; they wrote about the way in which, in Nazi Germany, the modern opera had "been practically killed . . . by the Hitler regime," and they reprinted

George Antheil's appeal to American composers and librettists. They also reported that Kay Boyle and Laurence Vail had "left their Riviera place at *Villefranche* and have gone to live in Vienna. Last heard from they were looking for a reasonable pension." ("Alas," the editors remarked. "If only there were one!") They concluded with a literary anecdote about meeting Eugene O'-Neill—about his telling them that he was once a short story writer himself and that *The Hairy Ape* was originally written as a story and was rejected by almost every magazine in America. "In despair (shall we say?) he then re-cast it in the form of a play."

Such notes and anecdotes—about the rise of fascism, about the success of *STORY*'s authors, and about their personal doings and whereabouts—become standard fare for the rest of the decade, and as the magazine succeeded and its enterprises expanded (they announced their first College Short Story Contest in the next issue, and Vanguard Press published their first anthology, *A Story Anthology, 1931–33,* at the end of the year), its tone became at the same time both more intimate and more expansive. They talked to their readers, at length, of their pride in having solicited stories from Ivan Bunin when he was unpublished and forgotten, shortly before he became the first Russian Nobel Prize winner. When he won the prize, *STORY* had thirteen of his manuscripts* (they finally chose, translated, and published three). And they even quoted, at excruciating length, from rejected manuscripts, in order to assure readers and writers, as they frequently did ("Every manuscript is read by the editors themselves") of the earnestness of their own labors.

> Another story, delivered in pain, heaven knows, and entitled "The Happy Parent," begins: "My friends wonder why I insist that I shall never have another baby. They do not know that I had twenty-five in one eternal night. . . ." Stories like

---

* In later years, Whit would expand that figure to thirty-five.

these are really read by the editors. Contrary to the theories of writers, who believe that their stories meet with a mere glance at the first three pages, such *contes* are eagerly eyed to the bitter end. . . . Authors, it might be said here, profit little from trying to trip up the editors by test-pages, annotations, etc., wilily inserted toward the end of the mss. to determine if the wan eye of the reader has seen that page. One memorable manuscript had a slip inserted at page seven, asking: "Did you get this far?" Another had a friendly insert of a bouquet of four-leaf clovers.

They noted, in a biographical sketch about William March ("the author of numerous stories, Mr. March yet finds time to be the vice-president of the Waterman Steamship Lines") that he and "William Faulkner used to play in the same backyard in the South occasionally, when they weren't scrapping"; they noted, with sadness, H.L. Mencken's retirement from *The American Mercury*, but they qualified their praise for him by lamenting his decision to "depreciate" the short story in favor of "the sociological article as *the* important form of literary interpretation of the American *mores*"; they noted the number of stories chosen by Edward O'-Brien from *STORY* for his annual *Best Stories* (four in 1931, and seven in 1932—the most ever chosen from one magazine by O'Brien, until, in 1934, he would choose nine from *STORY*), and stories selected for other anthologies (*O. Henry Memorial Prize Stories, Best British Short Stories,* and so on).

In the final three issues of 1933, *STORY* published work by, among others, Bunin, March, Faulkner, Peter Neagoe, Dorothy McCleary, Daniel Fuchs, Isaac Bein, Sherwood Anderson, E.P. O'Donnell, Eugene Jolas, Mary Heaton Vorse, and, in February 1934, the first published short story by a young Armenian writer from Fresno, California—a writer who would, within the next few years, become an acknowledged favorite ("The editors of *STORY* consider him their star discovery"). The writer was William Saroyan, and the story, which had arrived single-spaced on yellow paper, "The Daring Young Man on the Flying Trapeze," opened as follows:

SLEEP

Horizontally wakeful amid universal widths, praticing laughter and mirth, satire, the end of all, of Rome and yes of Babylon, clenched teeth, remembrance, much warmth volcanic, the streets of Paris, the plains of Jericho, much gliding as of reptiles in abstraction, a gallery of watercolors, the sea and the fish with eyes, symphony, a table in the corner of The Eiffel Tower, jazz at the opera house, alarm clock and the tap-dancing of doom, conversation with a tree, the river Nile, Cadillac coupe to Kansas, the roar of Dostoyevsky, and the dark sun.

Two issues later, they printed a letter from him to Martha. The letter, in part a meandering and detailed summary of Saroyan's reading of six long books of "cheap fiction"—he had at first considered burning them to keep warm—took up five double-column pages of the magazine, and began:

San Francisco
January 9, 1934

Dear Martha Foley:

I want you to know that it is very cold in San Francisco today, and that I am freezing. It is so cold in my room that every time I start to write a short story the cold stops me and I have to get up and do bending exercises. It means, I think, that something's got to be done about keeping short story writers warm. Sometimes when it is very cold I am able to do very good writing, but at other times I am not. It is the same when the weather is excessively pleasant. I very much dislike letting a day go by without writing a short story and that is why I am writing this meaningless letter: to let you know that I am very angry about the weather. Do not think that I am sitting in a nice warm room in sunny California, as they call it, and making up all this stuff about the cold. I am sitting in a very cold room and there is no sun anywhere, and the only thing I can talk about is the cold because it is the only thing going on today. . . .

Saroyan did, in fact, write and send to Martha a new short story every day for a month after she'd bought his first; she accepted a few, and tried to sell the others for him. (By 1941, according to a biographical sketch, Saroyan had written more than 500 stories.)*

In March 1934, *STORY* marked its first anniversary in America with much self-congratulation, noting that during the previous year "a total of 74 short stories were printed, the largest number of any of the three years and from two to four times as many as appeared in any other magazine in what is called the quality field." The editors prided themselves on the openness of their magazine to original and quality fiction, stating that, of the seventy-four stories published, "it is safe to say that hardly any of them would otherwise have seen print that year had they not been accepted by *STORY.* This, at least, was the feeling expressed by nearly every one of the contributors."

After having noted the names of both new and established

---

* In the Jaspersohn interview, Martha tells this story about Saroyan: "Edward and I were coming back to America by boat. He was coming over for a lecture tour. When the boat docked, I was so excited about Saroyan that I said, 'Oh Edward! We have discovered the most wonderful Armenian writer! And Edward looked very wise and said, 'No, you haven't. I have.' And so then we stopped off on the way to our apartment, where he was going to stay, at the Algonquin bar and sat around having drinks. And I said, 'What do you mean you have a story from Saroyan?' He said, 'That's not the name of my Armenian. The name of my Armenian is Tessiad, or something.' So he had an Armenian and I had an Armenian. And his Armenian had been publishing in the Boston Armenian paper, and my Armenian was going to be published in *STORY.* Then I read the Boston Armenian's story—I was having an awful lot of correspondence with Saroyan in those days—and I asked Saroyan if he knew that Armenian. And Saroyan wrote back and said, Yes. It was a cousin of his who'd been taking manuscripts out of Saroyan's wastebasket. Damned liar! He was writing under another name. Edward and I had been fighting over Saroyan, who was the Armenian in Boston and the Armenian in *STORY.* And O'Brien was telling me the Boston Armenian was better, and I was telling him the New York Armenian was better."

writers ("The stories were not only the work of new writers; many stories were the off-the-beaten-path productions of distinguished writers already known"), they went on to talk about what they saw as a virtual renaissance in the American short story, a renaissance for which, without undue modesty, they were prepared to claim a share of the credit. "The appearance of such an unprecedented number of interesting short stories in one magazine in such a relatively short time," they stated, "seems to have aided the trend in which public attention generally is turning to the short story as a vital art form. Even booksellers say that today they can sell a volume of short stories of literary integrity. Even publishers are ready to believe it." They went on to note that "the trend toward appreciation of the new short story has even affected the newspapers," and they cited the *Brooklyn Eagle,* in whose Sunday magazine section were printed stories by George Milburn, Erskine Caldwell, Kay Boyle, Thomas Mann, and Ivan Bunin. And, finally, they wrote that in England, two new magazines had appeared, "both avowedly dedicated to the same idea as *STORY.*" The first was *Lovat Dickson's Magazine* ("composed exclusively of short stories by such writers as H.E. Bates, L.A.G. Strong, Sean O'Faolain, Martin Armstrong, Walter de la Mare ... and to the work of authors without widely known names who have something new to say, and the skill with which to say it"); and the second, *New Stories,* whose editors stated that "the notable success of the experimental American magazine, *STORY,* has encouraged those who believe that a body of reader can, by similar methods, be found in England for short stories of outstanding literary merit and originality. . . ."

The next few years were *STORY*'s most glorious. By early 1935 circulation had passed the 21,000 mark;* they had pub-

---

* For the same year here are some other circulation figures: *The New Republic,* 25,000; *The American Mercury,* 31,000; *New Masses,* 32,000; *Scribner's,* 44,000; *Harper's,* 103,000; *The New Yorker,* 121,000.

lished their second anthology of stories from *STORY (STORY In America);** they had completed their first College Short Story Contest (won by nineteen-year-old James Laughlin, "the fourth in his family to bear that name, his family being the Laughlins of the steel industry in Pittsburgh"—Laughlin would later become the founder and publisher of New Directions Publishing Co.); and they had launched the first competition "for the Best Novel written by an Author who has had a story published in the magazine *STORY*." The $1,000 prize contest was co-sponsored by Doubleday, Doran & Company. The judges were Lewis Gannett; H.E. Maule of Doubleday; and Martha Foley.†

In mid-1935 *STORY* moved to new and larger quarters at 432 Fourth Avenue. The next six months were doubtless the most eventful in the magazine's history, for during this time Whit and Martha expanded both the magazine and the magazine's enterprises in ways that, perhaps, could only have taken place in America. The General Store atmosphere still prevailed—*STORY*'s writers and readers, despite their increased numbers, continued to be thought of as part of an extended family ("Our new quarters have a homey air. We are only fourteen floors above Michel's Tavern, at 29th and Fourth. Fourth Avenue is the heart of the American publishing industry. Michel's is the stomach.")—but the store itself was being enlarged at a quickening pace.

In early 1935 the magazine began a regular and expanded column of "End Pages," signed, usually, by Whit. He would later

---

* Vanguard Press
† Because, in March 1935 the judges could not "see a way clear to cast a deciding vote against either of [two] books," two one thousand dollar prizes were given: to Dorothy McCleary for *Not for Heaven* ("a lusty, gusty, warm-hearted, human portrait by an American woman Dickens of the most adorable, irritating and ingratiating old lady to appear in American fiction in many a day"), and Edward Anderson for *Hungry Men* ("The novel of the American jungle—of hungry men on the bum—of the whole dog-eat-dog world of America's last decade."). The novels were published in May, and, as would be the case with many books published by *STORY* authors (and by the Story Press), readers could buy autographed copies by making their purchases through *STORY* magazine.

collect these informal essays in a book, *The Literary Life and the Hell with It,* and the essays—mostly literary gossip and what can only be called "chit-chat"—ranged over a variety of subjects: Martha's attempts, in Paris, to learn to ride a bike and "how she scared the French Army"; Whit's meetings with famous writers such as Theodore Dreiser, George Bernard Shaw, and Frank Harris; his tales of a summer writer's conference he and Martha had taught at in Boulder, Colorado (where the other three teachers were Robert Frost, Robert Penn Warren, and Bernard De Voto); reports on Hemingway and others talking at Carnegie Hall before the American Writers' Congress, to enlist support against Franco; the results of a readers' survey on their favorite writers;* and personal and "cute" anecdotes of their family life —of David's eighteen imaginary playmates, of a trip to the West Indies, of the writers they entertained in their home or at their office.

In August 1936, with the establishment of the *STORY* Service Bureau, Whit and Martha, in a wonderfully American blend of idealism, optimism, missionary zeal, and capitalist enterprise, seemed ready to turn their magazine into an industry. The *STORY* Service Bureau provided six primary services to *STORY* Associates:

> 1—The STORY "Press-to-Reader" Service which enables members to order all current . . . books through the bureau, *and accumulate a cooperative rebate of 10%* which can be applied to other book purchases or to payment for *STORY* subscriptions. 2—The *STORY* Bureau Information Service about books, which will assist you in locating books and their publishers, will advise on the selection of books, will recommend

---

*   They were, in the summer of 1936, in order: Willa Cather, Pearl Buck, John Galsworthy, Ellen Glasgow, Sinclair Lewis, Sigred Undset, William Shakespeare, Dorothy Parker, Dorothy Canfield, Mark Twain, and Charles Dickens. Edna St. Vincent Millay was the favorite poet, Clarence Day the favorite humorist. Hemingway finished Whit noted, six votes ahead of Thomas Wolfe.

books—especially on the short story, will send publishers' catalogues on request. 3—The *STORY* Bureau Study Service, which will assist in the study of the Short Story, help study groups, classes and clubs, recommend books on the subject. 4—The *STORY* Bureau School Service, which will advise on the reputable schools and colleges offering the best course in appreciation, writing and the appreciation of modern literature. 5—The *STORY* Bureau Reading Service, which will recommend books for reading, select the most interesting stories in current periodicals (10 Short Stories of the Month) and otherwise assist in planning constructive reading. 6—The *STORY* Bureau "Best Seller" Service, which will print in the magazine each month the current best sellers in the bookstores throughout the country and the most popular books among *STORY* readers as indicated by their orders through the Service Bureau.

"STORY ASSOCIATES," their announcement concluded, "will become a powerful factor in assisting people to find the best contemporary literature. *STORY* was founded to present good stories. *STORY* now takes the next logical step forward in assisting the reading public to find and to buy the best in modern writing."

In the October 1936 issue, *STORY* announced that Dr. Kurt Simon (later spelled Semon), an exile from Nazism and formerly owner and publisher of the *Frankfurter Zeitung,* had joined the *STORY* organization as president. The editors, no longer getting office space from Random House, stated that the magazine was "on its own independent feet, concentrating solely on its own publishing," and that it was "now prepared to reach its widest possible audience, consonant with no loss in artistic integrity." And in the November issue, they inaugurated several new features "with a view to making [*STORY*] the most definitive magazine of its kind on the short story and contemporary writing in English."

The new features, which would run regularly until the end of the decade, were essays "on writing and writers . . . from the outstanding short story writers of the world"; regular columns of letters; best-seller lists; recommended reading; "Plus & Minus" —"a monthly survey of the reviews for and against the most significant books of the month." Again, after announcing the expansion, the editors reassured their readers that "these various additions are extensions of the magazine, on added pages, and not any encroachment on the regular number of pages which have been in the past, and will be in the future, devoted solely to distinguished short stories."

The new departures thrived. During the mid-Thirties, *STORY* published essays by Thomas Mann ("Measure and Value"), Sherwood Anderson ("Why Men Write"), Hendrik Willem Van Loon, Van Wyck Brooks, Eugene Jolas, James Laughlin ("New Words for Old: Notes on Experimental Writing"), Dorothy Thompson, George Bernard Shaw ("Fascism"), and semischolarly articles by less familiar names (e.g., "Chekhov's Middle Years," by Nina A. Toumanova).

And, finally, in April 1936—their Fifth Anniversary Issue— Whit and Martha announced the establishment of the Story Press, which, "in association with Harper & Brothers, expects to publish in America each year a limited number of books of high distinction." The books could be fiction or nonfiction, by "unknown writers" or "established authors." "Nothing," the editors assured their contributors and readers, "will influence the acceptance of a manuscript but its own vitality, freshness, and literary merit. A mere name or reputation for past performances will not count a hair's weight. Thus the new and unknown writer of talent is assured that his book will be given a warm welcome, a fair and sympathetic reading, and—when published—the greatest possible chance for recognition.

"Whit Burnett and Martha Foley, the editors of *STORY,*" the announcement went on, "will also edit the books for The Story

Press. It goes without saying that in the performance of their new duties they will give to the authors of books the same personal encouragement, the same discerning criticism and help, which has characterized their unique work in the field of the American short story."

They noted that Story Press authors would "not be limited to contributors to the magazine," and they urged writers who had not yet written their books but had an idea, "to feel free to consult with the editors for advice or help."

The Press's first book, published a year later, was Ignazio Silone's *Bread and Wine.* Its second book was *Song on Your Bugles,* by Eric Knight, a frequent contributor to *STORY* (a writer remembered today, if at all, for *Lassie Come Home,* but who was considered at the time—to judge from ads, blurbs, biographical sketches, and remarks in Whit's "End Pages"—to be as distinguished as Silone). Its third book, a collection of four long stories, was *Uncle Tom's Children,* by *STORY* discovery Richard Wright.

As I read through these mid-Thirties issues of *STORY,* I was impressed, naturally, with *STORY*'s wonderful optimism and excitement about fiction, with its continuing thrill in discovering new writers—and also with something simpler: with how much more important, to publishers and the public, fiction then seemed. During these years, there were dozens of advertisements in *STORY* from publishers, announcing large cash prizes for first novels. In addition to the *STORY*-Doubleday prize and Story Press books, the Book-of-the-Month Club offered four $2,500 awards a year to "unrecognized" authors; *The Atlantic* offered a $10,000 prize for a first novel; the W.P.A., in association with *STORY,* offered a $500 fiction prize (won by Richard Wright for what was to be his first published story, "Fire and Cloud"; the judges were Sinclair Lewis, Harry Scherman, and Lewis Gannett); and other publishers, including Knopf, Houghton Mifflin, Dodd

Mead, Little, Brown, Scribner's, and Harper's were also offering large sums, in prizes and fellowships, for fiction by "new" writers.

In 1980 some of these publishers will no longer consider unsolicited manuscripts, none of them offer annual prizes for new novels (if they offer prizes at all, they are invariably part of paperback tie-ins, etc.) While things are grim for the new writer, the plight of the established novelist seems especially dismal. As several editors at major New York publishers have admitted to me —after having turned down new novels by writers they admired and had been publishing—for the "established" writer of "quality" fiction it has, invariably, become an either/or situation: *either* a new novel by a writer whose previous one or two books have not been commercially successful is a "breakthrough" novel, *or* it will be rejected.* "In the old days," one editor said to me, "one would support the good writers on one's list with the best-selling writers. But those days are gone. Now that the conglomerates have taken over, it's every book for itself—with cost-accounting bottom-line thinking ruling all, and the writer's career be damned." The editor had, himself, recently felt forced to reject novels by his two favorite writers—writers whose new books, he said, were both their best-written and most ambitious. But, given the lack of commercial success of the writers' previous books, and the fear that the new books might be even less "accessible" to a general public than the previous ones, he'd felt he had no choice.†

To judge from the pages of *STORY*, things were different in the mid-Thirties. Martha and Whit were succeeding in their attempt to bring quality fiction to a wide audience. The magazine's

---

* In recent years only about 100 first novels a year have been published by all the major trade publishers combined, and one publisher, which, a dozen-or-so years ago had published 35 first novels in one year, last year published 5.

† Or, consider the president and publisher of one of America's most prestigious publishing companies—a man of excellent literary taste—saying to me, "You know, Jay, I've come to the conclusion that no novel today should be more than 270 pages long."

circulation stayed at around 20,000,* its books sold well (*Bread and Wine,* a Book-of-the-Month Club selection, went quickly to 100,000 copies), some of their discoveries (Saroyan, Caldwell, Farrell) were already reaching wide audiences, while continuing to publish—for twenty-five dollars a story—in *STORY,* and others were finding publishers. Whit and Martha noted in one column that six recent contributors had, owing largely to their appearance in *STORY,* sold first novels.

During these peak years—1934–1936—*STORY* published, for the first time in America, dozens of new writers, including Lewis Carliner, Villa Stiles, Edward Luchen McDaniel (a black elevator operator from San Francisco, who "told" his stories to a transcriber), A.I. Bezzerides (an Armenian who wrote to explain, at length, that he was *not* copying Saroyan), Peter De Vries (who "is interested in the short story as a medium for expressing the problems forced upon us all by this economic ruin"), Frederic Prokosch, Robert Traver, Jesse Stuart (who had just published a widely discussed book of 703 sonnets, *The Man with the Bull-Tongue Plow*), Elizabeth Hall, George Milburn, Jerome Weidman, Emily Hahn, John Cheever ("Of Love: a Testimony"), Edward North Robinson, Graham Greene, Elizabeth Janeway, Ignazio Silone, Nanette Kutner ("In Cold Blood"—"a depression story"), Paul Monash, Ludwig Bemelmans (with illustrations by the author), Rachel Maddux, and, in December 1936, a nineteen-year-old writer named Carson Smith ("Wunderkind"), who would soon change her name to McCullers.†

---

* A novel can, today, get on the *New York Times* national best-seller list without having sold 20,000 copies.

† About McCullers: "She is the daughter of a Columbus, Georgia, watchmaker. From six years on most of her energy was spent on music, with an aim toward a musical debut. A strenuous schedule of school and musical work was interrupted by illness at the age of fifteen, when she began to write and has been writing ever since. She has worked on her home town newspaper, the Columbus *Enquirer,* and, in New York, worked in a real estate office and on the editorial staffs, of two unmentionable comic magazines, and later as an accompanist and as a music-improvisor for some dancers."

During these years *STORY* also continued to publish work by writers who were already known or beginning to be known: Saroyan, Faulkner, Tess Slesinger, Peter Neagoe, Aldous Huxley, Wallace Stegner, Mari Sandoz, Paul Nathan, L.A.G. Strong, W.K. Wimsatt, Jr. (a teacher of "English and Latin in a New England preparatory school"), Rion Bercovici, H.E. Bates, Gladys Schmitt, Lord Dunsany, Chekhov, Morley Callaghan, Bernadine Kielty, Benedict Thielen, Edita Morris, I.V. Morris, Alvah Bessie, Mark Schorer, Nelson Algren, William E. Wilson, Frank O'Connor, Oliver Gossman, Meyer Levin, George Weller, Sean O'Faolain, Cornell Woolrich, E.A. Moll, Hal Borland, Vincent Sheean, William Harlan Hale, Madeline Cole, Ernest Brace, I.A. Kuprin, Alfred H. Mendes, Allan Seager, Romer Wilson, and Luigi Pirandello.

At the end of 1936, *STORY* also instituted a regular review column, "Firsts," by Horace Gregory, on the "new writers of today and their first books.* It emphasized too, its new commitment to publishing longer stories, for which it used—for the first time in English, according to Martha—the word "novella."

In connection with the newly introduced longer stories in *STORY,* for which there seems to be no word in the language except that cheap and banal one "novelette," which sounds like the potted novel it usually is or like something out of the war years vocabulary (like "farmerettes" or "flannelette"), we have gone somewhat far afield, and are bringing back the ancient and traditional Italian word novella for this neglected but highly important and eminently readable literary form.

In the next few years *STORY* would publish some forty novellas (by, among others, Howard Fast, Albert Maltz, Eric Knight, Ellis St. Joseph, Brewster Ghiselin, Robert Ayre, Max White, and

---

* In his first column Gregory reviewed *Green Margins* by E. P. O'Donnell, *Catalogue* by George Milburn, *Brief Kingdom* by Gerald Breckenridge, and *Divide the Desolation* by Kathryn Jean MacFarlane.

Helen Hull), and in 1938 the Story Press would publish a collection of five novellas, *The Flying Yorkshireman,* with "A Note on Novellas," by Whit and Martha.

Many of these short and long storywriters were then well known. Others (e.g., Alan Marshall, Lewis Carliner, A.I. Bezzerides, Martha Dodd, Edward Luchen McDaniel) were special favorites of the editors—discoveries they believed deserved and would get the audience and recognition attained by other *STORY* discoveries. To read through *STORY* during these years, then, is not only to remind ourselves of the great hope and excitement that writers, readers, magazine editors, and book publishers felt about fiction and new fiction writers—but about what time has done to this hope and excitement. It also shows what time has done to the work and reputations of many of these writers.*

During these years Martha and Whit were living in Croton-on-Hudson, and in their "End Pages" columns they often wrote about their family life there. In November 1936, Martha wrote her first signed column ("The regular End Pager being away in his native Mormon haunts of Salt Lake City, a humble substitute must take his place with all due apologies to his readers"), and in this column she reminisced freely about her career as a newspaperwoman—material that she would draw upon when writing her memoir forty years later.

---

* In the very first best-seller list *STORY* ran, in November 1935, the number one fiction best seller is *Vein of Iron* by Ellen Glasgow. Other authors in the top ten, in order: H.L. Davis, Temple Bailey, Hugh Walpole, Robert Briffault, Francis Brett Young, Warwick Deeping, MacKinlay Kantor, William McFee, and Willa Cather. The number one nonfiction best seller was Anne Lindberg's *North to the Orient.* And in the "Survey of Reviews," one finds, for example, Malcolm Cowley—later Faulkner's rediscoverer, writing in *The New Republic* of *Absalom, Absalom:,* "too often it seems that Faulkner, in the process of evoking an emotion in himself, has ignored the equally important task of evoking it in the reader." Clifton Fadiman, in *The New Yorker,* goes further, declaring the book "the most consistently boring novel by a reputable writer to come my way during the last decade. . . . It seems to point to the final blowup, of what was once a remarkable, if minor, talent."

I went to work on the *Journal* copy desk that evening. It was not a very busy night and about ten o'clock there was a lull in the amount of copy coming across. A blond young man around on the other side of the desk looked at me and I looked back at him. The *Smart Set,* then edited by Mencken and Nathan, was mentioned. He wrote short stories for it. I told him what I thought of Mencken. He told me what he thought of Mencken. We didn't agree about Mencken at all. We argued. And we've been arguing ever since, only we don't know any more whether it is a family argument or an editorial conference. The blond young man was Whit Burnett, your errant End Pager.

A few issues before, in his regular column, Whit had told once again the story he'd recounted in the very first issue of *STORY* —of the evening he spent with Frank Harris during Harris's last days in Nice:

Until the last, Mr. Harris kept a ruddy interest in the flesh, as well as the spirit. He was an Irishman and a Westerner. He insisted, when I marveled at his long life and hearty appetite, that I feel the biceps of his good right arm.
"Just like steel," he said.
"Just like steel," I said.
"I can eat anything," said Mr. Harris. "At 70-odd, too."
There was roast duck and *pommes soufflés,* Chablis with the *hors-d'oeuvres* and a good solid Chateauneuf du Pape with the duck. Afterward there were ices and coffee, and then armagnac and cognac. I think Frank took Calvados, which is stronger and more decisive as a drink than any apogee of applejack. It is a lovely, clearing drink. It is the white-heat poker of the spirits.
"Do you know how I do it?" asked Mr. Harris.
I confessed I did not.
"Every night," said Mr. Harris, "at ten o'clock, I take an enema."

* * *

The new features—letters, essays, best-seller lists, reviews—continued, for the most part, to appear regularly in the magazine for the rest of the decade, but from 1936 until Martha's leave-taking in 1941, the magazine initiated few other innovations, and most of them (for example, photo-essays and poetry) were quickly discontinued. In 1937 they began a series of adaptations of Broadway plays, with Margaret Mayorga's adaptation of Maxwell Anderson's *The Star Wagon.* "We believe," STORY announced, "that this effort to select from Broadway the most distinguished creative works each month will not only appeal to New Yorkers, who have the opportunity to see the plays and will like to refresh their memories on some of the wittier lines, but . . . it will have a major interest for all those drama-starved intelligent persons living remote from Broadway to whom a Broadway play never comes until it goes on the road or into the movies." But this project lasted for only three issues. (The other plays were Rachel Crothers's *Susan and God,* and Brian Doherty's *Father Malachy's Miracle.*)

The magazine devoted increasing space to antifascist essays and stories, as well as to a long anti-Franco poem by James Neugass ("Give Us This Day"), a poem that STORY reprinted and sold in a special forty-eight-page edition.* In May 1937, Martha wrote a column, "Emigrés All," about exiles from fascism —Thomas Mann, Ernst Toller, Ignazio Silone; and those fighting against fascism—Hemingway (who had "raised $40,000 on his personal notes to finance a fleet of Loyalist ambulances"), Ralph Bates, and André Malraux. She told of the first time Hemingway and Malraux met, at lunch in New York, and of an evening spent with Malraux:

---

* In January 1939, *STORY* published what was to be its most talked-about story, "Address Unknown," by Kressman Taylor [actually a husband and wife], a horrifying tale of Jews in Nazi Germany, abandoned by German and German-American friends. This story was reprinted as a separate book, by Simon and Schuster, and became, in its first week of publication, a national best seller.

A tense, vivid Frenchman, we met him the night he spoke at the New York dinner for *The Nation*'s Food Ship. In spite of the difficulty of having his speech broken up in paragraph-by-paragraph translation for him, a hard job which was valiantly performed by John Gunther, Malraux gave an excellent talk. With Malraux, John and Frances Gunther, Max Lerner and Anita Marburg, Louis Fischer, Malcolm Cowley and several others, we went after the dinner to the apartment of Clifton and Polly Fadiman where Malraux told more of his war experiences. He commands an *esquadrille* of Loyalist planes and once his plane bearing Malraux's own insignia was borrowed by another flier.

"This man was brought down," related Malraux. "He was killed in the crash. The rebels took his body, put it in a coffin and dropped it over Madrid. With it, they dropped a message, 'Here is your Malraux for you!'"

The magazine's college story contest continued through these years, as did the Story Press (which, in 1939, switched its association from Harper's to Lippincott), with books by Jerome Frank, Gladyss Schmitt, Whit *(The Literary Life and the Hell with It)*, Winthrop Sergeant, Mary Medearis, and best sellers by Frances Eisenberg *(There's One in Every Family)* and Mary O'Hara *(My Friend Flicka)*. But during these years, notice of the Story Service Bureau disappeared from the magazine's pages; the magazine returned (without explanation) in July 1938 to a bimonthly; there were—especially in 1938 and 1939—fewer essays by Whit and Martha, until, in 1940, there were none at all; and the magazine's circulation began to decline—to 17,000 in 1937 and 1938, and to 8,000 in 1940 and 1941.

In 1940 the magazine announced what was its only major new addition during these years—"Tonight's Best Story," a radio program broadcast on Tuesday evenings at 9:30 over New York station WHN. "This is the first attempt," Martha and Whit wrote, "to bring to radio listeners the same quality of vital literature that has made *STORY* the outstanding literary magazine of the day."

Rex Stout appeared in the opening show ("The Night Reveals," by Cornell Woolrich), and a few programs later Erskine Caldwell appeared to speak about Richard Wright's "Fire and Cloud." Other writers who had their stories adapted were Irwin Shaw ("God on Friday Night"), Kressman Taylor ("Address Unknown"), Eric Knight ("Sam's Little Tyke"), Saroyan ("Little Moral Tales"), Lord Dunsany, Seán O'Faoláin, Sherwood Anderson, and Martha ("What a Small World").

Though both the magazine's circulation and nonfictional "departures" declined during these years, the dedication to quality fiction by both new and established writers did not. During these years, *STORY* printed the first published stories of some of its most extraordinary finds: Richard Wright, twenty-one-year-old J.D. Salinger ("He is particularly interested in playwriting"),* Mary O'Hara, and Tennessee Williams.† The magazine's stories continued to be selected in large numbers for anthologies, especially for the annual *Best Stories* and the *O. Henry Memorial* volume, and it continued to publish the work—often the most original— of hundreds of new and established writers.‡

---

* In the same issue—March–April 1940—virtually all authors are under thirty years old.
† "I'm twenty-five, a native of Mississippi, descendant of Indian-fighting Tennessee pioneers," Williams wrote. "I've attended three universities, getting my B.A. degree last summer from the University of Iowa. While there, I worked as a waiter in the state hospital—waiting tables is my chief subsidiary occupation although I've also been employed in a shoe warehouse, office and retail store for short periods between my work at college. I've had two long plays presented in St. Louis by the Mummers of that city—they were 'Fugitive Kind' and 'Candles to the Sun.' I have two long plays in progress. Right now I'm doing chores and picking squabs for my board on a pigeon ranch in Los Angeles county and have just returned from a 440-mile bicycle tour of rural Mexico and the Southern California coast line. This spring I was given a Group Theatre prize for a one-act play."
‡ E.g., John Cheever ("He is at present at work on a novel"—this, twenty years before his first published novel), Alvah Bessie, Julia Davis, Paul Kunasz, Peggy Harding, Jesse Stuart, Saroyan, Roma Rose, Irwin Shaw, Liam O'Flaherty, V.G. Calderon. Meridel LeSeuer, Sherwood Anderson, Charles Angoff, Warren Beck, Erskine Caldwell, Guido D'Agostino, James T. Farrell, Emily Hahn, Dorothy McCleary, Edita Morris, Edde Tarjan, Constance Bestor, Stoyan Christowe, Robert Clurman, Steve Goodman, Hal Ellson, Louis L'Amour, William Negherbon,

The first issue of 1941—Martha's last year at *STORY*—contained stories by the Norwegian writer Eric Jens Peterson, Mary O'Hara, ("My Friend Flicka"), John Royston Morley, Anne Green, T.O. Beachcroft, Mary Medearis (college story contest winner), William Fifield, Eugene J. Hochman, Anne Brooks, R.H. Linn, and Irwin Shaw, and in the "Plus & Minus" section, among reviews of Hemingway's new novel, *For Whom the Bell Tolls,* we find Dorothy Parker saying "This is a book of all of us alive, of you and me and ours and those we hate," while Edmund Wilson remarks that "a master of the concentrated short story, Hemingway is less sure in his grasp of the form of the elaborated novel. . . . There is something missing that we still look for in Hemingway."

The next issue contained stories by old and new friends—Ellis St. Joseph, Frances Eisenberg, Warren Beck, Eric Knight, Nancy Wilson Ross, Joan Vatsek, and the first published stories of two new writers, James Ramsey Ullman ("Still Life") and Hallie Southgate Abbett ("Eighteenth Summer"), "one of the runners-up in *STORY*'s contest conducted among budding writers of the Junior League." Hallie would, in 1942, become the second Mrs. Whit Burnett, and she would from that year on, edit the magazine with Whit. (Her name first appears on the title page, as associate editor, in January 1944.)

The May-June issue of 1941 was the magazine's Tenth Anniversary Issue, and *STORY* observed the anniversary by reprinting "some of the most significant stories which have appeared in [its] pages since 1931." The editors reviewed the origins of *STORY,* as "a kind of proof-book of hitherto unpublished manuscripts"; they reviewed its successes, its history, its credo. "In ten years," Martha and Whit then wrote, "nearly a thousand short stories

---

Sean O'Faolain, James Pooler, Allan Seager, Charles Martin, Howard Melvin Fast, Angelica Gibbs, Travis Hoke, I.J. Kapstein, Manuel Komroff, Albert Maltz, Ted Olson, Katherine Anne Porter et al.

were published, hundreds of which have since been reprinted or anthologized elsewhere, a dozen of which are here presented, and if our readers differ with our choices, bear with us in our dilemma —it is no easy matter to select a dozen out of a thousand stories. The editors have chosen these stories not only for their literary quality but because in addition to being good stories they seem in one way or another, to illuminate the years in which they were published."

They noted that, for space reasons, they had chosen no novellas, and that they had originally picked forty-three "musts." The stories they finally chose—the stories that they believed were "almost a literary history of their time"—were:

"One with Shakespeare"by Martha Foley
"Rest Cure"by Kay Boyle
"A Day in the Country"by Whit Burnett
"Missis Flinders"by Tess Slesinger
"Death and Transfiguration"by Alan Marshall
"Winter"by Dorothy McCleary
"The Daring Young Man
on the Flying Trapeze"by William Saroyan
"The Captive"by Luigi Pirandello
"Solo on the Cornet"by Dean Fales
"Sacré du Printemps"by Ludwig Bemelmans
"Address Unknown"by Kressman Taylor
"The Old General"by Eric Knight

The issue was dedicated to two men who had died in the early months of 1941—Sherwood Anderson and Edward J. O'Brien. In the notes accompanying the stories we learn that Martha's had already been anthologized thirty-seven times; that "Rest Cure" was based upon Kay Boyle's meeting with D.H. Lawrence, and that, appearing in *STORY*'s first issue in 1931, it "struck a new note, not at all like the writing of the 'Twenties"; that "Missis

Flinders" was "the first forthright abortion story of literary stature ever to appear in an American magazine"; that "The Captive" was printed even though the author had won the Nobel Prize (which "has never been held against him"); that "Solo on the Cornet" was "the final word on the small town band and the wish of every American youth at one time or another to be a silver-tongued cornet player"; that Ludwig Bemelmans was "the only literary man who can so apportion his life as to write with one hand and paint with the other"; and that "The Old General" was "the single, new contribution" to the issue.

There remained two more issues of *STORY* for which Martha served as editor. The first, in July-August, contained stories by Fifield, Angoff, Neagoe, Flann O'Brien ("Flann O'Brien is a discovery of William Saroyan's, but further than that, at this moment, we know nothing except that he is not William Saroyan"), Robert Markewich, Sylvia Thompson, Virginia Moore, and James Ramsey Ullman. The second, and last, in September-October, was "a departure from the magazine's ten-year policy of exclusive devotion to the creative short story." It was an issue dedicated to Sherwood Anderson, "the greatest contemporary short story writer." The idea of the special issue originated with Paul Rosenfeld and Waldo Frank, and, in addition to selections from Anderson's work, contained contributions from Steiglitz, Dreiser, Gertrude Stein, Thomas Wolfe, Henry Miller, Saroyan, Jesse Stuart, Kenneth Patchen, Ben Hecht, Manuel Komroff, and others. "In the field of the short story," Martha and Whit wrote, "Sherwood Anderson set out on new paths at a time when the American short story seemed doomed to a formula-ridden, conventionalized, mechanized and commercialized concept. When *Winesburg, Ohio,* appeared in 1919 it was intensely influential on writers who either had lost heart or had not yet found their way. His vision was his own; his characters were people into whose hearts and minds he seemed intuitively to peer; and his prose was simple, deceptively simple, sensuous, rich and evocative."

And then, on page one of the November–December, 1941 issue, appeared the following, signed by Whit Burnett and Kurt Semon:

TO OUR READERS

With this issue, the name of Martha Foley disappears from the editorial title page of *STORY.* Miss Foley is on a leave of absence in order that she may edit the Edward J. O'Brien Memorial Anthology, *The Best Short Stories.*

They wrote of their desire to help continue O'Brien's "great and pioneering tradition" by relinquishing Martha, and they noted that having been co-founder and co-editor of *STORY* for ten years, "her experience during that period of reading and editing innumerable thousands of short-story manuscripts well equips her for her new task."

But the brief twenty-one-line announcement seemed—given all that had passed—strangely impersonal, amazingly cold and dry. "After ten years of daily association," it concluded, "it would be impossible in a few brief words here to express our gratitude for and appreciation of Miss Foley's work on *STORY.* We greatly regret her loss to the magazine and its readers, but we join with them in wishing her the very best in her new undertaking."

The *STORY* decade was over.

In the same issue in which Martha's departure was announced was printed the winner of *STORY*'s eighth nationwide college contest, "Greatest Thing in the World." It was written by an eighteen-year-old Harvard student ("probably one of *STORY*'s youngest contributors"), Norman K. Mailer. On how he had felt about appearing in *STORY,* Mailer later wrote, in *Advertisements for Myself,* that "probably nothing has happened in the years I've been writing which changed my life as much. The far-away, all-powerful and fabulous world of New York publishing—which, of course, I saw through Thomas Wolfe's eyes—had said 'yes' to me."*

"In those days," Mailer has written more recently, "for a young writer to be published in STORY was enough to give you the beginnings of a real inner certainty that perhaps you were meant to be a writer. Obviously it was one of the most important experiences of my life up to then."

STORY continued to give the kind of encouragement it gave to young writers such as Mailer, if intermittently, until 1964, and numbered among its "discoveries," after Martha's departure, Truman Capote, John Knowles, and Joseph Heller. Whit and Hallie edited it as a bimonthly until the summer of 1948, when it became, very briefly, a quarterly. It suspended publication from 1948 until 1951, when it reappeared for a while in book form *(STORY: The Magazine of the Short Story in Book Form)*† under Whit and Hallie's editorship, every six months. It ceased publication, again, through most of the fifties, and reappeared in 1960, under the partial sponsorship of the University of Missouri. "The editors," Whit wrote, "believe that there is even more demand now for a magazine of distinguished and readable short stories than there was when *STORY* first began nearly thirty years ago. . . . The short story is the most characteristic and durable fiction form

---

* "All the same," Mailer went on, "I'm embarrassed to read the story today. Crude, derivative of the kind of writing which was done in the thirties, I think it stands up only in its sense of pace which is quick and nice. Perhaps that is why it won—pace is found rarely in college writers. But how little real dedication it has! At eighteen Capote was already doing work which was beautiful, whereas 'The Greatest Thing in the World' reads like the early work of a young man who is going to make a fortune writing first-rate action, western, gangster, and suspense pictures."

Cf. Erskine Caldwell's statement about how "very pleased" he was "that Whit and Martha wanted to publish my early stories," for "publication of early work is what a writer needs most of all in life. By putting me into print when the commercial magazines and book publishers took no notice of what I was trying to do—they gave me the confidence to keep going in my own way instead of trying to write what editors want.' "

† published by the Story Press and A.A. Wyn, Inc.

America has produced. In the short story most writers of books first try their wings. Having seen contemporary writers through three decades, *STORY* enters the sixties confident there are many new writers of power and talent yet to be heard from. And to these as well as to all skilled and meaningful writers of our day, it opens its pages."

The belief and hope remained the same, but the times were different. *STORY* suspended publication again—for good—three and a half years (and twelve issues) later, in early 1964.* After *STORY*'s death, Whit, often with Hallie's collaboration, continued, as he had been doing, to put together many anthologies —*This Is My Best* ("self-chosen masterpieces of America's greatest living authors"), *The Seas of God* ("Great Stories of the Human Spirit"), *STORY: The Fiction of the 'Forties, Time to be Young, The Spirit of Man* ("great stories and experiences of spiritual crisis, inspiration and the joy of life"), *Two Bottles of Relish, A Pocket Story Book, The Modern Short Story in the Making, Firsts of the Famous, Sextet: 6 Story Discoveries in Novella Form, Black Hands on White Face,* and *Story Jubilee: Thirty-Three Years of STORY.* Whit died, at the age of seventy-four, on April 22, 1973.

When Martha left *STORY* (and Whit) in 1941 to assume the editorship of the annual *Best American Short Stories* anthology for Houghton Mifflin (Edward J. O'Brien was killed on February 24, 1941, during the blitz of London), the great period of her life was over. In the foreword to the 1941 anthology, she wrote of O'-Brien, "There was a moving humility in the way he set aside his own ambitions as a writer, denied his own great talent, to search

---

* By this time it was being partly sponsored by the University of Cincinnati, and, for its college prize, by the Readers Digest Foundation. In addition to Whit and Hallie, Richard Wathen was associate editor, William Peden was contributing editor, and Morley Callaghan, Allan Seager, and Allan Swallow were regional associates. J.D. Salinger tried to sponsor it also—by sending $200 of his own money to be used by *STORY* "for the encouragement of new writers"; he wanted the money applied to *STORY*'s college contest.

for, discover, and pay tribute for twenty-seven years to the achievements of others."

She might have said the same of herself. "For twenty-seven years," she wrote, "Mr. O'Brien dedicated himself to a unique task. From the transient pages of magazines he gathered short stories of literary value and gave them permanent publication in book form." To this task, for the remaining thirty-seven years of her life, Martha dedicated her labors. During some years, while simultaneously teaching (she taught for more than twenty years at Columbia University), lecturing, raising a child, editing three special *Best Stories* anthologies,* writing articles, and working on other projects (her memoirs, a textbook on the craft of writing, doomed attempts at a novel and short stories, a collection of novellas), she would read more than 8,000 short stories. Martha continued, despite *STORY*'s decline, to honor it in her forewords, and to choose stories from it (six in 1941, five in 1942, three in 1943). She also, through all her years as editor of this anthology, continued to make the two basic distinctions she had made when she'd edited *STORY:* between the new writer and the established writer, and between the large circulation magazines and the "little" magazines. "My own approach to the selection of the stories in this volume," she wrote in the foreword to the 1942 *Best Stories,* the first anthology that was completely her own, "has been to follow as closely as possible what O'Brien himself sought: literary distinction, integrity on the part of the author and a freedom from hampering, artificial restrictions." She found, in that year, "that the most exciting, if not always most finished, story writing was to be found in the small, regional magazines. It is here that new writers grope their way and, while their writing is often uncertain it is always freshly stimulating."

"All that any editor can say today is," she wrote—a statement

---

* *The Best of the Best: Short Stories 1915–1950, Fifty Best American Short Stories, 1915–1950,* and *200 Years of Great American Short Stories.*

she repeated thirty-five years later to a graduate writing class of mine, " 'These are the stories I myself liked best. I hope you will agree.' "

As O'Brien had, she dedicated most of the annual volumes to one of its authors (she refused, when asked, to autograph copies of the *Best Stories;* "Why should I?" she would state. "I wasn't the author!"), and in her introductions, she often noted trends, some that she lamented (for example, the deaths of magazines such as *STORY, The Kenyon Review, Collier's, The American Mercury, Tomorrow*) and the fact that the little magazines began to devote more space to critical articles—"It is much easier to be critical than creative," she wrote), and some that she praised (e.g., the advent of *New American Review* and *Antaeus,* the seeming death of certain kinds of formula stories in the slicks); she reminisced about her childhood, her own literary life (once, in 1968, with apologies to Edmund Wilson, in a witty and revealing self-interview), and often commented on the history of the American short story. From 1958 to 1971, her son David was listed as co-editor. He died in 1971. The last volume that Martha edited, in 1977, was dedicated "to the memory of Rex Stout." Her foreword began: "The most important literary event in the United States of America in the past year was not the writing of a great poem, story, play, essay, or history. It was writing of an entirely different kind but one that protects literary works and their authors. It was the legal wording of this country's first real copyright law. . . ."

She traced the history of copyright law in America, recalled the origin of *STORY* in Vienna, praised Stout for his lifelong labors on behalf of the copyright law (and, in passing, retold the story of the origin of his Nero Wolfe character), noted that during the past year "good humorous stories have been few and far between," urged editors of new magazines to send copies to her, and, as she always did, paid tribute to the memory of Edward J. O'Brien, who had founded the anthology in 1915.

To the end, then, she was the discoverer, nurturer, and protector of writers—and the lover of good stories. "In reading the innumerable stories published in our magazines throughout the year," she wrote in 1947, "I am in quest of literary adventure. When I feel that I have had an adventure in reading a story, when I think reading it has been a memorable experience, I hope that the readers of this volume also will find it memorable."

The full story of *STORY*, and of the annual *Best Stories*—of their significance, and of their influence on the American short story and on our literary history—remains to be told. Martha Foley—its staunchest advocate for almost fifty years—died at the age of eighty, in 1977. At the time of her death she was living in a small furnished apartment. She was in financial difficulties (she earned about $6,000 a year from the *Best Stories*). She was in constant pain, and she was still grieving over the loss of her husband and her son. Nonetheless, to her few friends, she was always cheerful, always full of wonderful stories, and she remained, to the day of her death, hard at work—reading stories, writing about them, and hoping to get through with her memoir, and on to the phantom novels that lay beyond.

For ten years of her life she had edited, with her husband, a magazine the like of which we shall never see again. For half a century—with extraordinary dedication, remarkable judgment, and a naïve and passionate singlemindedness that seems, in retrospect, almost childlike—she had devoted herself to what she loved most: to good short stories and to their writers. Rarely, if ever, had they had such a friend.

Index

Ballet mécanique (Antheil), 81n, 142
Bankhead, Tallulah, 183
Banks, Russell, 16
Barber, Will, 77
Bard, Josef, 212, 215
Barnaby Rudge (Dickens), 124–25
Barnes, Djuna, 114, 188n
Barnes, Eleanor, 42
baroque architecture, 93
"Bartleby the Scrivner" (Melville), 142n
Bates, H. E., 11, 141n, 180, 245, 247, 252, 260
Bates, Ralph, 11, 263
Baum, Frank, 38
Baum, Vicki, 232
Beach, Sylvia, 51, 63–64, 68–69, 131
Beachcroft, T. O., 266
Beauvoir, Simone de, 209
Beck, Warren, 11, 265n, 266
Becker, Stephen, 16
Beckett, Samuel, 114
Beggar's Opera (Gay), 235
Bein, Issac, 11
Being Geniuses Together (McAlmon), 188n
Bellow, Saul, 15–16, 23
Bemelmans, Ludwig, 8, 21, 259, 267
Beneš, Eduard, 95
Benét, Stephen Vincent, 141
Bennett, Hal, 16
Bennett, James Gordon, 67
Berlin Diary (Shirer), 106
Bessie, Alvah, 11, 414n, 247, 260, 265n
Best, Bob, 88–90, 107, 118, 158
Best American Short Stories, 7–8, 14–21, 23, 97–98, 100, 116, 117n, 131, 133, 151, 197, 204n, 211, 218, 237, 242, 249, 265, 271–72, 274
Best of the Best Short Stories 1915–1950, The, 15, 272n
Best British Short Stories, The, 105, 133, 249
Bestor, Constance, 265n
best-seller list, 10, 259n, 261n
Bezzerides, A. I., 14, 259, 261
Bialt, Elisa, 14
Big Man (Neugeboren), 20
Birchall, Gene, 71
Bird, William, 80, 122, 160–62, 188
Bisch, Louis, 216
Bishop, John Peale, 247
Bismarck, the Iron Chancellor, 91
Black Hands on White Face, 271
Black Heart, White Hunter (Viertel), 240
"Black Jesus" (Cowles), 245
black market, 166
Bleak House (Dickens), 117, 199

"Blessed Event in Vienna" (Foley), 156n
Bliven, Bruce, 154
Boas, Frank, 211
Bogan, Louise, 32, 165
Bolte, Mary, 218
Boni and Liveright, 40
Book-of-the Month Club, 198, 245n, 257, 259
Borland, Hal, 11, 260
Boston Herald, 35, 53
Boston Socialist party, 200–201
Boston Transcript, 35, 100
Bowles, Paul, 114
Boyle, Kay, 11, 23, 114, 130, 135, 141n, 188n, 245, 248, 252, 267
Brace, Ernest, 260
Bradbury, Ray, 15, 21–22
Branstetter, Otto, 36
Bread and Wine (Silone), 10, 257, 259
Brecht, Berthold, 226, 234–36
Breckenridge, Gerald, 260n
Breton, André, 71
"Bridge, The" (Crane), 66
Brief Kingdom (Breckenridge), 260
Briffault, Robert, 261n
Brisbane, Arthur, 56, 60
Britain, and Germany, 149–50
British Hawthornden Prize, 100
Britt, George, 90n
Brockway, George, 23
Brontë, Anne, 149
Brontë, Charlotte, 29, 149
Brontë, Emily, 29, 149
Brookhauser, Frank, 14
Brooklyn Eagle, 252
Brooks, Anne, 266
Brooks, Van Wyck, 10, 256
Broom, 211
Broun, Heywood, 90n, 219–20
Broun, Heywood, Jr. 219–20
Brown publishers, 258
Buchanan, George, 55
Buck, Pearl, 216
"Building of the Ship" (Longfellow), 205
Bullitt, William, 86, 111
Bunin, Ivan, 11, 248–49, 252
Burger, Dr., 152–54
Burke, Kenneth, 188n
Burke, Thomas, 228
Burnett, David, 12, 17–18, 20, 27, 154–55, 158, 166, 172–73, 176–80, 185–86, 191–93, 196–97, 206, 218–20, 225, 227, 230–31, 236–37, 242–43, 254, 273

Burnett, Hallie (Hallie Southgate Abbett), 266, 270–71
Burnett, Whit, 8–10, 12, 64, 82–83, 89, 92, 102, 115–22, 134–35, 143, 147–48, 152–54, 158–61, 164, 168, 170, 172, 190–93, 197, 206, 243–44, 266, 271
  and marriage to Martha, 136–38
  as newspaperman, 44–46, 50–51, 54, 63, 66–67
  and *STORY*, 128–29, 132–33, 174–75, 178–82, 202–3, 244–46, 248n, 253–54, 256–57, 261–62, 266–67, 270–71
  as a writer, 61–62, 72–74, 80, 99, 114, 116, 129–30, 141n, 162, 220–21, 264, 267
Burns, Robert, 105
Burrows, Dudley, 38
Burt, Maxwell Struthers, 14
Busch, Fred, 16
Butler, Frank, 16
Butler, Samuel, 148
Byrne, Donn, 14

Caballero, Gimenez, 141n
Caesar, Julius, 168
Calderon, V. G., 11, 265n
Caldwell, Erskine, 8, 21–23, 114, 141, 162, 180, 204–6, 245, 247, 252, 259, 265, 270n
Callaghan, Morley, 11, 260, 271n
Calmer, Edgar, 114
Camelots du Roi, 77–78
"Candles to the Sun" (Williams), 265n
Canfield, Cass, 103–4
Canfield, Dorothy, 254n
Cape, Jonathan, 246
Capote, Truman, 206, 270
"Captive, The" (Pirandello), 267–68
Carliner, Lewis, 14, 259, 261
Carroll, Lewis, 31
Carter, John Stewart, 16
Carver, Raymond, 16
"Casual Incident, A" (Farrell), 139, 140n
Catalogues (Milburn), 260n
"Catastrophe" (Musil), 134
Cather, Willa, 141, 254n, 261n
Céline, Louis-Ferdinand, 213
Century, 41, 100
Cerf, Bennett, 106, 198–201, 221, 245
Cervantes, Saavedra de, 191
Champska, Maria, 224
Chaplin, Charlie, 21, 64, 227–30
Chaplin, Oona, 229
Chaucer, Geoffrey, 119

Cheever, John, 8, 23, 210–11, 259, 265n
Chekhov, Anton, 9, 11, 73, 260
"Chekhov's Middle Years" (Toumanova), 256
Chicago Daily News, 102, 167–68
Chicago Tribune, 62, 71, 106, 190, 192
child labor law, 52–53
Childs, Marquis W., 247
Chopin, Frédéric, 183–84
Christian Socialist party, 87–88, 115, 123
Christians Only (Britt & Broun), 90n
Christowe, Stoyan, 11, 265n
Churchill, Douglas, 42
Clurman, Robert, 265n
Coates, Robert, 114
Cole, Madeline, 260
Coleridge, Samuel Taylor, 133
Colette, 184
College Humor, 209
College Short Story Contest, 10, 248, 253, 269, 271n
Collier's Magazine 11, 41, 119, 141, 273
Comfort, Will Levington, 14
Commentary, 12
communism, 74, 77, 95, 140n
"Confessions of an English Opium Eater" (DeQuincy), 89
Connell, Evan S., Jr., 16
Conrad, Joseph, 9
Conroy, Jack, 141
Consolidated Press, 80, 101, 122, 167–68, 188
Contact, 188
"Convalescence" (Boyle), 245
Coons, Carleton, 11
Coover, Robert, 15
Coppard, A. E., 11, 246
copyright law, 21, 85n, 273
Cosmopolitan, 141
Covici, Pat, 170
Covici-Friede, 170, 247
Cowles, John, 141n, 245
Cowley, Malcolm, 47, 261n, 264
Crane, Hart, 21, 65–66, 74, 148
Crawford, Cappy, 43
"Crime of Pessimism, The" (Balint), 130
Cronin, Bob, 49
Cronyn, George, 247
Crothers, Rachel, 14
Crown Prince Carol, 101, 107
Crown Prince Rudolph, 153
Czechoslovakia, 84, 95

D'Agostino, Guido, 265n
Dahlberg, Bror, 184

Index

Dahlberg, Mary, 184
Daily Mirror, The, 54–56, 58–63
Dance of the Machine (O'Brien), 148
Dangling Man (Bellow), 16
"Daring Young Man on the Flying Trapeze, The" (Saroyan), 267
"Dark Victory" (Dratler), 135
Darwin, Charles, 157
Davies, Marion, 55
Davis, H. L., 261
Davis, Julia, 14, 265n
Day, Clarence, 254n
"Day in the Country, A" (Burnett), 130, 133, 267
Deasy, Mary, 16
Death in the Afternoon (Hemingway), 189n
"Death and Transfiguration" (Marshall), 246, 267
Death in Venice (Mann), 134, 234
Debs, Eugene V., 36–37, 213–14
Decameron, 119
de la Mare, Walter, 252
Decline of the West, The (Spengler), 228
Decsey, Ernst, 130, 141n
Deeping, Warwick, 261n
Defense of Women, In (Mencken), 44
de Gaulle, General Charles, 70
Dehn, Adolph, 128
Dehn, Olivia, 128
depression, 12–13, 161, 171
    see also Great Depression
De Quincey, Thomas, 89
De Vries, Peter, 8, 13, 13n, 259
De Voto, Bernard, 254
Dickens, Charles, 29, 31, 41, 57, 117, 124–25, 195, 254n
Dietrich, Marlene, 134
Divide the Desolation (MacFarlane), 260n
Dodd, Martha, 247, 261
Dodd, Mead, 257–58
Doherty, Brian, 263
Dollfuss, Chancellor, 115
Donaldson, Don, 77
Donath, Ludwig, 224
Donath, Maria, 235
Donato, Pietro di, 141
Donoghue, Mort, 39–40, 42
Doolittle, Hilda, 187, 188n
Doran and Company, 253
Dorothy and Red (Sheean), 213, 215
Dostoyevsky, Fëdor, 250
Doubleday, 253
Douglas, Norman, 188n
Dratler, Jay, 232–33

Dreiser, Theodore, 57, 203, 217–18, 268
Dreiser Looks at Russia (Dreiser), 217–18
Ducks in Thunder (Dratler), 233
Duke of Windsor, 149–50
Duncan, Isadora, 81n
Dunsany, Lord, 260, 265
Duranty, Walter, 214–15
Dwyer, James Francis, 14

Eastlake, William, 16
Eastman, Max, 81n
economic determinism, 162
Education of Henry Adams, The (Adams), 162–63
Edward VIII, King, 149–50
"Eighteenth Summer" (Abbett), 266
"Eine Kliene Nacht" (DeVries), 13
Eisenberg, Francis, 14, 264, 266
election of 1920, 36
Eliot, George, 29
Eliot, T. S., 148
Elizabethans, 86
Elkin, Stanley, 15
Ellerman, Sir John, 187
Ellerman, Winifred, 187
Ellis, Havelock, 188n
Ellman, Richard, 187
Ellson, Hall, 265n
Emmanuel, King Victor, 149
"End of the Depression" (Bolte), 218
Enquirer, 259n
Epstein, Leslie, 16
equal rights, 52–53
Ernst, Morris, 207
Esquire, 11
Euripides, 32

Fabricant, Noah, 109, 141n
Fadiman, Clifton, 261n, 264
Fadiman, Polly, 264
Fales, Dean, 267
Fallon, Padraic, 11
"Family Vitriol" (Zoshchenko), 245
Fante, John, 141n, 245
Farrell, James T., 8, 139–40, 141n, 150, 162, 180, 259, 265n
fascism, 69, 87, 115, 149, 192, 228, 248, 263
"Fascism" (Shaw), 256
Fast, Howard, 11, 141, 266n
Father Malachy's Miracle (Doherty), 263
Faulkner, William, 11, 13n, 23, 141, 232–34, 246–47, 249, 261n
Fearing, Kenneth, 114
Fellowship of Reconciliation, 91

fiction
editors, 9–11, 203, 204n, 209, 237, 242, 256–58, 266–67
experimental, 112–13
publishing, 9–11, 41, 100, 257–58
see also STORY
Fiction magazine, 19n
Field, Marshall, 42–43
Fifield, William, 266, 268
Fifty Best American Short Stories, 1915–1965, 15, 272
film criticism, 10
Finnegan's Wake (Joyce), 51, 72
"Fire and Cloud" (Wright), 257, 265
Firsts of the Famous, 271
Fischer, Louis, 264
Fisher, Dorothy Canfield, 11
Fisher, Vardis, 16, 141
"Fisherman's Bride" (O'Neill), 245
Fitzgerald, F. Scott, 41, 141
Fleet Publishing Company, 271n
Flying Yorkshireman, The, 261
Fodor, M. W., 87–88, 95, 107–8, 118, 125, 160–61, 212, 223
Fodor, Martha, 88, 223
"Fog" (Jones), 135
Foley, Francis, 17
Foley, Martha, 79, 82, 92, 106n, 107, 111, 119–20, 147–48, 168, 170, 172, 191, 193, 206, 208, 253
as caption writer, 47–49, 53–54, 58
and childhood, 1–31, 02, 01, 273
as copy editor, 35, 43–44
death of, 7–8, 15, 17, 22, 274
as editor of *Best Stories,* 204n, 237, 242, 272–73
as editor of *STORY,* 8, 18–19, 21, 119–23, 127–38, 163, 174–75, 178–81, 196, 202–11, 242, 244, 253–54, 256–57, 266–74
as foreign correspondent, 65, 101
and marriage to Whit, 136–38
memoirs, 12, 14, 17, 22–24, 242
and motherhood, 152, 154–55, 158, 166, 172–73, 176–80, 185–86, 191–92
as newspaperwoman, 35–46, 53–55, 64–68, 70, 86, 97, 155, 196, 261
and politics, 32–33, 52–53, 91
as sports editor, 49, 54
as a teacher, 61, 240, 272
on women's rights, 21, 32–34, 52–53, 161
as a writer, 17, 22–23, 27, 80, 100, 111, 130, 133, 135, 141n, 163–65, 245, 264, 267, 273

Fool of Venus, The (Cronyn), 247
Ford, Ford Madox, 41, 71, 188n
Forum, 41, 99
For Whom the Bell Tolls (Hemingway), 266
Four Saints in Three Acts (Stein), 69
Four Winds Press, 271n
France, German occupation of, 69
Francis, H. E., 16
Franco, General Francisco, 74, 173, 193, 254
Frank, Anne, 69
Frank, Waldo, 141, 268
Frankfurter Zeitung, 255
Franz Joseph, Emperor, 153
French gothic architecture, 93
French Prix Femina, 100
french surrealists, 71–72, 74
Freud, Sigmund, 82, 104, 111
Friede, Ann, 168–70, 172
Friede, Donald, 142, 168–70, 172–73, 176, 193, 195
Frost, Robert, 254
Fuchs, Daniel, 249
"Fugitive Kind" (Williams), 265n

Gallico, Paul, 49, 54, 101
Gallic Wars (Caesar), 168
Galsworthy, John, 254
Gannett, Lewis, 197–98, 253, 257
Garbo, Greta, 21, 226–27, 230–31, 239, 241
Gass, W. H., 15
Gay, John, 135
Gentlemen's Agreement (Hobson), 142
Germany, 106–7, 150, 193, 223
American investing in, 65
and Anschluss with Austria, 90–91, 100, 123, 128n
and Britain, 149–50
and Treaty of Saint Germain, 90–91
Gerrish, Miss, 164–65
Gesta Romanorum, 119
Ghiselin, Brewster, 260
Gibbs, Angelica, 14, 266n
Gide, André, 205
Gilbert, John, 231
Gilbert and Sullivan, 107
"Give Us This Day" (Neugass), 263
Glasgow, Ellen, 141, 254n, 261n
Glaspell, Susan, 141
Glendale Evening News, 37
Goddard, Robert H., 157–58
"God on Friday Night" (Shaw), 265
God's Little Acre (Caldwell), 162, 205
Goebbels, Joseph, 224

Index

Goethe, Johann Wolfgang, 91
Gogarty, Oliver St. John, 147n–48n
Gold, Michael, 53, 141
Golem, The (Meyrinck), 85n
"Good-by New York" (Woolrich), 210
Goodman, Steve, 265n
"Good Man is Hard to Find, A" (O'Connor), 115
Gordon, Caroline, 141
Gossman, Heddy, 104–6
Gossman, Oliver, 11, 105, 122, 130, 133, 135, 141n, 260
Gotham Book Mart, 205
Grand Hotel (Baum), 232
Graves, Robert, 185
Great Depression, 63, 128, 140n, 166, 207, 218
"Greatest Thing in the World, The" (Mailer), 269, 270n
"Great Wheel, The" (Decsey), 130
Greek history, 69n–70n, 113, 148
Greek mythology, 113, 194
Green, Ann, 266
Greene, Graham, 11, 259
Green Margins (O'Donnell), 260n
Greenspan, Magistrate, 205
Gregg, Thomas, 14
Gregory, Horace, 260
Grey, Zane, 30
Griffith, D. W., 228
Guest, Edgar, 66
Gunther, Frances, 102–6, 116
Gunther, John, 11, 101–6, 120–21, 125, 137, 154, 158, 164, 167–68, 213–14, 264

Haardt, Sara, 203
Hahn, Emily, 8, 259, 265n
Hairy Ape, The, 248
Hale, William Harlan, 260
Hall, Elizabeth, 14, 259
Hall, Reverend Doctor, 56–59
Hall-Mills case, 56–59
Hamlet (Shakespeare), 205
"Hamlet's Dagger" (Komroff), 245
Hapsburg empire, 94, 108
Harding, Peggy, 265n
Hard Times (Dickens), 41
Hardwick, Elizabeth, 16
Hardy, Thomas, 29
Harper & Brothers, 10, 103, 256
Harper's Magazine 10–11, 41, 97n, 99–100, 246n, 252n, 258, 264
Harris, Frank, 130, 254, 262
Hartley, Marsden, 188n

Hartman, Joyce, 20
Harvey Swados Memorial Prize, 21
Hassell, Harriett, 14
Hasty Bunch, A (McAlmon), 187
Hawkins, Eric, 66
Hawthorne, Nathaniel, 57, 148
Haynes, Camille, 73
Hays, Arthur Garfield, 169
Hearst, William Randolph, 54–56, 59–60, 80
Hecht, Ben, 14, 268
Heller, Joseph, 270
Hemingway, Ernest, 21, 69, 80, 81n, 114, 116n–17n, 122, 141, 146–48, 165–66, 188n–89n, 208–9, 254, 263, 266
Hemingway, Hadley, 116n, 166
Henly, Linda, 246
Herald (San Francisco), 42
Herbst, Josephine, 114
"Herr Qualla" (Burnett), 129–30
Hertel, Elsa, 14
Hillman, William, 80
Hills, Lawrence, 67
Hitler, Adolph, 64–65, 87, 91, 94, 106–7, 123–24, 149, 193, 212–14, 216, 223, 228, 247–48
Hobson, Laura, 142
Hobson, Thayer, 142
Hochman, Eugene J., 266
Hoffenstein, Samuel, 239
Hoke, Travis, 266n
Hollinek, Herr, 128–29
Hollywood screenwriters, 232–34, 238
Hollywood Reporter, The, 43
Holocaust, 241
"Homage to Shakespeare" (Cheever), 210
Hoover Relief Commission, 212
Horthy, Admiral, 94–95
Houghton Mifflin, 15, 19–20, 34, 98n, 257, 271
Hound and the Horn, The, 11
Howard, Maureen, 16
How Like a God (Stout), 79
Hoyt, Jean, 183–84
Hugo, Victor, 29
Hull, Helen, 14, 260
Hungary, 95
Hungry Men (Anderson), 253
Hurst, Fannie, 14, 51
Hurston, Zora Neale, 11, 211–12, 246
Huxley, Aldous, 11, 236–37, 260

"Il Penseroso" (Milton), 31
Impromptu (Paul), 72
"Impulse" (Aiken), 245

"In Cold Blood" (Kutner), 259
"Indian Summer" (Caldwell), 162
Inside Europe (Gunther), 103
Irish, William (Cornell Woolrich), 210
Irving, Washington, 119, 148
I Saw Hitler (Thompson), 212–13
Isherwood, Christopher, 238
Italian-Ethiopian war, 77

Jabberwock, The, 30–32
Jack o' Lantern, 185
Jackson, Shirley, 15
Jacobs, Carl, 14
James, Henry, 71, 148
James, Polly, 233
Janeway, Elizabeth, 8, 259
Jarvis, Bernice, 8
Jaspersohn, William G., 97n–98n, 251n
Jews in Central Europe, 95–96, 123–24, 173, 222–23, 263n
Johnson, Arthur, 14
Jolas, Eugene, 10, 21, 68, 70–72, 74, 80, 112–14, 117, 130, 141n, 162, 249, 256
Jolas, Maria, 70, 72, 80, 112, 113n
Jones, Carter Brook, 135
Jordan, Josephine, 16
Jordan, Virgil, 14
Journal of the American Medical Association, 111
Joyce, James, 21, 41, 51, 63–64, 69, 72, 80, 81n, 147n, 166, 187, 188n, 191, 205

Kafka, Franz, 72, 95–96, 130, 134
Kantor, MacKinlay, 261n
Kapstein, I. J. 14, 266n
Keats, John, 29, 98
Kendall, Charles, 141
Kenyon Review, The, 273
Kerouac, Jack, 15
Khayyám, Omar, 16
Kielty, Bernadine, 246–47
"Kimono, The" (Morris), 135
Kirkland, Jack, 205
Klopfer, Donald, 198–99, 201, 245
Kneel to the Rising Sun (Caldwell), 206
Knight, Eric, 11, 14, 257, 265–66
Knopf, Alfred, 257
Knowles, John, 270
Komroff, Manuel, 11, 141n, 180, 198, 245, 247, 266n, 268
Kopf, Maxim, 216
Kotterdam "Mother," 39
Kreymborg, Alfred, 137–38
Kreymborg, Dorothy, 137–38

Krishnamurti, Jiddu, 237
Ku Klux Klan, 57, 59
Kulka, Max, 132, 136–38, 193, 195, 207, 222–223
Kunasz, Paul, 265n
Kun, Bela, 95
Kuprin, I. A., 11, 260
Kutner, Nanette, 233, 259

Ladies' Home Journal, 41, 141
Lady Chatterley's Lover (Lawrence), 79
"L'Allegro" (Milton), 31
L'Amour, Louis, 11, 265n
Laney, Al, 74n–75n
Larkin, Peter, 198–99
Lassie Come Home (Knight), 257
Latter-Day Saints, 120
Laughlin, James, 10, 253, 256
Lavin, Mary, 16
Lawrence, D. H., 41, 79, 130, 267–68
League of Frightened Men (Stout), 79
League of Nations, 32
Lenin, Nikolai, 201, 226
Lerner, Max, 264
LeSeuer, Meridel, 14, 265n
Let Us Now Praise Famous Men (Agee), 206
Levin, Meyer, 11, 260
Lewis, Sinclair, 203, 213, 215–18, 254n, 257
Lieber, Max, 205–6
Life and Death of a Spanish Town, The (Paul), 74, 193
Limehouse Nights (Burke), 228
Lindberg, Anne, 261n
Lindbergh, Charles, 60
Linn, R. H., 266
Lippincott, Bert, 211
Lippincott, J. B., 10, 211, 264
Literary Life and the Hell with it, The (Burnett), 220–21, 254, 264
"Little Moral Tales" (Saroyan), 265
Little publishers, 258
Little Review, The (Joyce), 63
London, Jack, 134
London Daily Express, 101, 155
London Times Literary Supplement, 130–31
Longfellow, Henry Wadsworth, 205
Lorre, Peter, 240
Los Angeles Daily News, 36, 38–43, 45, 49, 72, 97–98, 102, 155, 202–3
Lost City, The (Gunther), 104n
Lovat Dickson's Magazine, 252
Lowell, president of Harvard University, 90n
Low Run Tide (Paul), 73–74

Index

Lowry, Malcolm, 11, 204, 206–7, 246
Loy, Mina, 188n
Loyalists, 264
Luce, Clare Booth, 214–15
Lyon, Darwin, 157–58
Lyon, Harris Merton, 14
"Lyrical Ballads" (Wordsworth), 133

McAlmon, Robert, 80, 187–92
Macauley, Robie, 16
McCall's, 41, 214
McCleary, Dorothy, 8, 249, 253n, 265n, 267
MacCormack, John, 72
McCrindle, Joe, 20
McCullers, Carson, 8, 259
McDaniel, Eluard Luchell, 14, 259, 261
McDonald, George, 55–56
Macdonald, Ramsay, 88
MacFarlane, Kathryn Jean, 260n
McFee, William, 261n
McLaughlin, Robert, 58
MacMillan, Douglas, 72, 114n
McNamarra, John S., 246
Madden, David, 16
Maddux, Rachel, 259
magazines
    large-circulation, 9–10, 15, 41
    small circulation, 11, 41, 273
    see also specific magazines
Magyars, 95
Mahler, Gustav, 238
Mailer, Norman, 8, 269–70
"Maker of Signs, The" (Burnett), 162
Making of Americans, The (Stein), 69, 189
Malamud, Bernard, 15
Malraux, André, 263–64
Maltz, Albert, 11, 260, 266n
Manchester Guardian 87–88, 105
Manheim, Ralph, 141n
Mann, Heinrich, 134
Mann, Thomas, 10, 134, 227, 234, 252, 256, 263
"Man's Day" (Scribner), 211
Man with the Bull-Tongue Plow, The (Stuart), 259
Marburg, Anita, 264
March, Juan, 192–93
March, William, 249
Maria Theresa, Empress, 150
Marie of Rumania, 107–8
Mario the Magician (Mann), 134, 234
Markewich, Robert, 268
Marshall, Alan, 14, 246, 261, 267
Martin Charles, 266n

Martin Schuler (Wilson), 100
Marx, Karl, 162, 201
marxism, 64–65, 87, 140
Masaryk, Jan, 95
"Masses of Men" (Caldwell), 245
Maugham, Somerset, 238
Maupassant, Guy de, 29
Maule, H. E., 253
Mayer, Edwin Justus, 239
Mayorga, Margaret, 263
"Measure and Value" (Mann), 256
Medearis, Mary, 14, 264, 266
medical ethics, editorials on, 109–12
Meeter, George F., 14
Meeting Place, 204
Melville, Herman, 29, 142n, 147
Mencken, H. L., 40–41, 44, 109, 111, 114, 117, 136, 202–3, 249, 262
Mendes, Alfred H., 11, 260
Merrick, Rebecca, 14
"Metamorphosis" (Kafka), 72
Meyrinck, Gustav, 85n
Milburn, George, 247, 252, 259–60
Millay, Edna St. Vincent, 254n
Miller, Henry, 268
Mills, Mrs., 56–59
Milton, John, 165
Minot, Stephen, 16
"Missis Flinders" (Slesinger), 267–68
Moby Dick (Melville), 142n
Modern Short Story in the Making, The, 271
Moll, E. A., 14, 260
Monash, Paul, 259
Mooney, Tom, 36–37
Moore, A. E., 147n
Moore, George, 41
Moore, Marianne, 188n
Moore, Virginia, 267
Morey, Katherine, 34
Morgan, Berry, 16
Morley, John Royston, 266
Mormons, 53, 72–73, 120
Morris, Edita, 11, 236, 260, 265n
Morris, Ira V., 135, 141n, 146, 260
Mother Courage (Brecht), 235
Musil, Robert, 11, 134, 141n
Mussolini, Benito, 149, 192, 201
My Friend Flicka (O'Hara), 264
"My Friend Flicka" (O'Hara), 266
"My Mother's Goofy Song" (Fante), 245
"My Old Man" (Hemingway), 117n, 188n
Mystery of Edwin Drood, The (Dickens), 31
mystery novels, 79
mysticism, 113–14

Nabokov, Vladimir, 15
Nathan, George Jean, 40–41, 114, 260, 262
Nation, The, 208, 212, 264
National Socialist Workers, 64, 87
Nazis, 64–65, 69, 80, 87, 89–90, 123, 173,
    212, 227–28, 247–48, 255, 263n
Neagoe, Peter, 11, 114, 141n, 151, 249,
    260, 268
Negherbon, William, 14, 265n
"Neighbors" (Gorman), 135
Neugass, James, 263
Neugeboren, Betsey, 19–20
Neugeboren, Jay, 7–24
Newark Ledger, 35
New Directions, 10, 253
New Masses, 252n
New Republic, The, 16, 152, 252n, 261n
New Russia, The, (Thompson), 217
Newspaper Guild, 61
newspapermen
    and caption writing, 47–49, 53–54, 58
    and copy editing, 35, 43–44, 47–66
    and feature writing, 63, 66, 97–98
    managing editor, 35, 40, 47, 64, 66,
        70–71
    foreign correspondents, 65, 85–87, 89,
        104n, 125, 168, 212
    reporters, 35–67, 101, 212
    sports editors, 49, 54, 60
"New Words for Old: Notes on Experimen-
    tal Writing" (Laughlin), 256
New York Academy of Medicine, 109
New York Daily News, 47–50, 54–55, 70
New Yorker, The, 10–11, 185, 202, 261n
New York Globe, 35
New York Herald-Tribune, 65, 67, 131, 198
New York Sun, 167
New York Times, 42, 46, 50, 54, 61, 70–71,
    104n, 106n, 149, 206, 214, 259n
New York Times Book Review, The, 16, 47,
    130
New York World, 90n
Nightingale, Florence, 153
"Night Reveals, The" (Woolrich), 265
Nijinski, Madame, 238
Nobel Prize for literature, 134, 215, 234,
    248, 268
North German Confederation (1866), 91
North to the Orient (Lindbergh), 261n
"Notes of a Dangling Man" (Bellow),
    15–16
Not for Heaven (McCleary), 253n
"Nothing Can Stop It" (Wagner), 245
novella, 10, 73, 260
Noxon, G. M., 134–35

Noyes, Newbold, 14
nudism, 148–49

Oates, Joyce Carol, 15
O'Brien, Edward Jr., 8, 10, 17, 97–100,
    125, 116–19, 130–31, 133, 146–50,
    197, 222–23, 244, 249, 251n, 267,
    269, 271–73
O'Brien, Flann, 11, 268
O'Brien, Margaret, 233
O'Brien, Ruth, 222
O'Brien, Tim, 16
O'Casey, Sean, 147n
O'Connor, Flannery, 15, 23, 115
O'Connor, Frank, 260
"Ode to a Skylark" (Shelley), 31
Odets, Clifford, 141, 239
O'Donnell, E. P., 141n, 249, 260n
O'Faoláin, Seán, 11, 252, 260, 265, 266n
O'Flaherty, Liam, 11, 265n
O'Hara, Mary, 14, 264–66
O. Henry Memorial Prize, 18n–19n,
"Old General, The" (Knight), 267–68
Old Testament, 72, 152, 155
Olsen, Tillie, 16
Olson, Ted, 266n
O'Neill, Charles, 185, 245
O'Neill, Eugene, 229, 248
"One with Shakespeare" (Foley), 11, 99,
    130, 163, 165, 267
Orient Express, 107–8
Orphic Mysteries, 113
Ottoman Empire, 87
Outlines of History, 104
"Outward Bound," 188
Ozick, Cynthia, 16

pacifism, 52–53, 91, 151
Pacquita, 176–78, 186, 190–91, 193, 197
Paris Herald, 47, 62, 64–66, 69–70, 72, 74–
    75, 77, 80, 109, 195
Paris literary world, 68–70
Parker, Dan, 54
Parker, Dorothy, 21, 202, 254n, 266
Partisan Review, 16
Patchen, Kenneth, 268
Paterson, Isabel, 131
Patterson, Medill, 53
Paul, Alice, 33
Paul, Elliot, 72–74, 193, 195–96
Pavey, L. A., 141n
Pavlov, Ivan, 135n
Payne, Phil, 47, 49, 54–56, 59–60
Paynter, Henry, 59–60
Pearl Harbor bombing, 243

Index

Pearson, Drew, 103
Peden, William, 271n
Pegler, Westbrook, 49, 54, 101
Pen and Brush Club, 204
"Penny Whistle" (Gossman), 130
periodicals, 19
Perkins, Maxwell, 215
Perlman, Magistrate Nathan, 205
Peterson, Eric Jens, 11, 266
Petry, Ann, 16
Pharamond, Monsieur, 75
Philadelphia Public Ledger, 212
Phoenicians, 194–95
photo-essays, 10
"Piazza Tales" (Melville), 142n
Pictorial Review, 41
Pinck, Dan, 188n
Pirandello, Luigi, 11, 260, 267–68
Plaut, Elsie, 14
playwrights, 14
   see also specific playwrights
plays, publishing, 10
Plot in Central Europe (Fodor), 88
Pocket Story Book, A, 271
Podhoretz, Norman, 12
Poe, Edgar Allan, 119, 124–25
Poe Award, 210
poetry, 10, 41
Poetry, 13n
"Poetry Is Vertical," 113–14
politics and journalism, 74–75
Polizeibeamter, Herr, 131
Pooler, James, 266n
"Poor Everybody" (McLaughlin), 58
"Poor Relation, A" (Wilson), 130
Porter, Katherine Anne, 11, 114, 141,
   266n
"Portrait of a Contemporary at 70-odd"
   (Burnett), 130
Pound, Ezra, 64, 69, 81n, 90, 148, 188n
Powell, Dawn, 114
Powers, J. F., 15
Prague's Blue Laws, 136
Prater Violet (Isherwood), 238
Pratt, Theodore, 185, 246
Preparedness Day parade, bombing of, 36
printers and the union, 85n
Private Life of the Master Race (Brecht), 235
Professor Rat (Mann), 134
Prohibition (1933), 214
Prokosch, Frederick, 8, 259
"proletarian" stories, 12–13, 139–41
Proust, Marcel, 134, 213
Prunty, Patrick, 149
psychoanalysis, 82, 111

psychohistory, 111
Pulitzer prize, 77

Qualle, Herr, 83–84, 129–30, 173
quarterlies, 11, 19
Quarter, This, 130

Radio programming literature, 10, 12,
   264–65
Raisin, Abraham, 11
Random House, 198, 245, 255, 271n
Ravine, In the (Chekhov), 73
Razor's Edge, The (Maugham), 238
Reader's Digest Foundation, 271n
"Rear Window" (Woolrich), 210
Red Pavilion, The (Gunther), 103
Reichstag, Nazi invasion of, 103
Reinhardt, Elsa, 238
Reinhardt, Max, 238
"Rest Cure" (Boyle), 130, 133, 267
"Revolution of the Word Manifesto, The,"
   80, 113
Rhinelander family, 55
Riding, Laura, 114, 185
Rilke, Rainer Maria, 134
Rise and Fall of the Third Reich, The (Shirer),
   65, 107
Rivera, Diego de, 201
Robinson, Edward North, 259
Roderick Random, 68
Roosevelt, Eleanor, 49
Roosevelt, Franklin D., 86, 111
Roosevelt, Theodore, 90n
Rose, Roma, 14, 265n
Rosenblatt, Benjamin, 14
Rosenfeld, Isaac, 15
Rosenfeld, Paul, 268
Ross, Harold, 202
Ross, Nancy Wilson, 11, 266
Rossetti, Eugene, 65, 74–79, 84
Roth, Philip, 15
Rothberg, Abraham, 16
Royalist movement, France, 77–78
royalties on the short story, 21
Rumania, 107–9
Russell, Dora, 150
Russell, Bertrand, 150

Sacco-Vanzetti case, 53, 81n, 90n, 169,
   201
"Sacre du Printemps" (Bemelmans), 267
"Saint Katie and the Virgin" (Steinbeck),
   163
Salinger, J. D., 8, 23, 265, 271n
Salt Lake Tribune, 45

"Samarkand" (Foley), 135
"Sam's Little Tyke" (Knight), 265
San Francisco Journal, 36
San Francisco Record, 36–37
Sand, George, 183–84
Sandoz, Mari, 11, 260
Sappho, 69n–70n
Saroyan, William, 8, 21–3, 141, 202n, 250–51, 259–60, 267
Sarraute, Nathalie, 113n
Saturday Evening Post, 10, 41, 141, 212
Satyricon, 119
Saxl, Frau Doktor, 143
Scherman, Harry, 198–99, 201, 204, 245, 247, 257
Schiller, Johann, 91
Schmitt, Gladys, 260, 264
Schnitzler, Arthur, 85
Schober, Johann, 115
Schorer, Mark, 260
Schulberg, Ad, 227
Schulberg, Budd, 11
Schwartz, Delmore, 15, 151
Schwartzwald, Frau, 92, 143
Scopes "monkey trial," 168
Scott, John, 136–38
Scribner, Frederick, 211, 246
Scribner's, 10–11, 81, 100, 252n, 258
Seager, Allan, 11, 260, 271n
Seas of God The, 271
Second All Soviet Writers' Congress, 81n
Seipel, Monsignor, 115
Seizin Press, 185
Select, Madame, 65
Semitic race, 194–95
Semon, Kurt, 255, 269
Sergeant, Winthrop, 264
Sewanee Review, 41
Sextet: 6 Story Discoveries in Novella form, 271
sexual revolution (1930's), 111–12
Shakespeare, William, 29, 32, 69n, 134, 210
Shakespeare & Company, 51, 63, 131
Shaw, George Bernard, 10, 147n, 254, 256
Shaw, Irwin, 11, 230, 265–66
Sheean, Vincent, 213, 215
Shelley, Percy Bysshe, 31, 165
"Sherril" (Burnett), 52, 135, 162
Shirer, William L., 22, 65, 106–7, 118, 122, 158, 168, 171
short story
    as art form, 119
    definition of, 9

publishing, 10–12, 15, 100, 119, 130, 133, 139–41, 151, 204, 206–7, 256, 260–61
    see also STORY
Sidis, William James, 30
Silko, Leslie, 16
Silone, Ignazio, 10–11, 257, 259, 263
Simon, Kurt, 255, 269
Simon and Schuster, 263n
Sinclair, Upton, 134
Sippey, Dr., 111
Sitwell, Edith, 188n
Skinner, Ed, 43–45, 51
Slesinger, Tess, 8, 22, 141n, 260, 267
"Slight Mistake, A" (Zoshchenko), 151–52
Slovakia, 95
Smart Set, 40–41, 44, 114, 135, 164, 203, 211, 262
Social Democrats, 87, 91, 108, 123
socialism, 43, 52–53, 66, 87, 93
Socialist party, 32, 36
Socrates, 70n
"So Help Me" (Algren), 13, 207–8
Solari, Pietro, 141n
"Solo on the Cornet" (Fales), 267–68
Solotaroff, Ted, 7, 12
Sommerer, Resi-Frau Therese, 83, 85, 89, 92, 96–97, 99, 106, 116, 118, 121–25, 129–30, 133, 137–38, 145–46, 150, 152, 158–59, 166, 168, 173, 175
Song on Your Bugles (Knight), 257
Soupault, Philippe, 71
Southern Literary Messenger, The, 41
Southern Review, 41
South of Hitler (Fodor), 88
space age, early twentieth-century, 157–58
Spanish civil war, 74, 192, 196
Spellman, Cardinal, 49
Spengler, Oswald, 228
Spirit of Man, The, 271
Spock, Benjamin, 158
sports editors, 49, 54, 60
"Spring Evening" (Farrell), 140n
Stafford, Jean, 15
Stalin-Hitler pact, 217
Starhemberg, Prince, 87
Stark, Judy, 7–8, 17, 23
Star Wagon, The (Anderson), 263
Steele, Wilbur Daniel, 14
Stegner, Wallace, 11, 260
Stein, Gertrude, 11, 21, 68–70, 188n, 189, 247, 268
Steinbeck, John, 141–42, 163, 170
Stekel, Wilhelm, 104
Steloff, Frances, 205

Index

Steuerman, Mrs., 226
Stevens, Pembroke, 101, 155–56
Stevens, Wallace, 188n
Stieglitz, Alfred, 268
Stierhem, Eleanor, 119
Stiles, Villa, 14, 259
"Still Life" (Ullman), 266
St. Joseph, Ellis, 14, 260, 266
stock market crash, 81
Stone, Robert, 16
Stone Soldier, The: Prize College Stories 1963, 271n
STORY magazine, 7–8, 19n, 24, 36, 61–62, 97n, 119–23, 127–38, 201, 207, 216n, 220–21, 224, 248–49, 255, 257–58, 262–71, 273
    in America, 10–14, 201–216, 244–68
    authors published in, 11–12, 14, 130, 133, 135, 139–41, 151, 165, 180, 185, 204, 206–7, 210–15, 259–61, 265–70
    distribution of, 10, 131, 143–44, 264–65
    editing, 8, 18–19, 21, 119–23, 127–38, 163, 174–75, 178–81, 196, 202–11, 242, 244, 253–54, 256–57, 266–74
    first anniversary of, 9, 251
    joining Random House, New York, 201–16, 245, 255
    origins of (Europe 1931–32), 17, 117–23, 127–35, 139–45, 151–52, 162–63, 165, 168, 174, 180, 198–99
    production of, 128–29, 163, 174–75, 178–81
    Service Bureau, 254–55, 264
Story Anthology, A, (1931–33), 248
STORY: The Fiction of the 'Forties, 271
Story Jubilee: Thirty-Three Years of STORY, 271
STORY: The Magazine of the Short Story in Book Form, 270
Story Press, The 7, 10, 253n, 256–57, 270n
Story: The Yearbook of Discovery, 271n
Stout, Rex, 21, 75–79, 117–18, 265, 273
stream-of-consciousness writing, 113, 135
Strong, L. A. G., 141n, 180, 252, 260
Stuart, Jesse, 8, 259, 265n, 268
Studs Lonigan, (Farrell), 139
Sullivan, John L., 49
Sumner, John S., 205
surrealism, 71–72, 74
Susan and God (Crothers), 263
Swados, Harvey, 15, 21
Swallow, Allan, 271n
Swinburne, Algernon Charles, k6

Tab, 42
tabloid journalism, 47–60
    see also newspapermen
Taggard, Genevieve, 185
Tales (Chaucer), 119
Targan, Barry, 16
Tarjan, Edde, 265n
Taylor, Kressman, 14, 263n, 265, 267
Taylor, Peter, 15
television and sensational crime, 53–54
Tennyson, Alfred, 29, 128
Thackeray, William Makepeace, 29
"That Evening Sun Go Down" (Faulkner), 247
Theosophists, 237
There's One in Every Family (Eisenberg), 264
Thielen, Benedict, 260
Thilenius, Helen, 14
This Is My Best, 271
Thompson, Dorothy, 21, 101, 212–18, 256
Thompson, Sylvia, 268
Thompson, Virgil, 69
Three Lives (Stein), 69
Three Mountain Press, 80, 122
Three Stories and Ten Poems (Hemingway), 80, 122, 188n
Three Penny Opera, The (Brecht), 235
"Thunderstorm" (Vail), 135
Thurber, James, 195, 202, 208
"Time" (Bates), 245
Time to be Young, 271
Tobacco Road, (Caldwell), 162, 204–6
Toklas, Alice B., 68–69
Toller, Ernst, 263
Tolstoy, Leo, 29
Tomorrow, 273
Toumanova, Nina A., 256
trade unions, 65
Transatlantic Review, 20
transatlantic telephone, origin of, 92
Transatlantique (Antheil), 142
transition, 64, 68, 70–72, 74, 80, 99, 112–14, 117, 130, 162
transition *1927–1938* (MacMillan), 72, 114n
Traver, Robert, 259
Treaty of Saint Germain, 82, 90, 90n–91n, 100
Treaty of Trianon, 95
Treaty of Versailles, 90, 90n–92n, 100
Tree, Iris, 240
Trilling, Lionel, 15
Trotsky, Leon, 151
Try and Stop Me (Cerf), 220
Tucci, Niccoló, 16

Tulip Box, The (Thompson), 213
Turney, Douglas, 40–41, 45–46, 119
Twain, Mark, 254n
Two Bottles of Relish, 271
200 Years of Great American Short Stories, 15, 272n
"Two Men Free" (Burnett), 116–17

Ullman, James Ramsey, 8, 266, 268
Ultramarine (Cowley), 246
Ulysses (Joyce), 51, 63–64, 79, 81n, 187, 205
Uncle Tom's Children (Wright), 257
Undset, Sigrid, 254n
union organization, 36
United Press, 89
United States Congress, and copyright law, 21
United States customs, banning import books, 63–64
Updike, John, 15

Vail, Laurence, 135, 141n, 248
Vanderbilt, Cornelius, Jr., 38–39, 42–43, 170
Vanguard Press, 78, 117, 248, 253n
Vanity Fair, 11, 182
Van Loon, Hendrik Willem, 10, 256
Variety, 80–81
Vatsek, Joan, 266
Vein of Iron (Glasgow), 261n
Verdun, The Sacrifice (von Unruh) 151
Vetsera, Baroness Maria, 153
Vidal, Peire, 247
Vienna, 8, 17
    architecture of, 93–94
    and medicine, 109–12
    and secularization, 93n
    see also Austria
Viertel, Berthold, 238
Viertel, Gigi, 229–30
Viertel, Peter, 229–30, 240
Viertel, Salka, 225–26, 229, 231, 233, 238–41
Villa, José Garcia, 141n, 151, 247
von Berlau, Baroness Ruth, 224–26, 235
von Unruh, Fritz, 151
Vorse, Mary Heaton, 249

Wagner, Elizabeth, 245
Wagner, Herr, 83
Waiting for Lefty (Odets), 239
Walpole, Hugh, 261n
Warren, Robert Penn, 141, 254
Washington, George, 87

Washington Merry-go-Round, (Pearson), 103
Wathen, Richard, 271n
Weaver, Harriet, 51, 187
Weaver, Raymond, 147
Weidman, Jerome, 8, 259
Weigel, Helene, 235–36
Weill, Kurt, 235
Weimar Republic, 100, 115, 123
Weller, George, 104, 260
Wells, H. G., 104–6
Welty, Eudora, 15
Werfel, Franz, 238–39
West, Nathanaiel, 188
West, Rebecca, 105
Westcott, Glenway, 188n
"What a Small World" (Anderson and Foley), 265
White, E. B., 202
White, Eric, 14
White, Max, 260
"Who Killed Cock Robin?" (Wilson), 100
"Why Men Write" (Anderson), 256
Wilkinson, "Doc," 43
William Morrow Company, 142
Williams, Blanche Colton, 131
Williams, Tennessee, 8, 22, 204, 265
Williams, Thomas, 16
Williams, William Carlos, 11, 141n, 180, 187–88
Wilner, Herbert, 16
Wilson, Edmund, 266, 273
Wilson, Romer, 11, 99–100, 130, 149, 260
Wilson, William E., 16, 260
Wilson, Woodrow, 32
Wimsatt, W. K. Jr., 260
Wind and the Rain, The (Burke), 228
Winesburg, Ohio (Anderson), 268
"Winter" (McCleary), 267
Winter at Majorca, A (Sand), 183
Wiser, William, 16
Witt, Peter, 223
Wodehouse, P. G., 69
Wolfe, Thomas, 141, 254n, 268
Woman's Home Companion, 41
women's magazines, 41, 100
Woman's party, 32–34, 161
women's rights, 21, 32–33, 52–53
Wonderful Wizard of Oz, The (Baum), 38
Woods, R. C., 247
Woolcott, Alexander, 202
Woolrich, Cornell, 204, 209–10, 260, 265
Wordsworth, William, 29, 133
world economy, 1930s, 160–61
World Sex Congress, 111–12

Index

World War I, 16, 84, 86, 88, 90–91, 95, 123, 152, 157, 212
World War II, 70, 89–90, 95, 123, 192, 217
W.P.A., 10, 216n, 257
Wright, Richard, 8, 10, 21, 23, 68–69, 141, 209, 257, 265
writer(s)
   difference between "unknown" and "established," 8–9, 15, 258, 265
   discovered, 11, 14, 258, 265

Yeats, W. B., 147n
You Have Seen Their Faces (Caldwell), 206
Young Brett, 261n
Young Lions, The (Shaw), 204n
Young Lonigan (Farrell), 139

"Zelig," (Rosenblatt), 14
Zoshchenko, Mikhail, 11, 141n, 151–52, 245–46